SACRED GROUND

LEADERSHIP LESSONS FROM GETTYSBURG & THE LITTLE BIGHORN

JEFF APPELQUIST

ISBN 10: 1-59298-323-5
ISBN 13: 978-1-59298-323-0

Library of Congress Catalog Number: 2010901065

Printed in the United States of America

First Printing: 2010

14 13 12 11 10   5 4 3 2 1

Beaver's Pond Press, Inc.
7104 Ohms Lane, Suite 101
Edina, MN 55439–2129
(952) 829-8818
www.BeaversPondPress.com

BEAVER'S
POND
PRESS

To order, visit www.BeaversPondBooks.com
or call (800) 901-3480. Reseller discounts available.

This book is dedicated to
a business leader who was also
my first and finest professor of history,
my father,
Carl Allen Appelquist

I love you Dad

"Ye shall hear of wars and rumours of wars:
see that ye be not troubled: for all these things
must come to pass, but the end is not yet.
For nation shall rise against nation, and kingdom
against kingdom.... But he that shall endure unto the end,
the same shall be saved."

—Matthew 24:6–13—

"Once more unto the breach, dear friends, once more....
In peace there's nothing so becomes a man
As modest stillness and humility:
But when the blast of war blows in our ears,
Then imitate the action of the tiger.
Stiffen the sinews, summon up the blood,
Disguise fair nature with hard-favour'd rage.
Then lend the eye a terrible aspect."

—*Henry V* 3.1, l.1–9—

"Business is war."

—Countless Business Leaders Since Commerce Began—

Contents

PART ONE:
CREATE COMMON PURPOSE

PART TWO:
BUILD STRONG RELATIONSHIPS & TRUST

CONTENTS

List of Maps

Foreword

When I first decided to participate in a leadership development experience centered on a visit to the battlefield of the Little Bighorn, during the late, hot summer of 2008, I had few expectations it would serve as one of the most important and meaningful learning experiences of my life.

Upon arrival at the airport for my flight to Montana, I even privately wondered, "What am I doing here?" Such a mindset and attitude is not normally the basis for a transformational learning experience, but throughout my life, I've often been surprised to receive some of the most valuable gifts of knowledge, wisdom, and insights when I least expect them. I was unaware of all that was possible when venturing onto hallowed and holy ground, but now I know. So I will tell you, if your mind is open, your own personal learning and leadership journey will be greatly enhanced by the book you are about to read, *Sacred Ground: Leadership Lessons from Gettysburg and the Little Bighorn.*

Sacred Ground is the companion volume to the Gettysburg and Little Bighorn seminars facilitated by my friend Jeff Appelquist, but the book also stands proudly on its own. This insightful, ambitious, and creative collection of learning lessons not only pulls from the magnificent history of two of the most well-known American battles, but also helps us fast-forward to applications and connections with some of today's most successful leaders and organizations. I paraphrase a well-known quote that says, "He or she who does not know their history, is doomed to repeat it." The lessons from Gettysburg and the Little Big-horn are timeless gems available for us to examine today. We can learn from history, apply those experiences to modern-day challenges, and use our newfound knowledge to explore fresh and innovative ways to solve ongoing, as well as future, problems. We can pursue the greatest challenges that we each face—all with a higher degree of confidence, conviction, humility, and inclusiveness.

This wonderful book gives us enhanced perspective on the problems and issues we confront in the workplace today. The men and women who've come before us, perhaps unknowingly, gave their lives in order that their spirits and life-guiding principles might live on through us in smarter, more prosperous ways. Without a doubt, these lessons will inspire us to act in ways that will inspire others to follow our deeds in the future.

My experience of bonding and learning with my battlefield buddies in Montana will remain with me forever. Since the seminar, I have read many books on the subject of the Little Bighorn, I have participated in follow-up sessions, and I serve on an advisory board to further advance this unique experience. But my most meaningful moments occurred on the battlefield when tracing the various phases of the conflict and taking the time to debrief what happened and its relevance to me and my leadership style today.

My reading at the beautiful Indian Memorial of the moving words of the Sioux leader Ohiyesa—later known by his anglicized name of Charles Alexander Eastman—will serve for me as a lasting memory of the courage, spirit, and bravery of those who valiantly gave their lives. Immediately after I read Ohiyesa's heartfelt words out loud, at the very end of our battlefield tour, our group experienced a sudden, cold, and sustained wind on what had been an extremely hot and still summer day. This amazing and mystical occurrence touched me deeply and will forever serve as a reminder that we are all connected, and that our mutual life journeys always have been—and always will be—carefully intertwined.

I believe we all have an obligation to live each day to its fullest and in peace. We have an obligation to be the best leaders that we can be. We have an obligation to be citizens not just of America, or whatever nation we call home, but of the global community. We have an obligation to our children, and to future generations. The lessons from *Sacred Ground* can guide us in this quest.

The Sioux chief Ohiyesa said it well: "… as an ideal, we live and will live, not only in the splendor of our past, the poetry of our legends and art, not only in the interfusion of our blood with yours, and in our faithful adherence to the ideals of American citizenship, but in the living heart of the nation."

—Herschel R. Herndon—

Vice President Multicultural Relations,
Diversity and Urban Market Development

Best Buy Company, Inc.
September 2009

Introduction

MOMENT OF TRUTH

"If you don't find more Indians in that valley than you ever saw together, you can hang me."

—Mitch Boyer—

He was beyond weary after having spent more than twenty-four hours in the saddle. He had ridden nearly seventy miles to get to this point and cherished the thought of a few hours rest before duty called again. The night was black and cool, with countless stars high and bright in the sky. It was 2:30 a.m. When the scouting party finally unsaddled horses at the base of a hill beneath juniper and pine trees, he dropped exhausted to the ground and immediately fell into a deep sleep. Lieutenant Charles Varnum was a good soldier, a twenty-seven-year-old West Pointer serving in the Seventh U.S. Cavalry Regiment. That unit's commander, Lieutenant Colonel George Armstrong Custer, had thought enough of Varnum's abilities to appoint him chief of scouts. At dawn's first light, fellow guide Mitch Boyer shook Varnum out of his blissful slumber and beckoned him to follow. It was June 25, 1876, in the vast, rugged reaches of southeast Montana Territory. An immense Sioux Indian encampment, the largest Boyer had ever seen, lay just visible in the distance to the west.

1

Boyer, Varnum and two of Custer's Crow Indian scouts scrambled through the tall buffalo grass up a steep precipice to the high point known as the Crow's Nest. They looked down on the gap that bridged the divide between the Rosebud and Little Bighorn Rivers, at the Cha Tish, or Wolf Mountains. They were now in Crow country, and the Crow's Nest—named for the bird and not the tribe—had been used for years, perhaps centuries, as an observation post. This elevated ridge offered excellent, panoramic views both east and west. From this position, in the clear morning air, the Crow scouts had spotted the huge village, fifteen miles away to the west in the valley of the Little Bighorn. When Varnum, whom the Indians called Peaked Face, got to the top, they pointed westward. They could see the smoke of hundreds of morning campfires and, beyond that, an enormous herd of ponies.

Varnum's eyes were tired and sore from lack of sleep and his long ride in hard conditions. Try as he might, even through a telescope, his blurry vision prevented him from seeing what the others told him was there. The multilingual Boyer, who was half-Sioux and half-French, interpreted as the Crows coached Varnum, "Don't look for horses, look for worms. At that distance horses look like worms crawling on the ground." Varnum still failed the test, but he decided to trust his very capable professional colleagues. It was around 5:00 a.m. He wrote a note to Custer and sent two Arikara Indian scouts to find the Seventh Cavalry and its commander. This would not be difficult, as the smoke from the Seventh's morning fires rose lazily and very visibly in the distance eight miles to the east. The Crow scouts with Varnum could not contain their irritation and contempt. The Sioux could easily determine exactly where they were. Surely such carelessness would give their position away.

The one the Indians knew as "Son of the Morning Star" received the news at his bivouac at 7:30 a.m. Custer mounted his horse, Dandy, bareback and rode around the camp to alert his officers that the men should be ready to step off in half an hour. Custer's favorite scout Bloody Knife predicted anxiously, "We'll find enough Sioux to keep us fighting two or three days." Custer replied confidently, "I guess we'll get through them in one day." His plan was to cross the divide early on June 25, put the regiment in hiding, then conduct a thorough reconnaissance of the village and surrounding terrain. He would attack on the morning of June 26.

Custer now rode on ahead to the Crow's Nest. Gazing west through a spyglass, he experienced much the same frustration as Varnum. "Well I've got about as good eyes as anybody," complained Custer, "and I can't see any village, Indians or anything else." Out of frustration, Boyer said to Custer, "If you don't find more Indians in that valley than you ever saw together, you can hang me." Custer replied, anger rising in his voice, "It would do a damned sight of good to hang you now, wouldn't it." This was only the second time Varnum had ever heard Custer use profanity, proof of the commander's general exasperation with the situation.

Finally, through field glasses, after one more careful scan, Custer paused. He saw the dark formation of the gigantic pony herd kicking up dust. He knew what he was up against. But even when Varnum alerted him that the scouts had seen a pair of Indians a mile away, and also a small party of warriors watching them from a ridgeline in the distance, Custer intended to stick with his original plan. The frightened scouts vehemently disagreed and pressed him hard for an immediate attack. They were convinced the Sioux horsemen had seen the Seventh's campfires and would alert the village. The element of surprise would be gone. Custer pondered their advice as he continued to look out over the enormous expanse of terrain to his front. He was inclined to listen to his scouts. Shortly, his brother and subordinate officer Captain Tom Custer rode up with news that the regiment's back trail had been discovered as well. There were Indians to the front and Indians to the rear.

For George Armstrong Custer, this was his moment of truth as a decision maker. He knew he was outnumbered. Should he stick with his original plan, which involved being careful in his assessment of the situation, allowing his men and horses to rest, and attacking in due time? Or had circumstances now changed so dramatically that he must throw caution to the wind and move immediately? He had been a great hero of the American Civil War. Over four years of intense combat, he had made decisions quickly time and again and been rewarded for his audacity. He became the most famous Indian fighter of them all after the war and, again, had always acted boldly. Now, the fate of not only his entire command, but his place in history rested on this choice. He was a national figure, and there were many people who viewed him as a potential future candidate for the presidency. He could not afford a mistake. What decision would he make?

As leaders, we have all faced moments of truth throughout our professional careers. The stakes for us, most likely, have not ever been as high as those that confronted Custer and his Seventh Cavalry. Nevertheless, important decisions directly impacting the success or failure of our teams and organizations have sometimes rested in our hands. Is it possible that we could actually learn from historical examples how to make better decisions? Is it possible to use lessons from history to improve in other dimensions of our leadership as well? I believe the answer is a resounding yes.

What Can History Teach Us About Leadership?

"History does not repeat itself, but it rhymes."

—Mark Twain—

I love history. I have had a passionate interest in history since early childhood. I read lots of history books and have wanted to write one for as long as I can remember. But while this is undoubtedly a history book, it is not primarily so. This is a book about leadership, with history as the framework.

Let me explain, as I have been on a journey. Since the fall of 2007 I have taken twelve teams of approximately 180 business leaders to the Gettysburg and the Little Bighorn battlefields. We have had incredible experiences together while studying these momentous events through the lens of individual leadership and team dynamics. When I was employed as a human resources generalist at the Best Buy Corporation, the company was gracious enough to encourage me to develop my idea. The program was called "Learning Through History." Best Buy also, amazingly, allowed me to form my own limited liability company for purposes of marketing the program externally. This I have done with all my energy since I left Best Buy voluntarily in February of 2009. I am an entrepreneur at heart. It makes me profoundly happy to pursue what I love and make a living at it. I am eternally grateful to my "angel investor," the Best Buy Corporation.

At some point in this wonderful journey the light bulb lit up for me. I think I just woke up one morning and it came to me. I decided to write about the experience. What struck me again and again, based on personal observation and abundant feedback, was the power of history to teach. The lessons learned from these battles are very timely and highly relevant for leaders right now, especially in the tumultuous times in which we live.

These questions should sound familiar: How do we manage through profound change? How can we motivate our people in chaotic circumstances? How do we make good decisions despite imperfect information? How can we communicate more effectively? How do we see things from another person's point of view? How can we understand another culture in a global economy? How will we win or even survive in a highly competitive and uncertain world? The challenges leaders faced long ago are fundamentally the same as those that leaders confront today.

Based on a desire to get at these timeless challenges, we structure the seminar around a handful of important leadership dimensions. We will do the same in this book. These dimensions do not represent an exhaustive list or the final word on leadership or teams. There are as many ways of going about being a successful leader as there are successful leaders. This much was true in the 1800s, just as it is today. Nevertheless, outstanding leaders both past and present seem to consistently demonstrate these skills:

1. Great leaders **Create Common Purpose;**

2. Great leaders **Build Strong Relationships and Trust;**

3. Great leaders **Communicate Clearly and Share Information;**

4. Great leaders **Seek Self-Knowledge and Learning;**

5. Great leaders **Show Energy and Passion;**

6. Great leaders **Make Good Decisions.**

One of my favorite customers is Fresenius Medical Care. They are typical of many of the groups that have accompanied me to the battlefield. Fresenius is the world's largest integrated provider of products and services for people who are undergoing kidney dialysis. The Physician Strategies and Market Development Group from Fresenius, led by my friend Brian Gauger, has sent two teams to Gettysburg and one to Montana. Brian is one of those terrific leaders—of whom there are not enough—who recognizes that even in a tough economic environment he needs to invest in and develop his people. Brian has said, "These are the very individuals who are going to get us through the challenging times. We need to take care of them." He has brought members of his team from both the field and senior management in areas such as acquisitions, joint ventures, and market development. They are a very sharp bunch.

When a team such as Fresenius arrives on-site at the battlefield, we spend an initial half-day going through a series of preparatory exercises. We talk about the history of what happened there. We spend the entire next day touring the battlefield. We always hope for—and usually get—a warm and sunny day (knock on wood). We move from station to station in more or less chronological fashion. We do a reading from a historical source at each site, and then discuss the application of historical lessons to modern leadership and team challenges. The folks from Fresenius love to argue with each other. They get into it, but we are all usually smiling by the end of the conversation. We ensure we have at least one significant lesson learned from each location on the field. At the end of both the first and second days in Gettysburg we go out to dinner at restaurants that are on the National Register of Historic Places. They were private homes during the battle—some people say they are now haunted—but have been beautifully restored and are nationally renowned eateries. We have fun.

We spend a final half-day assessing what we learned together. We discuss what we saw and experienced, and how we might apply it to our own workplaces. We complete some exercises that provide us tools and action items to take back.

We also commit to a series of four follow-up Sustain and Build meetings (we were going to call them Build and Sustain meetings but then they would have been BS meetings and everyone has enough of those already). We conduct these conversations over the course of a year. We want to make sure the experience becomes more than just a one-time, event-based occurrence (everyone has had enough of those as well) with no lasting impact. The idea is to build on the powerful and memorable on-site adventure in a way that creates change and produces tangible business results.

The Fresenius team has spent entire days together, reviewing what we learned and how it applies. They have been especially focused on building their cross-functional relationships and better communication. They have made good progress in both areas. Brian Gauger says, "The follow-on work was key and helped me make several critical decisions about my organization. We saw an immediate improvement in business outcomes helping to drive our growth and leadership goals."

Despite the express focus on practical leadership skills and my assertion that this is not primarily a history book, there will be plenty of history here. You have already had a brief glimpse. I have gotten my fix (for the time being) in doing the research and writing. I have tried to focus on people, rather than dates, chronologies, and all the other things that made history so boring for many of us in school.

I regard history at its best as one unending, frequently unforgettable story about people who lived and breathed, and sometimes accomplished amazing things under great duress. While not everyone loves history, everyone loves a great story. And stories from the past still have power to inform our lives in the present. While history is undoubtedly the foundation, this book is written for today's business leader.

The book is divided into six parts that track our key dimensions. There are two chapters in each part, one on Gettysburg and one on the Little Bighorn. Our process will be to discuss the two battles in parallel fashion. We will move from site to site at each field just as we do in the seminar. After the battle narratives, we add a more current case study from the world of business to each chapter. I hope these short business stories help illuminate the enduring nature of the leadership lessons. Within the framework of the broader leadership dimension, each chapter ends with a specific leadership lesson. The book concludes with an argument for the relevance of history and a look at the battlefields today.

Frankly, you can learn everything you really need to know from this book by just looking at the leadership lessons that close each chapter—twelve chapters with twelve simple lessons. But you should dig deeper, because even easy concepts are often difficult to execute. By exploring further, you will see that the stories from history are fascinating, the parallels memorable, and the principles enduring. You may even be influenced to change the way you think, lead, and do business.

Finally, I characterize this as "one man's odyssey, with 180 of his special friends, to two sacred places in American history." For me these battlefields are as holy as any shrine, religious, historical, or otherwise, in the world. I have a special, other-worldly sensation when I visit them. I do not have adequate words to describe what happens. I feel electricity in the air. My wife asked me if I would tire of the routine of visiting these places again and again, but I said no, not ever. I am honored and humbled to be there, each and every time. I see something different and new, each and every time.

I have deeply enjoyed sharing the experience of this hallowed ground with many smart, energetic, perceptive people. They are good leaders and good citizens. They want to understand our past and figure out ways to make meaningful connections with their own busy lives. I believe they have taught me more than I have taught them. The leadership lessons presented ultimately have come from them and not from me. We have learned together, been inspired together, laughed together, and cried together. We have pondered the meaning of life and the mystery of death together. Perhaps most important, we have hoped for the future of our children together. It has been an amazing journey.

Maps

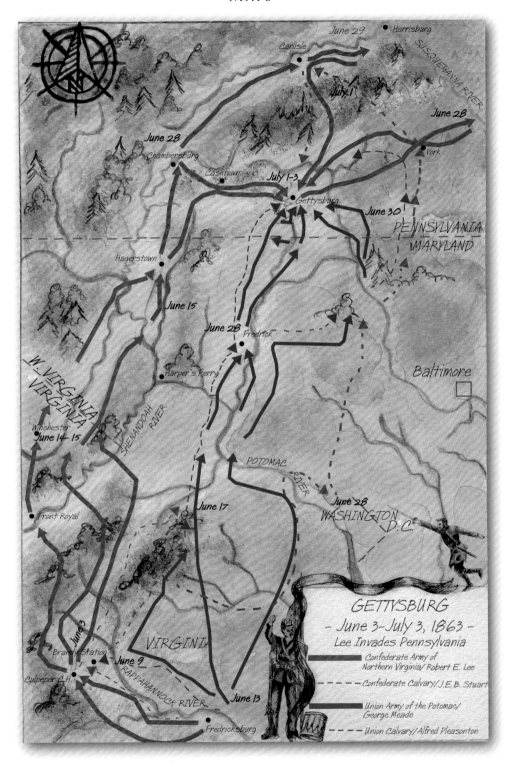

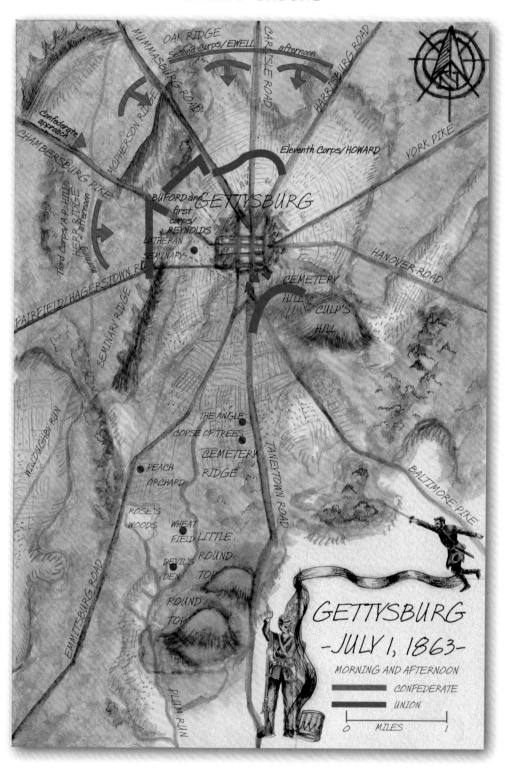

GETTYSBURG
—JULY 1, 1863—
MORNING AND AFTERNOON

First Corps/
LONGSTREET
APPROACHES

OAK RIDGE

MUMMASBURG ROAD

CARLISLE ROAD

HARRISBURG ROAD

Second Corps/ EWELL

YORK PIKE

CHAMBERSBURG PIKE

McPHERSON RIDGE

Third Corps/
A.P. HILL

HERR RIDGE

GETTYSBURG

HANOVER ROAD

FAIRFIELD/HAGERSTOWN ROAD

LUTHERAN
SEMINARY

SEMINARY RIDGE

CEMETERY
HILL

CULP'S
HILL

Eleventh Corps/
HOWARD

Elements of
Twelfth Corps/
SLOCUM

First Corps/
NEWTON

THE ANGLE

COPSE OF TREES

WILLOUGHBY RUN

CEMETERY
RIDGE

TANEYTOWN ROAD

BALTIMORE PIKE

PEACH
ORCHARD

ROSE'S
WOODS

WHEAT
FIELD

LITTLE
ROUND
TOP

Elements of
Third Corps/ SICKLES and
Twelfth Corps/
SLOCUM

DEVIL'S
DEN

EMMITSBURG ROAD

ROUND
TOP

PLUM RUN

GETTYSBURG
–JULY 1, 1863–

LATE EVENING

CONFEDERATE
UNION

0   MILES   1

ROSE'S WOODS

PLUM RUN

MILLERSTOWN ROAD

TANEYTOWN ROAD

LITTLE ROUND TOP

Fifth Corps/
Second Division/
Third Brigade/
WEED
● Fifth U.S. Artillery
HAZLETT'S BATTERY

Fifth Corps/
First Division/
Third Brigade/

VINCENT

140TH
NEW YORK/
O'RORKE

16TH MICHIGAN

44TH NEW YORK

83RD PENNSYLVANIA

20TH MAINE/
CHAMBERLAIN

48TH ALABAMA

47TH TEXAS

5TH TEXAS

4TH ALABAMA

47TH ALABAMA

15TH ALABAMA/
OATES

BENNING'S BRIGADE

DEVIL'S DEN

First Corps/
HOOD'S Division/
LAW'S and ROBERTSON'S
BRIGADES

(Law took command of the division
when Hood was wounded)

ROUND TOP

GETTYSBURG
- July 2, 1863 -

BATTLE FOR LITTLE ROUND TOP
LATE AFTERNOON

CONFEDERATE
UNION

0   1/4 MILE

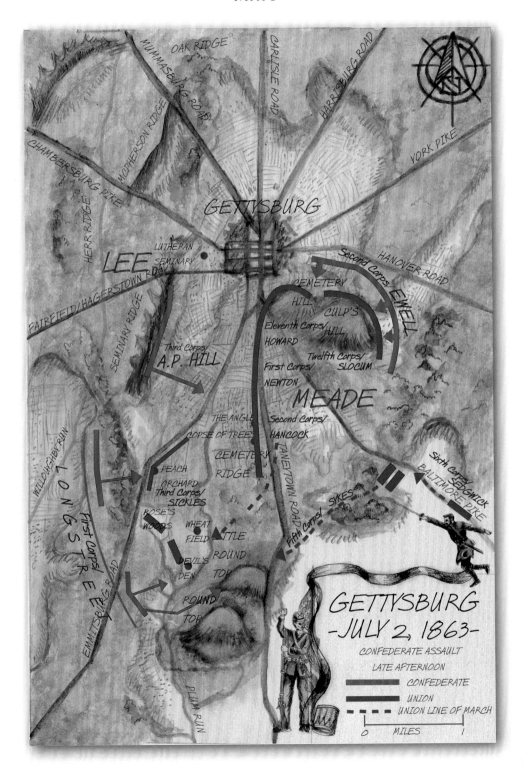

GETTYSBURG
—JULY 2, 1863—

CONFEDERATE ASSAULT
LATE AFTERNOON

CONFEDERATE
UNION
UNION LINE OF MARCH

0   MILES   1

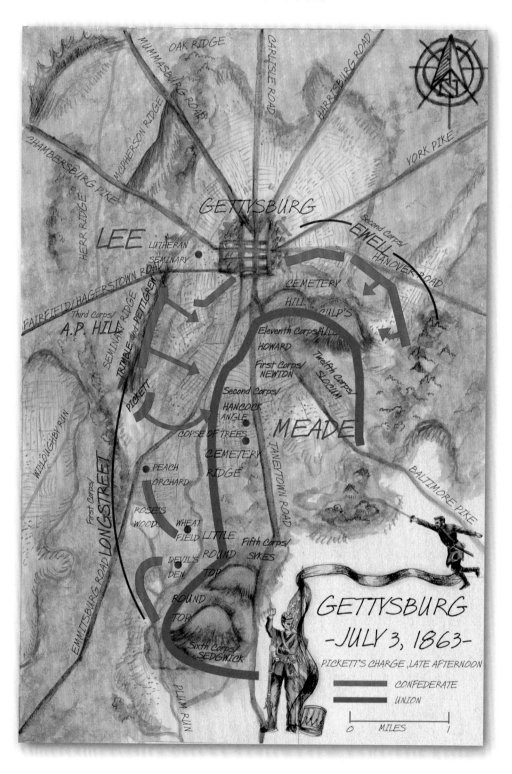

GETTYSBURG
—JULY 3, 1863—

PICKETT'S CHARGE, LATE AFTERNOON

Maps

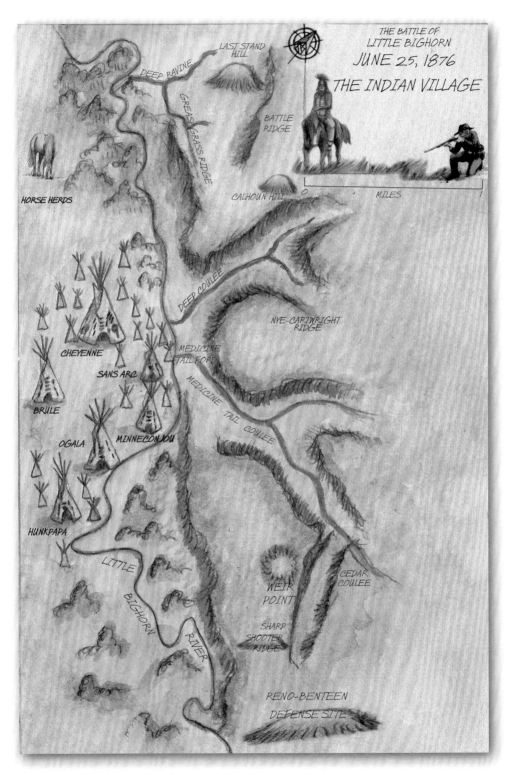

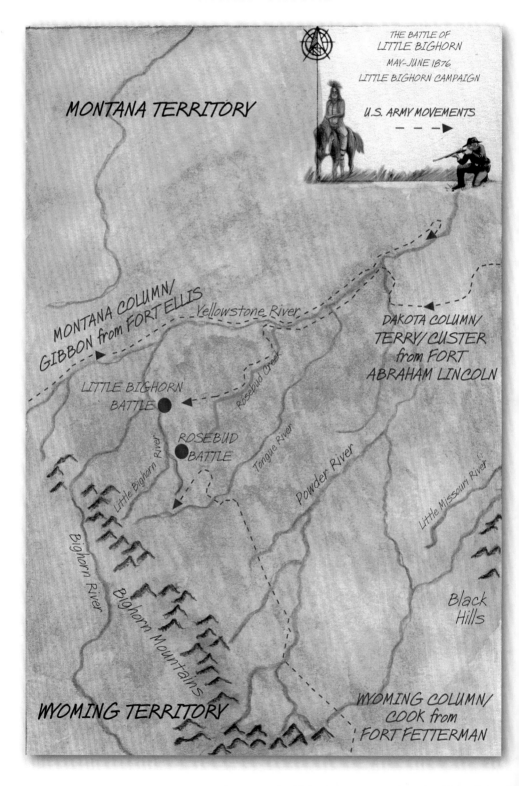

THE BATTLE OF
LITTLE BIGHORN
MAY–JUNE 1876
LITTLE BIGHORN CAMPAIGN

U.S. ARMY MOVEMENTS

MONTANA TERRITORY

MONTANA COLUMN/
GIBBON from FORT ELLIS

Yellowstone River

DAKOTA COLUMN/
TERRY/CUSTER
from FORT
ABRAHAM LINCOLN

Rosebud Creek

LITTLE BIGHORN
BATTLE

ROSEBUD
BATTLE

Little Bighorn River

Tongue River

Powder River

Little Missouri River

Bighorn River

Bighorn Mountains

Black
Hills

WYOMING TERRITORY

WYOMING COLUMN/
COOK from
FORT FETTERMAN

MAPS

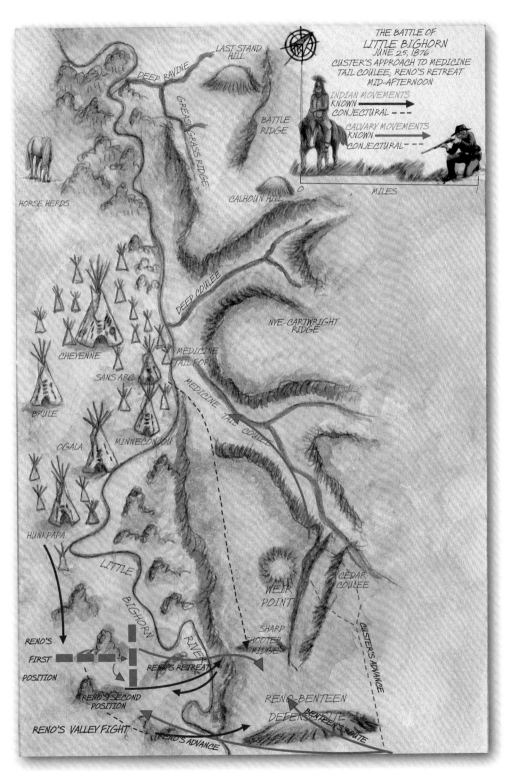

SACRED GROUND

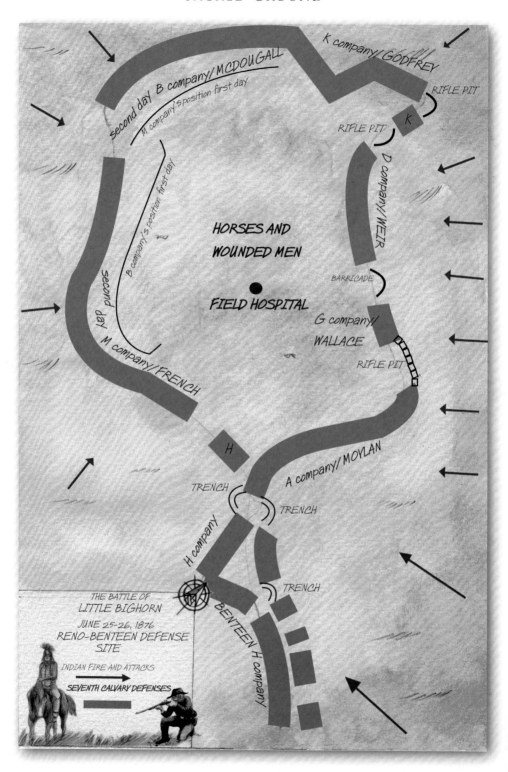

K company/ GODFREY

Second day B company/ MCDOUGALL

M company's position first day

RIFLE PIT

K

RIFLE PIT

B company's position first day

D company/ WEIR

HORSES AND
WOUNDED MEN

FIELD HOSPITAL

BARRICADE

Second day M company/ FRENCH

G company/
WALLACE

RIFLE PIT

H

A company/ MOYLAN

TRENCH

TRENCH

H company

THE BATTLE OF
LITTLE BIGHORN
JUNE 25-26, 1876
RENO-BENTEEN DEFENSE
SITE

INDIAN FIRE AND ATTACKS

SEVENTH CALVARY DEFENSES

TRENCH

BENTEEN H company

MAPS

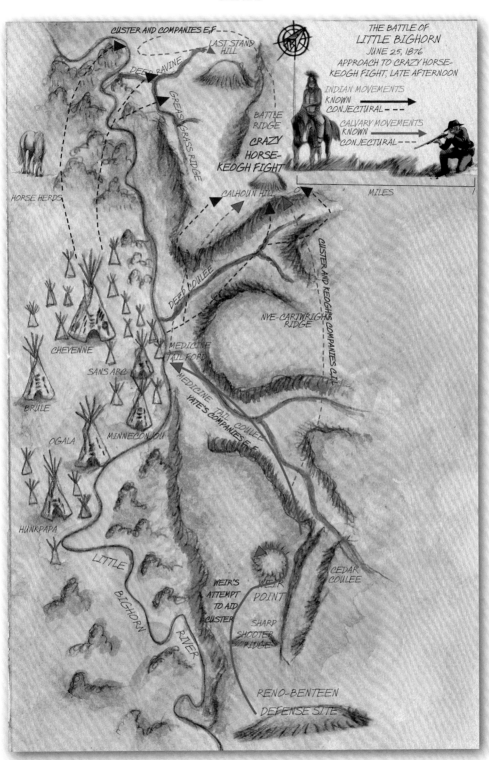

SACRED GROUND

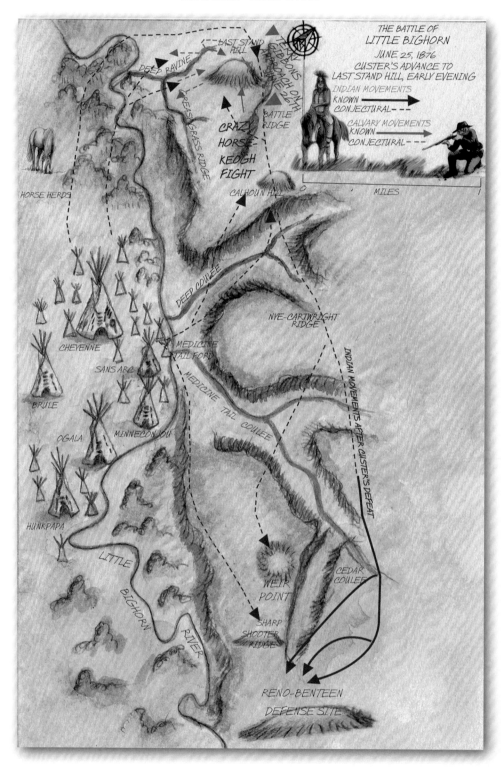

THE BATTLE OF
LITTLE BIGHORN
JUNE 25, 1876
CUSTER'S ADVANCE TO
LAST STAND HILL, EARLY EVENING
INDIAN MOVEMENTS
KNOWN →
CONJECTURAL - - →
CALVARY MOVEMENTS
KNOWN →
CONJECTURAL - - →

0   MILES   1

LAST STAND HILL

TERRY GIBBONS ON APPROACH ON 26TH

DEEP RAVINE

GREASY GRASS RIDGE

CRAZY HORSE-KEOGH FIGHT

BATTLE RIDGE

CALHOUN HILL

HORSE HERDS

DEEP COULEE

NYE-CARTWRIGHT RIDGE

CHEYENNE

SANS ARC

MEDICINE TAIL FORD

MEDICINE TAIL COULEE

BRULE

OGALA

MINNECONJOU

INDIAN MOVEMENTS AFTER CUSTER'S DEFEAT

HUNKPAPA

LITTLE

BIGHORN

RIVER

WEIR POINT

CEDAR COULEE

SHARP SHOOTER RIDGE

RENO-BENTEEN

DEFENSE SITE

Prologue

Historical Overview

"Now we are engaged in a great civil war, testing whether that nation ... can long endure."

—Abraham Lincoln —

From 1861 to 1865 the American nation suffered through a terrible civil war, North versus South. The Northern states, twenty-one in all with a total population of 22.5 million, realized a decided advantage in industrial and manufacturing capability. The eleven states of the Southern Confederacy, with a population of 8 million whites and nearly 4 million black slaves, relied on an economy whose output was 80 percent agricultural. Cotton, rice, and tobacco were the primary crops. There were also four border states (Missouri, Kentucky, Maryland, Delaware) with 2.5 million people, that permitted slavery but never seceded from the union.

The North sent just over 2 million men, about half of the eligible pool, to fight in the war. In the South slave labor could fill the void created back home when young whites were sent to serve. About 750,000 to 850,000 Southern men, representing 75 or 80 percent of the eligible pool, marched off to war. The average soldier on both sides was a native-born citizen, white, and Protestant. He was a farmer or laborer and young, generally between the ages of eighteen and twenty-nine. Twenty-five percent of Northern soldiers were foreign born, mostly Germans or Irishmen. Only 10 percent of Southern soldiers were born outside the United States.

The men were motivated to serve for different reasons: ideology, patriotism, peer or community pressure, a desire for adventure and to prove their masculinity, or the promise of a steady paycheck. They spent most of their time in camp, bored, where discipline was harsh and the food mediocre. They were armed with muzzle-loading, single-shot, rifled muskets that were capable of killing a man at 500 yards and beyond. In the hands of a skilled marksman, these weapons were consistently deadly from 300 yards and closer. A competent infantryman could fire three shots a minute. Because tactics had not fully evolved— at least early on the Napoleonic tradition of close order formations and frontal assaults predominated—they killed each other in droves. The worst loss of life, however, occurred in the camps. Diseases such as measles, chicken pox, mumps, and dysentery swept through and decimated the ranks.

In the end, of the nearly 3 million men who went off to war, Americans all, more than 620,000 never came home. A proportionate number to today's population would be 6 million dead. The country had never, before or since, experienced suffering and loss of this magnitude.

They fought over two controversial issues, state rights and slavery. Southerners viewed their way of life—rural and hugely dependent on slave labor—as time-honored and sacred. Their focus was on loyalty to one's state rather than the union of states. Southerners viewed themselves as inheritors of the legacy of the Founding Fathers: a group of states fighting a tyrannical central government that continually interfered in their internal affairs. The fundamental question became, does a state or group of states have the right to secede from the national union?

On the issue of slavery, while there were certainly some who advocated for the immediate abolition of the institution, the most significant point of conflict was the expansion of slavery into new territories. Politicians spent decades prior to the war debating this question. The challenge was complex because while slavery existed only in the South, racism ran rampant everywhere. Indeed, the full functioning of the Northern economy depended on slave labor as well.

In addition, only one in four white Southerners owned slaves or came from a family that did, so the vast majority of Southern soldiers were not slaveholders. These soldiers probably would not have said they were fighting to preserve slavery per se, but for the right of the South to be left alone. Even most Union soldiers, at least at the start, would not have said they were fighting to end slavery. Their goal was to bring the "ill-behaved rebels" back into the Union. Ultimately, the question of slavery could not be avoided and had to be decided. Slavery was the great American contradiction: how could a nation founded upon and dedicated to the proposition that "all men are created equal" allow human beings to live in bondage?

During the first three days of July 1863, at a small crossroads borough in Pennsylvania called Gettysburg, the Union and Confederate armies met accidentally, but with unspeakable fury. After much hard fighting, the Union prevailed and Robert E. Lee and his Army of Northern Virginia retreated south. The war would last almost two years longer, and there were more casualties after Gettysburg than there had been before, but Gettysburg proved a pivotal turning point.

In 1865, with Northern victory, the two burning issues were resolved: The United States would be one nation and the slaves were freed. The nation turned to the difficult business of rebuilding. The Southern economy was all but destroyed, with a third of its wealth gone. The country entered a period known as Reconstruction, which involved bringing Southern states back into the union and major but largely unsuccessful efforts to integrate freed slaves into society.

The great Union hero of the war, Ulysses S. Grant, was elected president in 1868. Unfortunately, he was a much better soldier than politician. His administration wrestled with the dual challenges of how to manage almost 4 million suddenly free African-Americans and also what to do about America's original inhabitants, the Native Americans of the Plains and other tribes. Those proud people occupied the abundant western reaches ambitious white civilization desired so desperately to dominate.

In 1876, America's centennial year, Rutherford B. Hayes was elected president. With Hayes's inauguration in early 1877 the Grant administration, riddled with incompetence and corruption, came to an ignominious end. Reconstruction also came to an end, with the goal of true equality for African-Americans still a distant dream for a faraway future.

For Native Americans, white efforts to civilize, Christianize, and eventually move them en masse to government-run reservations proved a largely hit-or-miss proposition. Tribal bands that for generations had known nothing but the unrestricted and nomadic life of the horseman, hunter, and gatherer were determined not to submit to the ways of the white man. Even George Custer himself said, "If I were an Indian, I often think I would greatly prefer to cast my lot among those of my people who adhered to the free open plains, rather than submit to the confined limits of the reservation...."

On June 25, 1876, on a small hillside near the Little Bighorn River in southeastern Montana, Custer and his immediate Seventh Cavalry command were wiped out by the angry young manhood of the Lakota Sioux and Northern Cheyenne nations. White America was shocked—the reaction was akin to our own modern-day horror, revulsion, and anger over the 9/11 attacks—and the response included a collective bloodlust for revenge.

While the Battle of the Little Bighorn represented the greatest victory ever by Plains Indians over white soldiers, the event tragically foreshadowed the ultimate end of the Indian way of life. Out of irreconcilable conceptions of land ownership, broken promises, profound mutual lack of trust, and deep hatred and cruelty perpetrated by both races, the whole sad story could only come to a violent and heartbreaking conclusion.

PART ONE

CREATE COMMON PURPOSE

Chapter One

GETTYSBURG

McPHERSON'S RIDGE: IF YOU ARE WITHOUT A COMMON PURPOSE, FIND ONE

"They will attack you in the morning and they will come booming— skirmishers three deep."

—General John Buford—

As dawn broke on Wednesday July 1, 1863, near Gettysburg, Pennsylvania, a Union soldier recorded the weather succinctly in his diary: "Rainy." Scattered showers soon gave way to the certainty of an oppressively hot summer day. Soldiers from the Union Army of the Potomac and the Confederate Army of Northern Virginia, about to initiate what would become the largest battle in the history of the Western Hemisphere, gazed eastward that morning and saw a menacing red sky.

John Buford, cavalry general and the senior Union commander on the scene, saw that same ominous crimson sunrise. But he was mightily distracted by other issues. He was virtually certain that Robert E. Lee and the entire Confederate army sat within easy hitting distance of his badly outnumbered division. Buford's weary troopers looked anxiously to him for leadership. Before the morning was over, Buford would demonstrate that leadership in memorable fashion by executing a plan, formulated overnight, which provided a common purpose for his team.

General Robert E. Lee did indeed reside, with the majority of his mighty host, within a few short miles of Buford. Lee had commenced an invasion of Union territory several weeks earlier. He had a number of strategic objectives in mind when he sought approval in May for his proposed plan from President Jefferson Davis and the Confederate cabinet. Lee wanted to seize the initiative and take control of the tempo of the war from the Yankees. He thought he could shock northern public opinion into clamoring for an end to the conflict. He sought to provide relief for the weary residents of war-ravaged Virginia by moving the scene of action to the enemy's turf. He wanted to feed his hungry soldiers and decrease demands on Southern farmers by foraging in the rich farmlands of Pennsylvania. There was a chance his invasion would relieve pressure on Confederate forces in the western theater of the war, where Union General U. S. Grant was slowly, inexorably moving to take the critically important city of Vicksburg, Mississippi. Finally and most important, Lee wanted a potentially war-ending battle with the Army of the Potomac.

Starting on June 3 from a position on the Rappahannock River near Fredericksburg, Virginia, Lee used the Shenandoah Valley as a corridor and the Blue Ridge Mountains to screen his movement. Lee and his approximately 75,000-man force strode purposefully northward. He had recently reorganized his army from two into three corps. Generals James Longstreet, Richard Ewell, and Ambrose Powell (A. P.) Hill were his three corps commanders (see the Appendix for information on army organization and the orders of battle for the Army of Northern Virginia and the Army of the Potomac).

Lee had also created a Grand Division of cavalry, led by the dashing Major General James Ewell Brown "Jeb" Stuart, with 10,000 veteran horsemen. But the infantry's movement north was ultimately hindered by a serious lack of information as to the enemy's whereabouts. Commencing on June 25, Stuart and three of his five brigades, tasked as always with serving as the "eyes and ears" of the army, went on a misguided and time-consuming ride around the Federal army to the east. Not until late on the second day of the Battle of Gettysburg would Lee, to his profound disappointment, be reunited with Stuart.

Despite the lack of accurate intelligence as they moved into enemy territory, Lee and his soldiers marched ahead with supreme confidence. They held the enemy in low regard. Since Lee had taken command of the Army of Northern Virginia in June 1862, they were together more or less undefeated. They had beaten the Yankees in the Seven Days Battles outside of Richmond and also defeated them at Second Manassas, Virginia. The first Confederate invasion of the North had ended at Antietam, Maryland, in a tactical draw. Fredericksburg had been a bloody massacre in favor of the Rebels. Finally, at Chancellorsville, Virginia, in May 1863, Lee executed his masterstroke. He broke all of the rules when he split his force in the face of a numerically superior enemy and executed a crushing flanking maneuver. The result was costly in manpower but a complete route of the Army of the Potomac.

Lee also had disdain for his Union counterpart General Joseph Hooker, whom the Northern newspapers had famously dubbed "Fighting Joe Hooker." Lee had beaten "Mr. F. J. Hooker," as he contemptuously referred to him, at Chancellorsville. He would beat him again. Lee's soldiers had come through for him time and again and he was heard to say to one of his officers prior to the Gettysburg campaign, "If properly led, these men can do anything."

The Army of the Potomac, on the other hand, was understandably demoralized by its string of setbacks. One commander after another (first George McClellan, then Ambrose Burnside, then Hooker) had failed to get the better of Lee. At the level of the rank and file, there was no lack of confidence in their fighting abilities. The troops simply felt that leadership had let them down. They were basically ready to look ahead to the next fight. But the officer corps was uniformly glum and at the highest levels maneuvered to undermine the current commander, General Hooker.

After complex political machinations, President Lincoln chose Fifth Corps commander George Gordon Meade to lead the army in the Gettysburg campaign. Meade was a West Pointer and engineer, with a volatile temper but cautious in his approach. He was competent and courageous, and would not back down from a challenge. He was appointed to top command only on June 28, so had a perilously steep learning curve.

By this same time in late June, Lee's army had reached the south central part of Pennsylvania (see Gettysburg Map Number One, June 3–July 3, 1863, Lee Invades Pennsylvania, in the List of Maps). Longstreet and Hill—with better than 40,000 infantry— occupied positions near Chambersburg west of South Mountain. Ewell's Second Corps (20,000 soldiers) had moved ahead to threaten the state capital at Harrisburg to the northeast, with one division also moving directly east toward York. Ewell's cavalry eventually reached to within shelling distance of Harrisburg, the farthest north that any of the Confederate forces ventured during the war.

Suddenly, however, Ewell was ordered to turn back and rejoin the main body of the army. Still blind with lack of reliable intelligence from his cavalry arm, Lee had received information from a civilian spy employed by Longstreet that some elements of the Union army might be close at hand. Lee determined that contact with the enemy could possibly occur in the vicinity of Cashtown or Gettysburg. He issued orders late on June 28 to consolidate his units but was clear with his leaders that they were not to initiate a general engagement with Union forces until the rendezvous was complete. Just prior to the battle, therefore, Lee's three corps occupied positions west, north, and east of Gettysburg, poised to move inevitably toward the place of destiny.

Not knowing how close the enemy lurked, Brigadier General John Buford rode into Gettysburg late in the morning on June 30 at the head of 2,950 tired cavalrymen. Buford was the senior Federal commander in the small crossroads town. He represented the vanguard of the Union army as it moved north, cautiously tracking Lee. He had received vague orders from higher command to "cover and protect the front" with his two cavalry brigades.

Buford, like President Abraham Lincoln, was born in Kentucky and raised in Illinois. Also like Lincoln he had relatives who served in the Confederate army. He was a hard-bitten cavalryman who had fought Indians out west. He drove himself and his men relentlessly. A reporter who met him described him as having "a good-natured disposition, but not to be trifled with." Buford had, "a tawny mustache and a little, triangular grey eye, whose expression is determined, not to say sinister." He was independent-minded and an excellent decision maker. Above all, John Buford was a talented professional soldier. He loved to fight and possessed a great tactician's eye for ground.

As Buford sauntered through Gettysburg, he noted the two critical features that made the place important. First, a series of ten roads ran from the town, like the legs of a spider, in every different direction. Historian Stephen Sears stated: "For anyone traveling (or marching) through south central Pennsylvania, it was hard to avoid Gettysburg." Second, cognizant of the military maxim that high ground always gives the defender an advantage, Buford spied several elevated ridges and hills that he knew would be critical geographic features in the combat to come.

To the west of town there were meadows and pastures, open country ideal for farming, and a series of long, low tablelands. These rounded heights contained three ridges running in a north-south direction. The most westerly and prominent of these was Herr Ridge, two miles from town. Next in line, one-and-one-quarter miles from town was McPherson's Ridge. Finally, three-quarters of a mile from Gettysburg and named for the Lutheran Theological Seminary that occupied its heights, lay Seminary Ridge.

Four prominent hills sat south of the town. The nearest was Cemetery Hill, one hundred feet in elevation and one-half mile from Gettysburg. Adjacent to Cemetery Hill to the southeast, three-quarters of a mile from town and higher in elevation, lay the heavily forested Culp's Hill. From Cemetery Hill, the earth sloped gradually downward and directly south forming one-and-one-half-mile-long Cemetery Ridge, where in some places there was no ridge at all as it reached ground level. Cemetery Ridge culminated in a rocky hill called Little Round Top. Farther south was taller, densely wooded Round Top Hill. Some who observed this unique topography likened it to a giant fishhook, with Cemetery and Culp's hills as the barb, Cemetery Ridge as the long shank, and the Round Tops as the eye of the hook (see Gettysburg Map Number Two, July 1, 1863, Morning and Afternoon).

Buford gained additional information on June 30 from unnerved citizens in Gettysburg. They excitedly reported the passage of a large body of Confederate troops headed eastward through town four days earlier, and the approach of additional elements from the west. Buford sought confirming intelligence by establishing numerous outposts several miles outside of town in a broad crescent from the northeast to the southwest. He carefully considered the reports of his scouts to the west along Chambersburg Pike (one of Gettysburg's network of roads that ran into town from the northwest) who had sighted Confederate infantry on the roadway in the distance earlier in the day on June 30. The scouts had also seen abundant enemy campfires that night toward Cashtown, eight miles from town to the northwest and also adjacent to Chambersburg Pike. Finally, reports came in warning of a large

Confederate force to the north as well, which was moving ominously in the direction of Gettysburg.

Buford needed a plan, and quickly. He had only sketchy guidance from high command. He had not seen this place before today. He knew he potentially faced a vastly superior enemy force. His men looked to him as they always had for confident leadership in a critical moment. His team needed direction and purpose. As the hours unfolded and the intelligence came in, Buford became determined to defend the town at all costs. His mission and the message he communicated to his men were simple: we will fight here until help arrives.

Buford's plans were in place as he waited to meet the Rebels, and for the arrival of infantry reinforcements under First Corps commander Major General John Reynolds. Buford wrote after the battle, "By daylight of July 1, I had gained positive information of the enemy's position and movements, and my arrangements were made for entertaining him until General Reynolds could reach the scene." Buford had, in short, created a common purpose for his team.

Specifically, Buford decided to fight using a defense in depth, and he delivered orders to that effect. The ridgelines to the west would allow him to conduct a delaying action with his cavalry dismounted. He would use his technology advantage in the form of single-shot breech loading carbines, which produced better than twice the rate of fire of the ponderous muzzle-loaders carried by the Confederate infantry. He deployed soldiers north of town as well as a sizeable group at Herr Ridge to the west. He positioned the bulk of his force closer to town astride Chambersburg Pike at McPherson's Ridge.

Despite the soundness of the battle plan and his determined decision to confront the enemy and impede his progress, Buford was as anxious on the evening of June 30 as his staff had ever seen him. He was unsure when help would arrive. When Colonel Thomas Devin, one of his brigade commanders, said that he would be able to handle any Rebel advance within the next twenty-four hours Buford became agitated. One can imagine the fire in his "triangular grey eye" as he replied, "No, you won't. They will attack you in the morning and they will come booming—skirmishers three deep. You will have to fight like the devil until supports arrive."

As for the highly regarded Major General John Reynolds and his First Corps of Union infantry, they too were poised to descend on Gettysburg on July 1 from their encampment near Marsh Creek five miles south of town (one of the ironies of Gettysburg is that Union troops approached from the south, while some Confederate units came from the north). Meade had designated Reynolds as a "wing commander," with responsibility not only for his own First Corps, but for Third and Eleventh Corps as well.

Over the last couple of days, all seven of Meade's corps (approximately 95,000 troops) had moved in parallel columns generally northward. Reynolds and his 11,500 First Corps soldiers were closest to Gettysburg. At 4 a.m. on July 1, Reynolds received orders from Meade's headquarters in Taneytown, fourteen miles south of Gettysburg, to advance north up the Emmitsburg Road to support Buford. With no particular reason to feel urgency, Reynolds allowed his men to sleep until sunrise. He intended to be in motion toward Gettysburg by 8 a.m.

What Reynolds could not have known was that as the sun came up, by 5 a.m., Harry Heth's division of Rebel infantry from A. P. Hill's Third Corps was already making its way southeast along the Chambersburg Pike toward town. They aimed to see what enemies might lie ahead, suspecting at best they would face local militia. From the high cupola of the Lutheran Seminary at 7 a.m., a Union signalman spotted Heth's troops in the distance and sent word to Buford. The grizzled Kentuckian hesitated to commit his troops fully either north or west until he had more information on the precise disposition and strength of the enemy.

At virtually the same moment in the hazy morning light further west, Illinois cavalrymen on duty at Herr Ridge also saw crimson Rebel battle flags approaching. They notified their detail commander, Lieutenant Marcellus Jones, who confirmed the sighting and sent word back to regimental headquarters. At 7:30 a.m. Jones dismounted and borrowed a carbine from one of the enlisted men. The young officer rested the weapon on a wooden fence and let loose a single, harmless round toward an enemy officer on horseback in the distance. Thus began the Battle of Gettysburg.

Precisely as Buford predicted, once under fire, the Confederate infantry came aggressively forward with a skirmish line three deep. Confederate artillery responded to the initial shots from the Union pickets, expecting them to scatter like the local militia they were supposed to be. But as resistance intensified from the blue-clad riflemen General Heth realized he was in for a fight. The Yankee cavalry had dismounted with every fourth man moving to the rear to hold the horses. The rapid-fire carbines gave the initial impression that Heth might be opposed by a potentially larger force, rather than vastly outnumbered cavalry.

Buford, now fully committed to this fight to the west, had posted 550 men to defend Herr Ridge. He stationed his main body at McPherson's Ridge, one brigade north of the Chambersburg Pike and one brigade south. He deployed his horse artillery battery (six guns) right next to the roadway so as to provide a clear shot straight at the enemy.

Buford's tactical purpose was to force Heth to take the time to deploy his infantry from column into line formation. In this, Buford succeeded. Heth halted his men and moved his two lead brigades into line, an exercise that required ninety precious minutes to complete. At around 9 a.m., fully arrayed for battle, the gray host finally advanced against Herr Ridge. There were 2,900 Confederates in line almost a mile from end-to-end. Buford had bought the critical time he needed, and his advance units now conducted a fighting withdrawal to the stronger line of defense at McPherson's Ridge.

At this same time, John Reynolds rode north with the lead division of his First Corps. He was still three miles from Gettysburg, with gunfire audible in the distance, when he received an urgent message from his friend Buford. The enemy was advancing in force along the Chambersburg Pike. A full-scale firefight was underway. Reynolds told his men to hurry forward, and he instantly galloped off with a few staffers to reach the scene as quickly as possible.

As he rode rapidly through Gettysburg, Reynolds, also with a veteran soldier's eye, took note of all the same topography that had made such an impression on Buford the day before. Once he spied Buford at his headquarters on McPherson's Ridge, Reynolds shouted out, "What's the matter, John?" Buford responded, "There's the devil to pay." He quickly briefed his superior officer. Reynolds recognized the significance of the confluence of roads and the nearby ridges and hills. He liked the defensive ground Buford had chosen.

Reynolds told Buford to continue the fight, and that the infantry was close at hand. Reynolds dispatched a rider to Meade at Taneytown to tell him "the enemy were coming on in strong force, and that he was afraid they would get the heights on the other side of town before he could; that he would fight them all through the town, however, and keep them back as long as possible." With that, Reynolds galloped back south to urge his infantry forward.

Reynolds soon reached the lead division and personally hurried his blue-clad warriors into town. They moved off the Emmitsburg Road, past Seminary Ridge and into position on McPherson's Ridge in relief of Buford's beleaguered cavalrymen. Reynolds rapidly directed one brigade to the right and the other to the left. Time was of the essence. It was 10 a.m. Buford's men were at the end of their endurance, and Confederate riflemen poured over the high ground in front of them.

In a fateful personal decision, Reynolds deliberately placed himself in the eye of the storm. He felt no doubt that his men needed to see him at this moment and to feel the inspiring effect of his own physical courage. He sat his horse amidst the terrible combat that swirled about him. He turned in his saddle to the troops behind him and shouted, "Forward, forward men! Drive those fellows out of that! Forward! For

God's sake forward!" Those were his last words. At that moment, he toppled from his horse and lay still on the ground. His orderly wrote later, "a Minnie ball struck him in the back of the neck, and he fell from his horse dead. He never spoke a word, or moved a muscle after he was struck. I have seen many man [sic] killed in action but never saw a ball do its work so *instantly* as did the ball which struck General Reynolds." Despite Reynolds' sudden demise, his support of Buford in the critical choice of ground was hugely important.

After continued fierce fighting at McPherson's Ridge, Confederate forces temporarily withdrew to Herr Ridge to regroup. The Yankees had held the line for now. There was a lull in the combat, but in the meantime fresh units from both armies continued to pour into the area in a steady stream. Most significantly, lead elements of Richard Ewell's Confederate Second Corps arrived from the north in the early afternoon. Union troops moved rapidly through town to meet Ewell but, after much ebb and flow, the Yanks were outnumbered and outfought. Lee had a temporary advantage and, though he had not wanted to fight at this time or in this place, now committed all of his available forces to the effort.

As the day wore on with the action moving back and forth, the sheer weight of the Confederate onslaught from both the west and now the north eventually caused Union units to break and retreat in chaos through the town. Fortunately, a contingent of the Eleventh Corps of the Union army moving toward Gettysburg—under prescient orders delivered that morning from Reynolds—had begun to fortify the critical high ground of Cemetery Hill. It was at Cemetery Hill that the retreating Union soldiers regained their composure late in the afternoon, turned again to face the enemy, and began to dig in. They would never be dislodged from those positions.

The Confederates won the first day of the Battle of Gettysburg. But the Yankees held the high ground, thanks to John Buford. His courageous decision making ensured that the ultimate outcome, whatever it may be, would be determined on this field.

As the senior leader on the scene on June 30, Buford faced great uncertainty. Direction from on high was sketchy. He knew he needed a plan, and quickly. He gathered relevant data through his own powers of observation and from other sources, both internal and external. He relied on his own highly developed military sixth sense and his veteran team. He realized that if he could delay the Confederates west and north of town he might buy sufficient time for Union reinforcements to secure the hills to the south. Only then was victory possible. He did not need someone to help him decide, and he knew his hard-fighting cavalrymen looked only to him for the answer. The plan was simple and straightforward: Fight a delaying action until help arrives.

What Buford asked his men to do was risky and difficult, but achievable. They may not have liked it and probably grumbled, as soldiers always do, but they knew their mission. What John Buford gave them, when they needed it most, was a common purpose.

★ ★ CASE STUDY ★ ★

JACK WELCH AND GENERAL ELECTRIC: NUMBER ONE OR NUMBER TWO—FIX, SELL OR CLOSE

On April 1, 1981, John Francis "Jack" Welch Jr. became the youngest chairman and CEO in the history of the General Electric Corporation. Born in 1935, Welch was an engineer with a Ph.D. who toiled for two decades at GE before ascending to the top job. He had a reputation as an informal maverick who achieved results. During his twenty-year run at the helm of this multifaceted conglomerate, GE's revenues improved from $27 billion to $130 billion. Market value jumped from $12 billion to $410 billion. Welch presided over more than 600 acquisitions and aggressively pushed GE to enter newly emerging markets. By the end of Welch's tenure, GE was the largest and most valuable company in the world. In 1999 Welch was named "Manager of the 20th Century" by *Fortune* magazine. Many of the business methodologies and leadership concepts he espoused continue to be emulated by corporate executives the world over.

Did Welch accomplish all this on the basis of a sweet and warm personality? No. Did he achieve consistently stellar results by establishing a common purpose for his team? Yes.

General Electric was founded by the famed inventor Thomas Edison. Edison was noted for the prolific and eclectic variety of his inventions and innovations, including the phonograph, incandescent electric lamp, and wide-spread electric power generation and distribution. In 1890 Edison established the Edison General Electric Company to consolidate his varied business interests. Two years later Edison merged his company with a competitor called the Thomson-Houston Company to form General Electric. By 1896 GE was one of twelve original companies listed on the Dow Jones Industrial Average, and the only one still listed to this day.

Over time GE grew into a behemoth with a staggering array of functional businesses and a reputation for creativity and innovation, but also for bureaucracy. GE produced everything from the first electric toaster to the first electric locomotive. The portfolio came to include businesses as varied as radio and television, plastics, and aviation technology. By the time Jack Welch took over, GE contained forty-two strategic business units: appliances, lighting, transportation, motors, medical materials, industrial electronics, aerospace, financial and information services, and more.

The profound challenge for Welch became how to develop a common vision for such seemingly disparate disciplines. He said, "We were in so many different businesses. In those days, if you were in a business that was profitable, that was good enough reason to stay in it. Changing the game, getting out of low-margin, low-growth businesses and moving into high-margin, high-growth global businesses was not a priority. At that time, no one in or outside the company perceived a crisis. GE was an American icon...."

In December 1981, eight months into his new job as CEO, Welch delivered a message to Wall Street analysts around his vision for GE. He acknowledged later that it "was a bomb." He said, "At the end, the reaction in the room made it clear that this crowd thought they were getting more hot air than substance." Nevertheless, the blueprint Welch outlined that day became the common purpose and rallying cry for GE throughout his storied tenure.

In his speech Welch quoted at length from a letter to the editor of *Fortune* magazine written by a Bendix executive on the subject of strategic planning. Interestingly, that letter cited the nineteenth-century German military theorist Karl Von Clausewitz, who wrote the classic book *On War,* in making an express comparison between the challenges faced by war and business planners. As quoted by Welch, the letter summed up Clausewitz: "'Men could not reduce strategy to formula. Detailed planning necessarily failed, due to inevitable frictions encountered: chance events, imperfections in execution, and the independent will of the opposition. Instead, the human elements were paramount: leadership, morale, and the almost instinctive savvy of the best generals.

"'The Prussian general staff.... perfected these concepts in practice. They did not expect a plan of operations to survive beyond first contact with the enemy. They set only the broadest of objectives and emphasized seizing unforeseen opportunities as they arose.... *Strategy was not a lengthy action plan. It was the evolution of a central idea through continually changing circumstances* [emphasis added by Welch].'"

The letter, and Welch, went on to assert, "'Business and war may differ in objectives and codes of conduct. But both involve facing the independent will of other parties. Any cookbook approach is powerless to cope with independent will, or with the unfolding situations of the real world.'"

At that time, Welch believed inflation would slow worldwide economic growth in the decade of the '80s. He tied the concept of developing a central idea vs. a detailed strategy into his worldview by saying: "The winners in this slow-growth environment will be those who search out and participate in the real growth industries and insist upon being number one or number two in every business they are in—the number one or number two leanest, lowest-cost, worldwide producers of quality goods and services or those who have clear technological edge, a clear advantage in a market niche."

Welch also said, "... On the other hand, where we are not number one or number two, and don't have or can't see a route to a technological edge, we have got to ask ourselves [management guru] Peter Drucker's very tough question: 'If you weren't already in the business, would you enter it today? And if the answer is no, face into that second difficult question: What are you going to do about it?'" Welch's simple ultimatum was that those businesses would be fixed, sold, or closed.

Welch concluded, "We believe this central idea—being number one or number two—more than an objective—a requirement—will give us a set of businesses which will be unique in the world business equation at the end of this decade." Welch described the number one or number two idea as the "hard" message, but also believed GE needed to incorporate "soft" concepts (a sense of reality, quality, excellence, and the human element) into its culture in order to succeed over time. Indeed, he became well known for his intense focus and abundant time spent on developing talent. Welch desired to cut through bureaucracy, eliminate the sense of comfort and entitlement that came with the notion that profitability was good enough, but to also give employees free reign—in the spirit of Thomas Edison—to innovate, try different things, and learn from mistakes.

Welch did his best to sell the idea: "... I repeated the No. 1 or No. 2 message over and over again until I nearly gagged on the words.... The organization had to see every management action aligned with the vision." But while the concept passed the simplicity test, and while most employees understood it and agreed to it intellectually, the emotional leap was a more difficult process. Those who were not in a top-performing business worried incessantly.

Welch spent a good deal of time over the next five years earning the nickname "Neutron Jack" (he left buildings intact but the people were gone). One quarter of GE's employees left the company during this period, 118,000 in total. Of that number, 37,000 people worked for businesses that were sold. As Welch himself acknowledged, "The turmoil, angst, and confusion were everywhere."

But Welch stuck to the message, underscoring the reality that people don't necessarily need to like or agree with the common purpose as long as they understand it. Welch admitted the strategy was not perfect. Some businesses realized no particular competitive advantage in being one or two, especially those that were highly commoditized. Some huge businesses with global reach, such as financial services, might still be worth holding even if not one or two. Some people simply objected to Welch's style as he led the effort, asserting he was demanding and abrasive.

Yet Jack Welch, like him or not, boldly led GE through a golden era of growth and profitability almost unmatched in the annals of corporate America. He did it by finding and clearly outlining a simple but powerful vision, early in his tenure, that guided his thinking and actions every day. His team's common purpose—one or two in everything we do, or fix, sell, or close—represented the evolution not of a complex strategy but rather a clear central idea that survived through continually changing circumstances over two full decades.

Leadership Lesson One:

IF YOU ARE WITHOUT A COMMON PURPOSE, FIND ONE

Teams without common purpose are rudderless and have no hope of achieving at a high level over time. If you are a leader, ask yourself, does my team have a common purpose? If you are unsure or the answer is no, find a common purpose and communicate it soon.

I can speak to the importance of this fundamental lesson from personal experience. In a twenty-five-year career that has spanned military service, legal practice, and business (I have been an entrepreneur and worked for a combined sixteen years at the Target Corporation and then Best Buy), I have observed teams without a common purpose. I have been a member of teams without a common purpose. I have been the leader—shame on me—of teams without a common purpose. Those teams do not work.

In contrast, teams that know with confidence what they are about can become juggernauts. They are led by men and women who make a point of finding a common purpose and sticking with it.

Perhaps my favorite and most memorable personal example of a common purpose was the creed that bound me and my fellow infantry Marines: "To seek out, close with, and destroy our enemy, through fire and maneuver." No ambiguity there. Not coincidentally, the U.S. Marine Corps is by far and away the best team with which I have ever been associated.

Common purpose doesn't have to be complex or blindingly original. To the contrary, it should be simple and reflect common sense. It does not have to come from on high, although it might. It can come from you.

The purpose can be risky: John Buford's plan involved risk. The purpose can be edgy: Jack Welch's plan had edge. Not everyone needs to like the message. Some of John Buford's men lost their lives executing against his purpose. Many of Jack Welch's employees lost their jobs as an outcome of his purpose. Nevertheless, the ultimate result in both cases was victory.

Use your own business savvy in the discovery process. Read and study. Consult with your team and other valued advisors. Take advantage of both internal and external resources. But in the end, you must find a purpose that is compelling and makes sense for your team. You must communicate that purpose until you nearly "gag on the words." You must stick with the message. Finally, follow through to make sure that your team acts to carry out that purpose. You may not be named "Manager of the Century," but you will see improved business results.

Chapter Two

LITTLE BIGHORN

THE INDIAN VILLAGE: A UNIFIED VISION MUST PERMEATE THE TEAM

"I would rather die an Indian than live a white man."

—Sitting Bull—

In late June of 1876, a band of perhaps 7,000 Plains Indians, with 1,500 to 2,000 warriors, gathered near the Little Bighorn River in southeastern Montana Territory. They came to the lush valley of this clear and cold waterway, which they knew as the Greasy Grass, under the leadership of the great and charismatic Hunkpapa Sioux chief Sitting Bull.

In his book *Lakota Noon: The Indian Narrative of Custer's Defeat*, historian Gregory Michno described Sitting Bull's encampment early in the day of June 25 (see Little Bighorn Map Number One, The Indian Village):

"The scene was reminiscent of a thousand similar mornings. The east-facing lodge openings admitted arrows of light from the red-orange sun making its appearance over the bluffs. A few wandering dogs yipped here and there, rummaging for scraps of food. Ponies grazed on the luxuriant grasses, watched over by a few sleepy boys. Early risers began to cook their breakfasts.... There would be nothing extraordinary about this image were it not for the fact that this was an unusually large combined village of Lakota and Cheyenne, mostly, currently engaged in a struggle for the continued existence of their way of life. Although such was the case, the villagers had no inclination that today would be their Armageddon, their Götterdämmerung. Realization comes only long afterward, with the benefit of hindsight, when chroniclers peer through elegiacal mists to ascribe hours and minutes of universal import to events that participants could only view as just another day. As they carried on with routine decisions—whether to sleep a little while longer, to go fishing, to round up the ponies, to dig for some wild turnips—an entire way of life was about to come to balance on the fulcrum of this one day."

The saga of Sitting Bull and the events leading up to June 25 and the Battle of the Little Bighorn provides a classic historical example of a leader who developed a unified vision that permeated his team. Sitting Bull had sent word via messengers in the spring to any agency Indians (those who lived on the reservation) to come join him on the Rosebud River. Non-treaty Indians (those who still roamed free) were of course welcome as well. From the most veteran chieftain down to the last young, untested warrior, Sitting Bull's people knew their mission: They must fight the white man to defend their homelands and the continued existence of their way of life.

Native Americans and whites had clashed over numerous issues for hundreds of years, from the time of the arrival of Christopher Columbus in the New World in 1492. One of the critical points of contention and cultural difference became two widely divergent opinions about land ownership. To the Indian, land could only be held in common by the tribe. To the Indian the land provided not only subsistence but gave spiritual meaning to his very existence on the earth. The Indian was a part of the land, the land a part of him. The Iroquois traditionally referred to the land as their Mother, who therefore could not possibly be bought or sold. One could not own the land any more than one could own the air.

For whites, who held strict and legalistic views of property, this idea was unfathomable. To whites, land ownership for an individual was a civil right. The person who legally paid for and held title to land had the right to work it, protect it, and dispose of it as he pleased. Whites regarded the Indian point of view as a serious hindrance to the very necessary work of developing the American continent to its fullest potential. In 1817, President James Monroe wrote, "The hunter or savage state requires a greater extent of territory to sustain it, than is compatible with the progress and just claims of civilized life ... and must yield to it."

Explosive white population growth coupled with the idea of the inevitability of westward development led to incredible pressure on Native peoples. White America had grown from a population of 4 million colonists occupying a relatively narrow strip of land on the Atlantic coast in 1789, the year George Washington assumed the presidency, to more than 12 million by the time of Andrew Jackson's ascendency to the White House in 1829. A desperate need for more land was pressing.

In addition, the prevailing mindset of the day was that Native people were morally inferior, lacking the energy and instinct for progress, and that they had no claim to stand in the way of developing civilization. The idea of "Manifest Destiny" was articulated as early as 1845 in an editorial in the New York *Democratic Review,* which said it is "our manifest destiny to overspread the continent allotted by Providence for the free development of our yearly multiplying millions." Senator John C. Calhoun of South Carolina stated, "Our great mission is to occupy this vast (continental) domain." Ambitious white adventurers, opportunists and frontiersmen looked west in search of riches and unbounded freedom. But the original inhabitants of that immense, abundant, breathtaking territory stood squarely in their way.

By the middle 1800s, the Native American tribes known as the Plains Indians came to occupy the broad belt of land west of what we now call the Midwest all the way to the Rocky Mountains, and from the Canadian border deep into the desert Southwest. The two primary Plains tribes that fought Custer's Seventh Cavalry at the Little Bighorn were the Lakota Sioux and Northern Cheyenne. There were also a small handful of Arapaho participants among Sitting Bull's warriors. Custer employed Indian scouts of the Crow and Arikara (also known as Ree) tribes, who were dread enemies of the Sioux and Cheyenne. So, in a civil war of sorts, Indians actually fought Indians at the Battle of the Little Bighorn.

The Sioux, originally known as Dakota, Nakota, or Lakota depending on their region and dialect, were far and away the largest and most powerful tribe. Whites took to calling this nation of people Sioux, a shortening of the North American French word "nadoues-sioux," which in turn derived from the Ojibway Indian word "notow-essiwak," which means "little snakes." Many Sioux detested the name but, ultimately, at least some came to answer to it. The earliest known home of the Sioux was located in what are now southern Minnesota, northeastern Iowa, and northwestern Wisconsin. Exactly when the Sioux began to move to the Great Plains is unknown, but it was at some point during the second half of the eighteenth century. The transition from a farming and woodland hunting people to nomadic buffalo hunters was swift and dramatic.

The Sioux dominated an enormous territory from Minnesota to the Yellowstone River in the west and Canada to the Platte River in the south. Generally, the Dakota occupied the eastern, the Nakota a small portion of the central, and the Lakota the western reaches of the empire. Altogether, the Sioux probably numbered between twenty and twenty-five thousand people at the height of their power.

The main body of the Sioux was the Teton, who were of the western or Lakota grouping. The Teton in turn were broken into seven main tribes: Hunkpapa (Sitting Bull's branch), Oglala (Crazy

Horse's branch), Blackfeet, Brule, Miniconjou, Sans Arc, and Two Kettle. Of these seven divisions the Oglala was the most important and prestigious. The Sioux, of whatever division or branch, were widely known for their unsurpassed courage and resourcefulness in war and raiding, and admired as well for the sophistication of their social and religious rites.

The brethren and allies of the Sioux were the Cheyenne. The name Cheyenne comes from the Teton Sioux "Shahiyena," which means "People of Alien Speech." The Cheyenne originated from what is now Minnesota. They eventually migrated to North Dakota sometime in the late seventeenth century where they continued to live a generally agricultural existence. From there, over time, they were driven further west by none other than the Sioux, and ended up first in the Black Hills and ultimately near the upper branches of the Platte River.

In 1825 the Cheyenne divided into northern and southern nations, with the southern Cheyenne moving to the Arkansas River region of Colorado. The northern Cheyenne stayed put at the headwaters of the Platte and Yellowstone Rivers. By this time, the Cheyenne were expert horsemen and buffalo hunters. After an ongoing period of conflict the Cheyenne made peace with the Sioux shortly after the Cheyenne divided, and the two tribes remained reasonably friendly going forward. There were probably 3,000 to 3,500 members of the Cheyenne nation at its height. Like the Sioux, the Cheyenne were known as superb and fearsome warriors.

Indeed, Plains Indian males were bred from a very early age to be warriors. Sioux boys, for example, played a game called "throwing them off their horses." The boys chose sides, stripped naked, and charged at each other, with the objective of tossing another boy off his pony. Once on the ground, that boy was "dead" and out of the game. The boys may have been bruised (both physically and emotionally) after the game, but over time they developed collectively into the warrior horsemen that Army General George Crook called "the greatest light cavalry in the world."

The highest prestige for a Plains Indian came through raiding and war. War was not a game, but a very serious matter. Killing, however, was generally not the point. True bravery was demonstrated through "counting coup" (from the French word for "blow"), which involved either touching or striking an enemy, whether dead or alive, with a hand or a weapon. The most meaningful accomplishment was to count coup within an enemy camp. Whoever counted coup most frequently and with the greatest bravado and daring was the best warrior and the hero of the battle. (Wouldn't war be less costly if this were the standard for battlefield courage everywhere?)

Plains Indians were also perfectly capable of conducting war in a lethal manner if necessary, and in the heat of a pitched battle relied on such weapons as bows and arrows, lances, knives, clubs, and tomahawks. These weapons were still in use by the time of the Battle of the Little Bighorn in 1876, but as early as the 1850s the rifle (especially late-model repeaters) had begun to replace the bow and arrow as the most desirable weapon for fighting from horseback or at long range. Despite being armed with rifles, most Indians failed to develop into particularly effective marksmen.

Sioux and Cheyenne military tactics consisted of raiding, dividing of forces, hit and run, and decoy and ambush techniques. These methods would today be described as guerilla or asymmetrical warfare. The Indians did not fight the kind of set-piece battles that had characterized the combat of the American Civil War, not only because they had no formal command structure that could provide coordinated discipline, but also because they could not afford to take serious losses. They also used their intimate knowledge of terrain to their profound advantage. They struck when and where they wanted, then drifted away with lookouts posted to cover their back trails. If pursued, they would disintegrate into smaller groups and move into rocky territory where they could not be tracked. Army cavalrymen experienced endless frustration as they rode their mounts to exhaustion in fruitless pursuit of a shadowy enemy. These indirect guerilla tactics were particularly maddening—just as they were with the stealthy Viet Cong during the Vietnam War and are with the elusive terrorists of today—to American soldiers trained in the classical methodologies of war.

While white soldiers could frequently bring superior numbers and firepower to bear, they were generally seriously mismatched on an individual level. The army downsized massively after the Civil War; by the early 1870s, there were barely 25,000 men in service. Only a small number of these soldiers, a few thousand at best, served on the Western frontier. They came from all levels of society. Many were uneducated, could not get a job in the civilian sector, or were foreigners who did not speak English. Some were outright criminals or chronic deserters. They were poorly fed, equipped, and trained. They were often inept horsemen and terrible marksmen. They did not match up well man against man versus their Plains Indian opponents who were to the saddle, the hunt, and warfare born. The Sioux and Cheyenne proved a ghostly and formidable enemy.

These two famous tribes, the Sioux and the Cheyenne—with their prowess as warriors, colorful history, and proud traditions—came together in massive numbers to the valley of the Little Bighorn in the summer of 1876. They gathered to protect themselves and their free-roaming way of life in defiant response to an order from the U.S. government in late 1875 that directed all Indians nationwide who had not already done so to surrender to the confinement of reservations by January 31, 1876. They gathered, unified in their purpose, at the behest of one man, the great and magnetic Sioux chieftain Sitting Bull.

Sitting Bull was probably born in 1831 on the Grand River in South Dakota, and he would have been forty-five years old at the time of the Little Bighorn battle. He came into life the scion of a prestigious Hunkpapa family. He was known as Jumping Badger as a boy. He went hunting buffalo for the first time at age ten, and at fourteen participated in his first raid against the hated Crow enemy, after which his father honored him by naming him Sitting Bull. His skill as a hunter and warrior only increased as he grew older.

He lived in a society that valued and cultivated four critical traits in its men: bravery, fortitude, generosity, and wisdom. Over time Sitting Bull came to represent the very embodiment of these attributes in the minds of his people. Many believed in Sitting Bull as a Wichasha Wikan, or holy man. It was said he had the gift of prophesy, and saw things in dreams and visions that came true. Prior to the Little Bighorn battle, he spoke of a dream in which white soldiers who were upside down on their horses came falling out of the sky in great numbers into an Indian encampment. This dramatic vision foretold of a great victory for the Sioux.

The Sioux did not compartmentalize their spiritual world and had no word for religion. Instead, their beliefs and rituals permeated all dimensions of life at all times. Sitting Bull not only understood the beliefs and rituals of his culture, but also comprehended the natural phenomena out of which they arose. He developed a deep kinship with the natural world and an understanding of how it worked. He communed on an ongoing basis with Wakan Tanka, the omniscient, ubiquitous, spiritually holistic force that ran through all things. He spent much time in meditation and contemplation concerning how best to use his special powers to help his people.

Sitting Bull was, therefore, the rarest of combinations in Sioux culture: a superbly brave and skillful warrior, and a deeply mystical and visionary holy man. He nevertheless made his way in life in humble fashion, foregoing the relative comforts of the material world that his skill as hunter and warrior and prestigious place in the tribe entitled him to enjoy. He behaved like a common man in his interpersonal relations. He made no show of his high rank or exalted status. He was particularly kind and attentive to those who were not at the top of the tribal hierarchy: women, children, and the elderly. The great chief was generally taciturn but on occasion spoke extensively and openly. He had a deep bass voice that commanded attention, and he was even known for his singing and composing. He was a polite listener who never interrupted another who was speaking. Like Abraham Lincoln, he was good-humored and laughed heartily once in a while, but he was also known to withdraw into periods of quietness and even depression.

Sitting Bull's personal life was turbulent and sad. He became married for the first time in 1851 to a woman probably named Light Hair. Light Hair gave Sitting Bull a son, but she died in childbirth and the boy in turn died of disease at age four. Sitting Bull subsequently took two spouses—multiple wives being acceptable in Sioux society—who were named Snow-on-Her and Red Woman. Snow-on-Her gave him two daughters, and Red Woman a son. Unfortunately, the two women jealously detested one another and bickered constantly. Sometime in the late 1860s, Sitting Bull decided he could no longer tolerate the incessant arguing. He judged Snow-on-Her to be mostly to blame, so banished her from the tipi. Red Woman died in 1871, leaving Sitting Bull as a single parent with three children in his care. In 1872, he again took two wives, who were siblings named Four Robes and Seen-by-the-Nation. These two women got along in fine sisterly fashion, and this arrangement lasted until Sitting Bull's death in 1890.

As with any generally revered leader, in any time or place, Sitting Bull knew the support and love of many but also had serious detractors. Ultimately, whether beloved or not, Sitting Bull has come to be seen as the towering figure in the history of the Sioux nation. His people regarded him as the very embodiment of Indian resistance to the white man, known as "wasichu," and listened carefully when he spoke. He had been heard to say, "The white people are wicked."

In 1876, Sitting Bull was at the height of his power and influence. When the U.S. government issued its ultimatum commanding Indians to move to the reservation by January 31, the order was largely ignored. Sitting Bull knew there was little food at the agencies and also thought it unlikely that the government would send soldiers to enforce the edict.

The situation changed when in March a band of mostly Cheyenne—a peaceful group led by Chief Old Bear—was attacked by white cavalry as the Indians encamped along the Powder River in southern Montana. The Indians fought back and casualties were light, but the white soldiers succeeded in burning the village. Old Bear led his followers along the Powder until they reached the small camp of the Oglala Sioux chieftain Crazy Horse. These combined villages then rode to Sitting Bull's camp to the northeast.

The Sioux and the Cheyenne had an alliance and, while Sitting Bull initially advocated for peace—or at least avoidance of conflict—he also made it clear that his people would fight to defend themselves and their allies. Their home territories, their families, and their way of life would not be compromised. Sitting Bull had been known to say "I would rather die an Indian than live a white man." Sitting Bull's message of defiant self-determination spread rapidly among Native populations who would be inspired to connect with him.

In the spring, the increasingly large group of Cheyenne and Oglala and Hunkpapa Sioux moved farther to the northwest. They were joined in the journey by additional free-roaming bands including, among others, more Cheyenne, Minneconjous, Sans Arc, Blackfeet, Santees, and Yanktons. By early summer, there were 500 lodges and perhaps 1,000 warriors, with many more moving to unite in the cause.

In particular, young warriors were eager to preserve their free way of life and show off their prowess in battle with the wasichu. They were especially motivated and inspired by stories they had heard of the magical leader with the simple but compelling message: We will fight to defend our homelands and our way of life. They were told Sitting Bull was not just an extraordinary warrior chieftain but communed with Wakan Tanka and could see the future. Who would not want to follow such a man?

By late June, the massive gathering had moved to an encampment in the valley of the Greasy Grass. There, on June 25, the powerful vision that brought them together would be severely tested by the wasichu.

★ ★ CASE STUDY ★ ★

MAGIC JOHNSON ENTERPRISES: WE ARE THE COMMUNITIES WE SERVE

In March 1979, in one of the most memorable college basketball games ever played, Earvin "Magic" Johnson and his Michigan State Spartans defeated Larry Bird and Indiana State to win the NCAA title. If his name had not been a household word before then, this dramatic contest catapulted Magic Johnson into the national consciousness. He went on to a thirteen-year Hall of Fame career with the Los Angeles Lakers, which included five NBA titles and three league MVP awards. He was particularly noted for the pure joy and energetic passion with which he played. As his career progressed, Johnson became determined, once his playing days were over, to become just as successful in business as he had been in athletics.

Over time and with much hard work, Johnson built a multifaceted business that still reflects the vision of its founder. His simple message, "We are the communities we serve," is clearly communicated at all levels of his organization and promotes the importance of providing goods and services for traditionally neglected communities. Magic Johnson provides a superb example of a leader whose unified vision permeates his team.

Johnson was born in 1959 in Lansing, Michigan, where he grew up one of ten children. His parents worked hard and expected the same from their kids. Johnson's father worked as many as three jobs to support his family, including owning his own trash hauling business. From this example and through association with other local African-American entrepreneurs who served as mentors and role models, Johnson became intrigued at an early age with the idea of running his own business. His initial goal—by his own admission—revolved around making as much money as possible. As he matured, however, he became convinced that he could do much more by acting as a catalyst for change in underserved communities.

During his years in the NBA, as he and the Lakers traveled the country, Johnson saw visions of urban blight at its worst. He said, "Riding in the team bus to the arenas in Chicago, Detroit, and other cities, I'd see boarded up storefronts and houses where black businesses had once operated and where hardworking black families had once lived. Poverty, crime, and hopelessness had driven them out and taken over. Despair dominated every block.... The lost lives and empty buildings made no sense to me.... Time after time as we drove through those desolate city landscapes, I'd think, *Someday, I'm going to do something about this. Someday, I'm going to come back here and help rebuild these neighborhoods.*" [Emphasis added by Johnson].

Johnson had identified his niche. "Some call my target market 'urban America'" he said, "or 'emerging markets' or the 'inner city.' All of these descriptions apply to underserved minority communities, where my heart lies. My goal is to do well financially while creating jobs and providing goods and services for the people we serve in those areas."

Abundant research underscores the power and growth potential of "underserved minority communities." Minority populations in the United States are growing seven times as fast as the white majority population. According to the U.S. Census Bureau, Hispanics are the largest minority group, with more than 45 million people (15.1 percent of the total population) and growing. Half of the nation's population growth from 2000 to 2006 came from Hispanics. There are more than 40 million African-Americans in the United States (13.5 percent of the population). By 2012, these two groups combined will have more than $2 trillion in spending power. In addition, the growth rate for minority-owned businesses far exceeds that for all U.S. businesses. Johnson summarized, "When I tell corporate leaders about the opportunities to serve and work with minorities in urban America, they listen because my partners and I have proven that investing in minority communities makes sense."

Johnson formed Magic Johnson Enterprises in 1987. He acknowledged there were serious challenges early on. He reflected on those days: "The urban American market was not an easy sell initially. The corporations behind the big brands had their own proven business models, and they targeted the suburbs. They knew they could make money in sprawling, outlying areas populated mostly by middle—and upper-income white families. They were slow to grasp the economic viability of investing in places such as Harlem and South Central.... Back then, I had to overcome the skepticism of bankers and corporate leaders. They seemed to think I was just a jock playing around in a new game. So in my early ventures I had to take most of the financial risk."

Also, understandably, Johnson himself realized a steep learning curve as a businessman. One of his first ventures, the Magic 32 retail store, was a flop. Magic 32 launched in 1990 in Los Angeles to sell licensed athletic gear. Johnson said, "This was my first big retail venture.... We never made it beyond the first store.... The major factor was our crazy main buyer, who ordered the clothing *he* liked rather than stocking up what our customers might buy. Did I mention that *I* was the main buyer? Big mistake.... There were other factors, but what really killed the Magic 32 retail chain was my lack of vision for it."

Lesson learned. Every great team needs a unifying vision. And every person on the team must understand the vision.

In 1994 the Johnson Development Corporation entered into a partnership with Sony Retail Entertainment to purchase the Baldwin movie theater in a run-down area of South Central Los Angeles. Johnson said, "The Baldwin project was about entertaining people and providing something of value to the community; *something that had been lost.*" Ultimately, the theater became one of the highest grossing venues in the country, and Johnson and his partners (Sony eventually merged with Loews and then Loews merged with AMC) built additional multiplexes in Los Angeles, Atlanta, Houston, Cleveland, and New York City.

By this time, Johnson had clearly articulated the vision for his company, "Developing businesses in urban neighborhoods for the benefit of underserved communities—our communities—is a mission with deep meaning for me and for the more than twenty thousand people who work for me. Our motto is 'We are the communities we serve.' That isn't just a catch phrase designed to impress people. It is from the heart. Our mission frames everything we do... I make sure no one forgets it. Everything we do is aimed at serving people who have not been well-served by the business community in the past. Call them urban Americans, emerging markets, or minority communities; they are why we do what we do—in everything we do. I remind team members every day of our mission because it helps them understand that they are part of something important, something that can change the world."

Today, Magic Johnson Enterprises is an approximately $700 million empire with three primary divisions: Business Venture, Capital Management, and Consulting and Licensing. The Business Venture unit runs Burger King Restaurants in the southeastern United States and partners with Sodexo to provide food and facilities management to underserved communities. Through a unit called Urban Coffee Opportunities, Johnson is the sole franchisee of Starbucks coffee shops, with hundreds of outlets. In addition, the company runs thirteen 24 Hour Fitness Magic Johnson Sport Clubs and an independent venture called Magic Workforce Solutions that provides staffing and career services. Finally, since 1998, Business Ventures has owned and operated a T.G.I. Friday's restaurant—in partnership with Carlson Restaurants Worldwide—in Ladera, California.

The Capital Management Division invests heavily in urban communities. The division operates three funds: a private equity growth fund that provides money for urban businesses, one of the largest private equity real estate funds in America with $1 billion in committed capital, and a fund that focuses on urban residential areas. This group has constructed or repositioned over 2 million square feet of retail space, generated thousands of jobs, and emphasized environmental responsibility.

The Consulting and Licensing Division deploys the Magic Johnson brand and enjoys partnerships in the health care area with Aetna and Abbott. This group formed a multi-year partnership with the Best Buy Corporation to help the world's largest consumer electronics retailer strengthen its presence and relationships in urban communities. Consulting and Licensing also operates the AMC Magic Johnson theaters.

In keeping with Johnson's vision and deep commitment to the idea of community the Magic Johnson Foundation, founded in 1991, provides funding focused on educational, health, and social needs in underserved areas. The Foundation has donated more than $1 million to organizations working on HIV/AIDS education and prevention (an area of special concern and passion for Johnson who was diagnosed HIV positive in 1991, cutting short his basketball career). The Foundation also has provided 800 college scholarships to minority students and supports numerous other community-based initiatives.

Through the ups and downs, good days and bad days, and triumphs and failures in a more than two-decade adventure in business, Magic Johnson and his team have stayed true to the vow that, "We are the communities we serve." Any person at Magic Johnson Enterprises can recite the motto. Every person knows what is expected. That is the simple power of a noble and unified vision, well-communicated and universally understood.

Leadership Lesson Two:
A UNIFIED VISION MUST PERMEATE
THE TEAM

Regardless of the verbiage used—vision, mission, goal, strategy, identity, purpose—no team operates effectively over time without the benefit of a single compelling idea that drives it forward.

Even the pithiest, well-thought-out, inspiring vision is worthless if it exists only in the mind of the leader. I vividly recall a personal situation where a leader with whom I worked as human resources support was convinced that his direct reports understood their goals and objectives for the fiscal year. He was certain, and assured me, that he had communicated clearly in this regard. We came to find out, as his team was asked to prepare their self-appraisals in anticipation of annual reviews that they—to a person—had only the vaguest idea what the boss expected of them. They worked hard all year, but frequently on the wrong stuff. What a mess.

My mistake was not checking in earlier and more closely with the team, on their supervisor's behalf, to ensure mutual understanding. Painful lesson learned for the HR guy. The boss made the mistake of assuming his "communication" had been clear and understood. No unified vision permeated the team. The result was frustration all around, wasted effort, loss of credibility, and lousy business results.

The objective, of course, is to develop your team's vision and then share it. Don't assume that people understand and buy in just because you put it out in an e-mail three weeks ago. They don't understand. They don't buy in. But they might. Your job is to communicate, again and again, at every level of the organization. The vision can't just apply to certain team members; it must apply to everyone. Every person—including the last part-timer in the mailroom—must be clear and easily able to call out what the team is working toward. If you aren't sure as their leader whether they have such clarity, ask them.

The vision might be thrust upon you by external events or conditions. There could be a big change in the organization, or some kind of financial issue, or a severe challenge from a strong competitor. For Sitting Bull, the stakes were clear. External forces had determined his fate, and the fate of his people. He would not submit, and resistance to the white man was the defiant call to action he conveyed to everyone who would listen and join his cause.

Magic Johnson, on the other hand, had to discover his vision. His vision developed over time as he matured, observed the world, and then determined where his energy and passion were best placed. But his vision, once he hit upon it, was no less compelling: We are the communities we serve. And he has been masterful in sharing the vision with his team in a way that helps them understand the higher cause that their work honors.

So seek and establish your vision in whatever way is appropriate. Make it your foundation. Communicate. If it is simple, sincere, and permeates the team, all other things are possible.

PART TWO

BUILD STRONG RELATIONSHIPS & TRUST

Chapter Three

GETTYSBURG

LONGSTREET MEMORIAL: CHERISH PEOPLE WHO GIVE YOU HONEST FEEDBACK

"I consider it a part of my duty to express my views to the commanding general."

—General James Longstreet—

Confederate Army commander Robert E. Lee and his First Corps commander James Longstreet enjoyed a long and close professional relationship. They had endured many hardships and fought many battles together. They possessed deep respect and warm regard for each other as fellow members of the brotherhood of soldiers. Due to the strength of this bond, Longstreet, probably singularly among Lee's subordinates, did not hesitate to provide Lee with sometimes brutally honest input. Longstreet sincerely regarded it as his duty and obligation to tell his chief the honest truth as best he could see the truth.

Longstreet's idea of the way the campaign and battle of Gettysburg should be conducted differed dramatically from Lee's. Longstreet repeatedly advocated for his point of view. There is no doubt that throughout the entire war, Lee listened carefully when Longstreet spoke. Lee cherished Longstreet's frank counsel. But in the end, at Gettysburg, Lee dismissed Longstreet's arguments and proceeded with his own plans. The controversy arising out of Lee's momentous decision to ignore Longstreet's advice persists to this day.

Robert Edward Lee was born in January 1807 at spacious Stratford Hall, the Lee family home in Westmoreland County, Virginia, along the Potomac River. He was the son of Ann Carter and Henry "Light Horse Harry" Lee. Light Horse Harry had earned his sobriquet as a great hero of the American Revolution, and he later became governor of Virginia and a U.S. congressman. He was also financially irresponsible and dishonest, speculating in land and neglecting to pay his debts. He did a poor job supporting his family, spent time in debtor's prison, and paid little attention to his five children.

When Robert was three years old the Lees moved to more modest accommodations in Alexandria, Virginia. When he was six, his father—in poor health and financial duress—left the country and set sail for Barbados, never to see his family again. Harry Lee died a broken man when Robert was eleven. Raised by his mother, who was a strong-willed woman but who suffered ill health herself, Robert became in effect the man of the household at an adolescent age. One can only imagine the impact on the young boy of this unsettled upbringing, and the famous but distant father whom he barely knew and who had brought such embarrassment to the family.

Whatever his inner turmoil, and thanks to the love and influence of his mother, by all accounts Robert grew into a highly intelligent, stable, courteous, and mature young man. He entered the U.S. Military Academy at West Point in June of 1825 to pursue the profession of arms. At the Academy he compiled an impressive record. He served as cadet adjutant (the highest rank in the corps), graduated second in the class of 1829, and, amazingly, navigated the entire four years without receiving a single demerit for any infraction of West Point's rigorous code of conduct. He was terrifically handsome, possessed tremendous discipline, had outstanding military bearing, and so fairly earned the nickname from his classmates, "The Marble Man."

Lee received an assignment upon graduation as second lieutenant to the Corps of Engineers. For the next several years, he served at a number of posts pursuing various military construction and public works projects. While stationed at Fort Monroe, Virginia, in 1831, Lee married Mary Anna Randolph Custis (a great-granddaughter of Martha Washington) at Mary's majestic family home in Arlington, just across the way from Washington, D.C. Mary possessed wealth and status. She gave him seven children, but the match proved less than a perfectly happy one for Lee. Mary was spoiled and unable to fully carry out her responsibilities as wife and mother. In time she developed arthritis, which rendered her an invalid for the rest of her life. Lee loved his wife and remained steadfastly faithful to her throughout the marriage. He was nevertheless known to generally adore women (and they him), and he carried on flirtatious correspondences with a number of pretty young females in later years.

During the Mexican War (1846–1848), Captain Lee served with great distinction on the staff of army commander Winfield Scott. On several occasions, Lee pursued risky reconnaissance missions in which the intelligence he gathered proved crucial to a battle's outcome. Lee was commended again and again for his bravery and skill by Scott, one of the great soldiers of American history and a man whom Lee admired tremendously. Lee came out of the war with the rank of brevet colonel (brevet ranks were conferred in wartime as an honorary promotion to reward gallantry in action), but still held the permanent regular army rank of captain.

Lee also came out of the war convinced, as a result of his firsthand observation of Scott's brilliant campaign against Mexico City, that offensive action was the key to success in warfare. Lee perhaps learned this lesson too well. As biographer Emory Upton stated, "Lee and many of his contemporaries accepted their experience of offensive success in Mexico as universally valid. The Mexican experience confirmed Napoleonic teaching and rendered reliance upon offense an article of faith in the military mind. What veterans of the Mexican War forgot or failed to emphasize were the factors which allowed attackers to succeed in Mexico—the poor state of [Mexican commander] Santa Anna's army and the use of muskets as primary infantry weapons." In other words, in a future war against a motivated enemy armed with longer range rifled weapons, the offensive might not always fare so well.

After the war, Lee resumed his engineering duties but in 1852 was appointed superintendant of West Point. Lee proved a highly progressive leader of the Academy. He improved the campus infrastructure and course curriculum and focused attention on the well-being of cadets. Lee maintained his contacts with General Scott and also spent time in study, expanding his own professional horizons. Lee may have been influenced by his association with Professor Dennis Hart Mahan, an instructor at West Point who taught tactics to a number of future Civil War leaders during his long tenure. Among other things, Mahan emphasized that field fortifications, or trenches, were important in modern war. Despite his bias for the offensive, there would nevertheless be times in his career when Lee, the talented engineer, would heed defensive military principles as well.

In 1855 Lee was appointed lieutenant colonel of the Second U.S. Cavalry, changing his branch of service from engineers to the arm of cavalry. He had for some time longed to command combat troops rather than serve in a support function. His first duty was at a lonely outpost called Camp Cooper, Texas, protecting settlers from the raids of Comanche and Apache Indians. In 1859, when abolitionist John Brown and a small band of followers seized the federal arsenal at Harper's Ferry, Virginia, Lee was selected to lead a detachment of militia, soldiers, and U.S. Marines to subdue the uprising. After a short skirmish, in a small-scale precursor to the intense emotion and violent action that would soon sweep the nation, Lee and his men captured Brown.

With the firing by Confederate artillerists on Fort Sumter, South Carolina, in April 1861, the Civil War commenced. Lee, recently promoted to colonel in the regular army, and still highly esteemed by Scott (who would start the war as commander of all U. S. forces), was offered command of all field forces of the army that President Lincoln had called to serve. Lee, ever loyal to his beloved Virginia, refused the entreaty. With Lincoln's request for 75,000 troops to put down the rebellion, Virginia seceded from the union. Lee, who agonized over the decision in his reluctance to take up arms against the government he had faithfully served for thirty-two years, resigned his commission. He soon accepted command of the military forces of Virginia with the rank of major general.

After a series of initial missteps while leading troops in north-western Virginia and a stint helping to prepare Confederate coastal defenses, Lee became principal military advisor to President Jefferson Davis in the capital city of Richmond, Virginia. In June of 1862, after General Joseph E. Johnston was seriously wounded as he fought Union General George B. McClellan's Army of the Potomac during the Peninsula campaign, Robert E. Lee assumed command of the Army of Northern Virginia. Some historians assert that no single round of artillery ammunition fired by Union forces during the entire war did greater damage to their own cause than the shot that put shrapnel into the chest of Joe Johnston, thus paving the way for "The Marble Man."

"The assignment of General Lee to command the army of Northern Virginia was far from reconciling the troops to the loss of our beloved chief, Joseph E. Johnston, with whom the army had been closely connected since its early active life. All hearts had learned to lean upon him with confidence, and to love him dearly. General Lee's experience in active field work was limited to his West Virginia campaign against General Rosecrans, which was not successful. His services on our coast defences were known as able, and those who knew him in Mexico as one of the principal engineers of General Scott's column, marching for the capture of the capital of that great republic, knew that as military engineer he was especially distinguished; but officers of the line are not apt to look to the staff in choosing leaders of soldiers, either in tactics or strategy. There were, therefore, some misgivings as to the power and skill for field service of the new commander."

These words were written many years after the war by the man who, over time and despite his initial misgivings, became Robert E. Lee's most trusted lieutenant and closest advisor. He was born in South Carolina but raised in Georgia, and his father had nicknamed him "Peter"—which in biblical parlance means rock—for his sturdy nature. His name was James Longstreet.

Longstreet was born in 1821. When he was nine, his parents sent him to live with relatives in Augusta, Georgia, in pursuit of better educational opportunities and with hopes of a military career. Longstreet received an appointment to West Point in 1838 where, unlike the scholarly and controlled Robert E. Lee, he compiled a poor academic and disciplinary record. He finished fifty-fourth out of sixty-two cadets in the class of 1842. He was, however, well-liked and made friends easily, many of whom would either serve by his side or oppose him in the Civil War. Longstreet's best friend was also a poor student, a shy young man from Ohio who was a year behind him named Ulysses S. Grant. Longstreet served as best man at Grant's wedding in 1848, where the bride was Longstreet's fourth cousin, Julia Dent.

Longstreet entered the infantry and was assigned to duty at Jefferson Barracks near St. Louis in 1842, where Grant joined him one year later. In 1844 Longstreet met the post commander's daughter, Maria Louisa Garland, and they wed in 1848. Like Lee, Longstreet served with great distinction in the Mexican War, seeing combat in virtually all of the major engagements and ultimately winning the brevet rank of major. At the Battle of Chapultepec in 1847, he was wounded in the leg as he carried the regimental colors up a hill. Before he fell, he handed the flag off to his good friend Lieutenant George Pickett. After the war, Longstreet fought Indians out west, ultimately rising to the regular army rank of major by 1858.

When the Civil War broke out, Longstreet—like Robert E. Lee and many other Southern officers—reluctantly resigned his commission to take up arms against the country he had loyally served for nearly two decades. He received an assignment as brigadier general, serving as a brigade commander in the war's first major battle at Manassas. He was soon promoted to major general and given command of what eventually became the First Corps of the Army of Northern Virginia, with six brigades and about 14,000 men. He was working in this capacity during the Peninsula campaign at the moment, immediately after the Battle of Seven Pines, when Robert E. Lee became his new boss. Longstreet distinguished himself in the successful Seven Days Battles that ensued near Richmond, prompting Lee to call him the "staff in my right hand."

In early 1862, Longstreet suffered a devastating personal tragedy. An epidemic of scarlet fever swept through Richmond, Virginia, where his wife Maria lived with their four children. In the span of a week three of the four siblings—a one-year-old girl and two boys, ages four and six—succumbed to the fever. An older boy barely escaped with his life. The parents were so despondent that Longstreet's friend George Pickett had to make the funeral arrangements. On campaign up to that point, Longstreet's headquarters camp had always been known as a place of fun, where a good stiff drink and a hand or two of poker were always permitted. Longstreet himself was a skilled poker player who loved to join in the games. After his unbearably sad loss, he became withdrawn and somber, and while camp life continued, Longstreet now only observed quietly from the shadows. We can only speculate as to the effect this sad event had on his mental and emotional state.

At the Battle of Antietam on September 17, 1862, after the long and bloody day's fighting had ended, Longstreet approached Lee's headquarters to deliver his report. Longstreet said, "General Lee walked up as I dismounted, threw his hands upon my shoulders, and hailed me with, 'Here is my old war-horse at last!'" Longstreet had continued to prove his calm steadiness and military skill up to and through the Antietam campaign. In October 1862 Lee recommended that Longstreet and Stonewall Jackson be promoted to the new rank of Lieutenant General, with each man to command a "wing" of Lee's army. Longstreet's unit was formally designated as First Corps and Jackson's as Second Corps in November.

Longstreet, militarily ahead of his time, favored a tactical defensive mode of warfare. He understood the lethality of modern weaponry and the general futility of frontal assaults under most conditions. Longstreet's men manned the walls of Marye's Heights at Fredericksburg on December 13, 1862. Six head-on attacks were hurled back with more than 12,500 Union casualties, against 5,300 for the defenders. Interestingly, though Longstreet was not present for Lee's daring masterpiece at Chancellorsville in May 1863, the "old war horse" later described Chancellorsville as "an instance of an offensive battle, where we dislodged the Federals, it is true, but at such a terrible sacrifice that half a dozen such victories would have ruined us." That sacrifice also included the death of Stonewall Jackson.

Lee, the gambler, clearly demonstrated his inclination for the offensive at Chancellorsville. He had also by this time fully developed his management style, which was in some respects decidedly modern. He worked to develop an overall strategy for his team, and then depended on his commanders to execute against his orders. Lee said, "I think and work with all my power to bring the troops to the right place at the right time; then I have done my duty. As soon as I order them into battle, I leave my army in the hands of God." He believed that if he were to actively intervene in the midst of the chaos of combat that it "would do more harm than good. It would be a bad thing if I could not rely on my brigade and division commanders."

Historian Emory Upton said, "Here was the military expression of traditional Southern honor, state rights, and individualism; the commanding general planned and launched the army into battle, but then left the conduct of combat to those who commanded component units of the army. In one sense Lee abdicated his authority once he committed his army to battle." Lee's propensity to rely on his own intuition to put an overarching plan into place for his team with an emphasis on aggressive offensive movement, and then sit back and watch the results, played itself out in classic fashion at Gettysburg.

When Lee and Longstreet initially discussed the idea of a second invasion of the north Longstreet was in favor of the concept but argued vehemently that certain conditions be met. He said, "...I was never persuaded to yield my argument against the Gettysburg campaign, except with the understanding that we were not to deliver an offensive battle, but to so manouevre that the enemy should be forced to attack us—or, to repeat, that our campaign should be one of offensive strategy, but defensive tactics."

Lee undoubtedly agreed that the ideal scenario would involve artfully maneuvering into a position where, as at Fredericksburg or even Second Manassas earlier in the war, the enemy would be forced to attack on ground of Lee's choosing. Any competent commander would hope for such an ideal situation. Nevertheless, it seems highly unlikely that Lee would have committed himself to fighting with primarily defensive tactics, despite Longstreet's later protestations that he would not have gone along with the plans under any other circumstance. Lee would have been unnecessarily and irresponsibly tying his own hands in agreeing to such a future course of action. Lee's later comment in response to Longstreet's assertion that Lee pledged only a defensive battle was that he "had never made any such promise, and had never thought of doing any such thing." That idea, he said, was "absurd."

Lee, aggressive soldier though he was and as contradictory as it may seem, was notoriously conflict-avoidant in his interpersonal relations. He was courteous to a fault, considerate of people's feelings, and simply hated a blunt conversation. Whatever the truth of the interactions between them, Longstreet felt sure that he and Lee had a clear understanding as to the conduct of the northern invasion. In Longstreet's defense, this would not be the last time in the war that one of Lee's subordinates would misinterpret communication from him.

As the Army of Northern Virginia commenced its march north, therefore, Lee's true and ultimate intention—in keeping with his overall strategic plan and bias for aggressive offensive action—was to seek out and destroy his enemy. By the end of the first day's fighting at Gettysburg on July 1, Lee saw his opportunity. He still lacked specifics as to what lay before him, but his men had carried the day through skillful fighting and weight of numbers. Lee might be able to defeat the Union army before Meade could bring all his forces to bear. In Lee's mind, time was a critical factor.

Lee consulted his lieutenants at the end of the initial day of battle. At this time, Longstreet first suggested a specific course of action based on his understanding of the agreed-upon idea for the campaign. Longstreet used field glasses to spy the formidable enemy defensive works on Cemetery Hill. He may have held visions of Fredericksburg in reverse as he told Lee, "We could not call the enemy to position better suited to our plans. All that we have to do is file around his left and secure good ground between him and his capital." Lee did not dismiss Longstreet's suggestion out of hand—he always listened when Longstreet had something to say—but quickly decided he must attack. Lee pointed to Cemetery Hill and said, "The enemy is there. If he is there tomorrow I am going to attack him." Longstreet bluntly shot back, "If he is there, it will be because he is anxious that we should attack him; a good reason, in my judgment, for not doing so."

Longstreet continued to hammer at Lee with his alternate scenario throughout the three days of battle. His first idea involved a broad flanking maneuver designed to position the Rebel army squarely between the Yankees and Washington, D.C. This was a bold move that would have involved a march of many miles. Meade would be forced to react to re-establish his supply line and, more importantly, defend the capital city. At a later point, in a simpler proposal, Long-street suggested a more limited tactical flanking movement that would position troops behind the Round Tops to imperil the Union line. He said, "I thought that we should move around to his left, that we might threaten it if we intended to maneuver, or attack it if we determined upon a battle." Lee would have none of it. His response was to give Longstreet principle attack responsibility, per the commander's plans, on both Day Two and Day Three. Longstreet was thus put into the unenviable spot of having to lead assaults with which he vehemently disagreed and which ultimately failed.

Lee and Longstreet were angry with each other at Gettysburg. Lee undoubtedly felt frustration with Longstreet's continued insistence on his own suggested course of action. At some point, Lee no doubt thought, once a subordinate has voiced his opinion and a contrary decision has been made, it is time to salute sharply and carry out orders. For Longstreet, Lee's unwillingness to consider another route to victory bordered on recklessness. Longstreet clearly visualized a path to success, but felt he was not being heard. Longstreet's chief of staff wrote later that his superior, "did not want to fight on the ground or on the plan adopted by the General-in-Chief. As Longstreet was not to be made willing and Lee refused to change or could not change, the former failed to conceal some anger. There was apparent apathy in his movements. They lacked the fire and point of his usual bearing on the battlefield."

Lee was never directly critical of Longstreet's conduct during or after the battle. After the war, Lee became president of Washington College in Lexington, Virginia (later Washington and Lee College). He proved to be an excellent and enlightened leader of that institution and continued to be revered throughout the South. He died of heart failure just five years after the war in 1870.

Longstreet asserted in his memoirs many years after the war that he and Lee maintained the utmost respect for each other until "political differences" caused a split in 1867. Longstreet came under tremendous criticism after the conflict, and especially after Lee's death, when the stories came to be rewritten. He had committed multiple "crimes." He was viewed by many as having been negligent in his conduct of the battle of Gettysburg. There was a perception that he was angry with Lee, did not support the commander's chosen course of action, and was indolent in execution. And there was more to be added by Longstreet's detractors. Longstreet was a good friend of U.S. Grant, whom he had befriended when they were both humble and academically inept cadets at West Point. Grant was the great Union hero of the war and was elected president in 1868. Grant's wife, the former Julia Dent and America's first lady, was Longstreet's cousin. Longstreet joined the Republican Party—Grant's party—and he accepted jobs in the Grant administration.

Most infamously, Longstreet had the temerity to criticize Robert E. Lee—a Southern icon then and to this day—in his memoirs. Longstreet stated that, in effect, Lee had been off his game at Gettysburg and that Lee had acknowledged multiple times after the fact that he should have listened to Longstreet's alternate battle proposal. If Lee had listened to him, Longstreet argued, the war may have turned out differently. Whether adoption of Longstreet's flanking plan would have resulted in a Confederate victory will of course never be known. It is interesting to note, however, that in a letter written in 1870 concerning Gettysburg, Union commander George Meade said, "Longstreet's advice to Lee [to move around the Yankee army's left flank and to disrupt communications and supply in the rear] was sound military sense; it was the step I feared Lee would take...."

Only in more recent years, with the publication of Michael Sharra's Pulitzer-prize-winning book *Killer Angels* (1974) and the release of the movie *Gettysburg* (1993), has Longstreet's reputation been somewhat rehabilitated. He was portrayed in those vehicles as a common-sense leader (albeit with an extraordinarily bad beard in the case of actor Tom Beringer in *Gettysburg*) who had the best interests of his troops and the cause for which they fought in mind. The controversy continues.

Longstreet said in a letter to a relative written three weeks after the battle, "I consider it a part of my duty to express my views to the commanding general. If he approves and adopts them, it is well; if he does not, it is my duty to adopt his views, and to execute the orders as faithfully as if they were my own." Whether Longstreet worked fully and energetically to implement Lee's orders is open to question. Whether Lee should have accepted Longstreet's plan, and whether that approach might have worked, is also subject to debate.

We do know that Robert E. Lee was blessed with a lieutenant who spoke his mind freely at all times, especially when he disagreed. Whatever elements of Lee's character were at work, to his credit, he obviously created an environment in which at least one person felt safe telling him the truth. Lee always listened, irritated though he may sometimes have been. He never dismissed Longstreet out of hand. However, Lee also owned the incredibly difficult responsibility of the final decision maker, and obviously reserved the right to take the course of action he deemed best. Despite the drama of the great dispute at Gettysburg, to the end of the conflict Lee still cherished his relationship with Longstreet. As the two warriors parted ways at Appomattox in April 1865, Lee said to Longstreet's aide, "Captain, I am now going to put my old war horse under your charge. I want you to take good care of him."

★ ★ CASE STUDY ★ ★

MEG WHITMAN AND EBAY:
LISTEN TO YOUR CUSTOMERS

In 1995, California computer programmer Pierre Omidyar created an online auction place for his girlfriend to buy, sell, and trade Pez dispensers, which she collected. The site was known as Auction Web and interest soon ran well beyond mere Pez dispensers. On the site, for a minor fee, people could post items for sale. The highest bidder for any given product secured the purchase. Omidyar also received a small commission for each sale and soon began to generate profits. Buyers and sellers had an opportunity to rate each other, which introduced an element of integrity and quickly weeded out most scammers. From this simple concept, the juggernaut now known as eBay was born. A huge community of aficionados developed and, by 1997, the site was one of the most heavily visited marketplaces on the web. The operation soon became too big for Omidyar to manage on his own. The search began for a professional business leader who could appreciate the technological challenges, but who also had an astute sense of the importance of the customer experience in sustaining success. That executive turned out to be Meg Whitman.

Whitman, while at the helm of eBay, provided a dramatic example of a leader who not only cherished feedback, she could not function without it. She listened carefully, mostly to her customers but also to anyone else who offered a useful point of view, and used what she learned to create a unique and powerful success story.

Margaret Cushing Whitman was born in 1956 in New York. Her father was a businessman, and she grew up in an affluent neighborhood in Cold Springs Harbor on Long Island. Her mother stayed home to raise Meg and her two siblings and possessed an adventurous streak. Margaret Whitman Sr. had served in New Guinea during World War 2 as an airplane and truck mechanic for the Red Cross. She was a great inspiration to Meg and told her daughter that she could achieve anything she wanted out of life. Meg Whitman was a talented athlete and student in high school. She enrolled at Princeton University, earned an economics degree, and then followed with a Harvard MBA.

Whitman's first job out of graduate school was with Procter & Gamble, where she became a brand manager. She met and married her husband, a medical doctor, and the couple relocated to California. She secured a consulting position with Bain & Company in San Francisco and worked there eight years. She moved to the Walt Disney Company, attaining the level of senior vice president and acquiring key marketing experience. Next there came another cross-country move to follow her husband's medical career. She found success as a division president of shoe maker Stride Rite in Lexington, Massachusetts, overseeing the revival of the venerated Keds brand of sneakers. She briefly served as president and CEO of Florists Transworld Delivery and then moved to Hasbro as a general manager. Her two young sons appreciated her work on Mr. Potato Head while she was chief of the preschool toys division. Throughout her varied and peripatetic career, Whitman became known as a hands-on executive with an intense brand and customer focus.

In the autumn of 1997, Whitman received an inquiry through a headhunter from a small California e-commerce startup looking to expand. Whitman researched Auction Web, and its site consisted of not much more than simple classified ads. She related, "I remember sitting at my computer saying, I can't believe I'm about to fly across the country to look at a black-and-white auction classified site." She did travel to see this little company with thirty employees and $4.7 million in revenue. She sensed something in the spirit of the place that she liked, and saw enormous potential in the business model. Omidyar and his leadership team were of course impressed with her marketing, customer, and big business background. Whitman came aboard as CEO in March of 1998.

Any number of skeptics felt that Whitman was not qualified to run eBay for lack of technical expertise. She quickly demonstrated her willingness to roll up her sleeves and learn. In mid-1999, the eBay site crashed for twenty-two hours, and weeks of uncertainty and instability followed. Whitman sat through endless technical discussions to get at root causes, pulled all-nighters with the team, and when she did sleep, she slept on a cot in the office. She hired a technology chief whom she promptly fired when solutions did not come rapidly enough. The problems were fixed, and Meg Whitman had impressed everyone, including her detractors, by acknowledging what she did not know and working tirelessly to educate herself.

Whitman also brought her vaunted customer focus to bear. She was quick to credit eBay's success to its enormous community of buyers and sellers, who in essence run the business by determining which transactions will take place, and by managing inventory and shipping. The power of the business model, said Whitman, "is in the community of users who have built eBay."

Whitman spent considerable time monitoring feedback from buyers and sellers by perusing discussion boards. She said, "The great thing about running this company is that you know immediately what your customers think." She organized annual member conferences that brought thousands of eBay customers together to swap ideas and learn how to more effectively use the site. She spent time during these events on the floor interacting with as many customers as possible. Numerous sellers have been able to make a handsome living trading on eBay full-time, and Whitman enjoyed interacting with them. Whitman declared, "Actually, most of these sellers know more about eBay than [eBay] employees. They use it every single day. They're the experts.... The businesses that have been built on this platform are remarkable."

While taking the time to listen to her customers, Whitman also made a series of executive decisions that vastly improved the company's growth potential. After overseeing eBay's IPO in 1998, she sought to improve the user experience by encouraging merchants to establish fixed prices in addition to selling at auction. This move sped up the pace of activity on the site by attracting new kinds of buyers, and fixed price sales now account for a significant percentage of eBay's transactions. She also engineered the purchase of PayPal, a payment process service that allows eBay customers to reimburse merchants immediately, while avoiding the inconvenience of putting a check in the mail.

Whitman oversaw explosive expansion at eBay. In 2002 revenues rose 62 percent to $1.1 billion, with an earnings jump of 172 percent to $249 million. The company's growth slowed in relative terms and profitability tailed off in the final three years of her decade of tenure. Nevertheless, by the time Whitman resigned her position in 2008, eBay had 15,000 employees, just under $8 billion in revenue, and 300 million registered users. Meg Whitman was honored as *Fortune's* most powerful woman in business in both 2004 and 2005. Much of what she accomplished can be attributed to her desire to hear what people were telling her, learn from it, and take appropriate action based on that new knowledge.

Even now, as of this writing, as she undertakes a run for the California governor's office, Whitman continues to solicit input from multiple sources. She has traveled to consult with a number of Republican governors across America to seek out best practices and policy advice. She visited Governor Rick Perry of Texas to talk about the economy. She tapped Jeb Bush, former governor of Florida, to discuss education. She also sought advice from economists at Stanford University to help her with the issue of job creation. Whether she will be successful in her next great career venture remains to be seen but, whatever the outcome, Meg Whitman's ongoing willingness to seek feedback, listen, and adapt will hold her in good stead.

Leadership Lesson Three:

CHERISH PEOPLE WHO GIVE YOU HONEST FEEDBACK

Most of us grasp intellectually the importance for success in business of giving and receiving honest feedback. Why so few of us do it well is because it's difficult to do.

Many of us are averse to hurting someone's feelings (think Robert E. Lee) and consequently are reluctant to deliver the full truth as we see it. We are also generally loath to receive feedback ourselves. It can be embarrassing and unpleasant. How many people (both supervisors and employees) actually enjoy the annual review process, which is all about feedback? Not many that I have met.

With all of that said, I am still struck at how often in my ten-year career in human resources I came across even very senior leaders who would not give straightforward feedback when they should have, nor were they at all interested in what anyone had to say about them. This fundamental unwillingness to provide or hear honest feedback costs organizations dearly over time.

As a leader, if you arrive at a point where you lose interest in receiving feedback (if you ever had interest in the first place), or you say you want feedback but create an environment that is clearly not safe for providing it, you cannot succeed over the long haul.

Good leaders foster a culture in which it is okay to speak up, even if the message might be painful. Robert E. Lee, frustrated though he may have been with James Longstreet's continued attempts to achieve a different outcome at Gettysburg, always respectfully listened and considered Longstreet's point of view. Lee made it clear by the way he behaved and treated his trusted subordinate that, despite the occasional vehement disagreement, he always expected Longstreet to speak his mind honestly.

The very best leaders not only accept feedback, but they actively seek it out. They could not function without the information they receive, virtually always from multiple sources. It is like the air that they breathe. They use that data to drive change in themselves and in their organizations. Meg Whitman constantly sifted through countless bits of information, especially from her customers, the buyers and sellers who were the foundation of eBay's success. She used what she learned to create one of corporate America's all-time great growth stories.

Two final questions are key: 1. Do you have someone in your professional life—at least one person who is your Longstreet—who pushes you and provides you with genuinely honest feedback? If the answer is yes, that's good news for you and your organization; 2. If you don't have someone like Longstreet, why not, and what will you do about it?

Chapter Four

LITTLE BIGHORN

CUSTER'S ADVANCE: WITHOUT TRUST THE BATTLE IS LOST

"I'm only too proud to say that I despised him."

—Captain Frederick Benteen—

On the third day of the Battle of Gettysburg, a young Union cavalry leader saw his fill of combat. He had just been promoted to lead a brigade and directed his men in action against Confederate horsemen, commanded by Jeb Stuart, on open, rolling ground (today known as East Cavalry Field) three miles east of the main fighting. Stuart had been ordered by Robert E. Lee to attempt a disruption in the enemy rear. On two separate occasions during the melee, the dashing Yankee officer was heard to shout to his Michigan troopers, "Come on you Wolverines. Follow me!" as he led them from the front in headlong charges. The great cavalry duel took place more or less concurrently with Confederate General George Pickett's doomed late-afternoon assault against the Federal center, and resulted in Stuart's ultimate

75

withdrawal from the field to join the main body of the Army of Northern Virginia in preparation for its retreat from Pennsylvania.

The youthful Union officer was unusual in several respects, and not just for his propensity to put himself in mortal danger and revel in the sound, fury, and violence of battle. He was only twenty-three years old. A few days earlier he had been a mere captain on the staff of General Alfred Pleasonton. But top leadership saw something very special in him, and leapfrogged him over many more senior officers in promoting him to brevet brigadier general. He dressed flamboyantly, wearing a velveteen jacket with gold decorations on the sleeves, a dark blue sailor shirt with a red tie, and a soft Confederate hat that he had scrounged up from a battlefield. He was a superb horseman and a natural athlete. He was ruggedly handsome with deep blue eyes, slender, and just under six feet tall. His hair, golden and luxuriant, reached nearly to his shoulders in flowing curls. He was adored by women throughout his lifetime and occasionally gave female admirers locks of his hair. He became known as the "Boy General." His name was George Armstrong Custer.

Custer's career spanned the entire Civil War and a decade of Indian fighting after the war. Publicity and, especially later in his life, controversy seemed to follow him wherever he went. He was multidimensional and complex. Like all of us, he was human and therefore possessed good traits and bad. Without a doubt, during his service with the Seventh Cavalry after the war, one of his supreme deficiencies was his lack of ability to create a team bonded by trust. This deeply unfortunate failure of leadership on his part would be his demise.

Custer was born in December 1839 to a middle-class, Methodist family in New Rumley, Ohio. His father, Emmanuel, was a hardworking blacksmith and a staunch Democrat. Emmanuel and his wife Maria had both lost spouses and brought young children to this, the second marriage for each. The first two children they conceived together died as infants. The entire blended family therefore rejoiced when George was born healthy and full of energy. He was the favorite by far, and he became the ringleader of the four additional siblings who were born to this happy, loving, rambunctious clan. For his entire lifetime, Custer deeply cared for his parents and all of his brothers and sisters, and they for him. Custer developed an especially close relationship with his older half-sister Lydia Ann, who helped substantially in the raising of the young ones.

Though his father had aspirations of a career in the ministry for "Autie" (Custer's childhood mispronunciation of his middle name) Custer was an incurable romantic who dreamed of the glory of life as a soldier. Emmanuel was the Captain of the New Rumley militia, and when the unit drilled, young Autie would march with them, toy gun over his shoulder, in a uniform made by his mother.

When Custer was twelve, after finishing six years of formal schooling, he moved to Monroe, Michigan, to live with his half-sister Lydia and her husband. There, Custer attended the Stebbins Academy for Boys. He became well-known at this prestigious institution not for his scholarship—though he was clearly very bright and devoured adventure novels—but for his outgoing personality, sense of humor, and practical jokes. He was also by this time an accomplished horseman who loved the outdoors. At fifteen, Custer moved back to Ohio to be with his parents, who had purchased an eighty-acre farm near New Rumley. The life of a farmer was not for Custer, so he attended a training school for teachers. He soon accepted a position as a teacher in Cadiz Township, seventy-five miles away.

In 1856, Custer secured an appointment to West Point where, once again, he became famous not for academic achievement but for his personal charisma and mischievous streak. He prided himself on his ability to accumulate demerits for myriad infractions (eventually setting records in that dubious category) right to the point where he might be expelled, and then straightening up just in time to make it till the end of the term. He engaged in late-night shenanigans at Bennie Haven's, a nearby tavern that was strictly off limits to cadets. He pursued his passion for women, contracting venereal disease during a furlough in 1859, which required treatment when he returned to the Academy. He was without a doubt the most popular man in his class ("we all loved him," said one cadet), as much for his devotion to fun as anything else. During a Spanish class, Custer politely raised his hand and requested that the professor translate the phrase "class is dismissed" into Spanish. When the instructor did so, Custer promptly stood up and marched out with his bemused classmates in tow.

For all of his light-hearted antics, Custer knew as well as anyone that deadly serious storm clouds were gathering over the United States that would have profound implications for every cadet at West Point. A moment of reckoning was coming. When Abraham Lincoln was elected president in November 1860, a trickle of southern students left the Academy. Several more departed when South Carolina seceded in December of that year. Most of the remaining boys from the South left to volunteer their services to their new government when the Confederate States were formally established in February 1861. In total, thirty-two young men from Custer's class resigned. Custer understood the dilemma faced by his southern counterparts, many of whom had become his close friends at the Point, but he also knew his loyalty lay with the Union.

In those days the course of instruction at West Point lasted five years. Custer's class was due to graduate in the summer of 1862. But because of the demand for officers to provide training for the vast multitudes of brand-new citizen soldiers that would fight this war, schedules were accelerated. The class of 1861 graduated in May, and Custer's class—after a herculean effort to cram a year's worth of learning into thirty days—became the second class of 1861, finishing in June. Not surprisingly, Custer graduated as the goat of his class, thirty-fourth out of thirty-four. He seemed to take a peculiar pride in this accomplishment (such as it was) telling a classmate that since he couldn't be at the "head" of his class, he might as well end up at the "foot." His worst grade came in cavalry tactics.

Custer received his commission as a second lieutenant and on July 20, upon his arrival in Washington, D. C., was assigned to the Second Cavalry. His unit had marched west with General Irvin McDowell's army toward a place called Manassas, Virginia, near the Bull Run creek, in anticipation of the first major engagement of the war. Custer secured a horse and rode hard all night to join his new comrades near dawn on July 21. The two armies fought furiously that day, but Custer's unit played only a reserve role. From a hillside, Custer watched as what looked to be a certain Yankee victory turned into an ignominious and chaotic retreat. In what Confederates subsequently labeled "the great skedaddle," the Union army practically ran all the way back to the capital city. Custer, however, was commended for his bravery in the conduct of rearguard actions.

Custer had experienced his first taste of action, and he loved it. He came to enjoy the turbulence of war as few others did. He possessed the heart of a warrior. Despite the fact that as a West Pointer he was tapped for staff work with several different generals, he continually volunteered for reconnaissance and other missions that would bring him in harm's way. He received acknowledgment for his competence and bravery, eventually garnering the attention of General George B. McClellan, commander of the Army of the Potomac. Custer joined McClellan's staff and quickly made a strong, positive impression. When Lincoln fired McClellan in November, however, Custer went home to spend the next several months in Monroe, Michigan.

While on his extended leave, Custer met a Monroe belle named Elizabeth Bacon. Her family and friends knew her as "Libbie." She was intelligent, vivacious, and gorgeous, with lustrous dark hair and dazzling, penetrating eyes. She captivated Custer from the moment he saw her, and she quickly came to adore him in return. She was also the daughter of a prominent local citizen, Judge Daniel Bacon, who very much disapproved of the brash young military officer from humble beginnings. For Custer, no prize was more hard-won during the Civil War years than the hand of Libbie Bacon. They carried on a clandestine correspondence. As Custer's wartime fame grew, Judge Bacon's resistance to the match seemed to dissipate. The couple was married in an elaborate ceremony in February 1864.

Libbie Custer, for the remainder of the Civil War and during all of the years her husband served out west, spent as much time with him in the field as possible. The harsh and trying conditions of the military camp must have seemed a far cry from her comfortable and affluent upbringing in Monroe, but she never wavered in her desire to be at Custer's side. He fascinated her. He loved music and could whistle the melodies from an opera after hearing them just once. He loved to participate in amateur plays, was a serious thespian, and later in his career while stationed on the frontier once wrote, "I wish we had someone competent to give us lessons in private theatricals." He played silly practical jokes on friends and family and then laughed hysterically. Custer had given up drinking during the Civil War, and he worked hard to curb his use of profanity, but he had a lifelong addiction to gambling that he was never able to master. He was a poor public speaker with a high voice, who sometimes talked so rapidly he could barely be understood. He was a boring conversationalist, but developed into a competent writer. His autobiography, *My Life on the Plains*, is still in print. He was an ardent hunter, loved horses, and owned many pets, especially dogs. He had limited ability to concentrate, could barely sit still to read a book, required little sleep, and drove both himself and his men mercilessly. He had what today might be diagnosed as attention deficit disorder. But Libbie Custer cared for him deeply, faults and all.

When Libbie and George were apart they exchanged long, flowing, and frequently titillating letters, playfully using pet names for various parts of their bodies. In one letter Custer wrote her, "Come as soon as you can. I did not marry you for you to live in one house and me in another. One bed shall accommodate us both." On another occasion he penned an eighty-page missive to his beloved. When they were together in garrison, they would chase each other through the house playing tag, laughing and shouting with delight. They clearly loved and were devoted to each other.

The marriage, like any other, suffered from minor irritations around finances, small jealousies and the like. Both Libbie and George were strong-willed and opinionated. The couple was also childless—to their great disappointment—which some historians speculate may have resulted from the possibility that Custer was sterile due to the gonorrhea he contracted as a West Point cadet. In her old age, Libbie admitted that the two great tragedies of her life were her husband's death and their childlessness. Libbie nevertheless devotedly supported her husband, even long after his demise at the Little Bighorn. She never remarried, spending her entire widowhood traveling, lecturing, and writing best-selling books about her life with George Armstrong Custer. She died at age ninety in 1933, having done all in her power to guard his reputation and refute those who questioned his conduct at the Little Bighorn.

After meeting his future bride, Custer returned to service in the Army of the Potomac in the spring of 1863. In the interim, the army had seen commanding General Ambrose Burnside fall by the wayside after the debacle at Fredericksburg in December 1862. The new leader, Joseph Hooker, worked to reorganize his forces, including the cavalry arm. The Union cavalry had never quite been a match for the gifted horsemen of Jeb Stuart's legions. Hooker determined to unify his cavalry into one corps of three divisions and to improve their training and leadership. Alfred Pleasonton was given command of the newly formed corps, and he recommended the promotion to brigadier general of three young captains—Elon Farnsworth, Wesley Merritt, and George Custer—who were "officers with the proper dash to command Cavalry." New Potomac army commander George Meade approved these promotions on June 28, the day he took the job, and Custer was handed a brigade of Michiganders in Judson Kilpatrick's division. The crucible of Gettysburg, where Stuart's grand division and the rest of the Army of Northern Virginia were eventually bested, followed shortly.

Again and again as the war progressed Custer proved his skill and courage as a leader of men. His troops revered him and followed him into combat without hesitation. The Michigan Brigade won a reputation as the best cavalry unit in the army, and General Pleasonton called Custer, "the best cavalry General in the world." Custer's propensity to lead aggressively from the front in reckless charges belied his skill as a tactician. He became extremely adept at sizing up a situation quickly and acting appropriately based on his assessment. There is no doubt that he favored the offensive, and came to believe in his own charmed existence—"Custer's Luck" it was called. He had no fewer than eleven horses shot out from underneath him during the war. Historian Larry Sklenar wrote: "All in all, he was a bit of a wild boy, thoroughly convinced that in following his instincts, he would find his destiny as dictated by the God of Battles. In this sense alone, he was a fatalist, as men in combat must always be." Custer wrote after Gettysburg, "I believe more than ever in Destiny."

In September 1864 Custer was given command of a cavalry division and a short while later promoted to brevet major general. His national fame grew. He continued to play an instrumental role in the waning months of the war at such battles as Tom's Brook, Cedar Creek, Waynesboro, Five Forks, and Sayler's Creek. He was present in the vicinity of Appomattox Courthouse, Virginia, when Generals U. S. Grant and Robert E. Lee signed the articles of surrender on April 9, 1865. Union General Philip Sheridan, who was a huge fan of his "youngster" Custer, gave Mr. McLean a $20 gold coin for the table on which the surrender documents were executed. Sheridan presented the memento to Libbie Custer shortly thereafter with a note that read, "There is scarcely an individual in our service who has contributed more to bring about this desirable result than your gallant husband."

With the war's end Custer spent most of the next year with a cavalry division in the south, where a strange transformation came over him in the way he treated the men in his charge. During the Civil War, he had been generally beloved by his troops. He was solicitous of their well-being and quick to praise their accomplishments—and sometimes downplay his own—in his official reports. He now adopted a style of iron discipline that included floggings for various misdeeds and even executions for the crime of desertion. He seemed indifferent to his men and quickly achieved notoriety as a tyrant. He became intensely disliked by many of the soldiers in his command. This reputation as a rigid martinet dogged Custer for the remainder of his days. He wrote to his wife in 1869, "I never expected to be a popular commander in times of peace."

Custer's transformation from a charismatic, inspiring, caring leader to an authoritarian, despotic task-master (whatever the reasons behind it) represented an unfortunate turning point in his career. Never again would he enjoy the full and unbridled support of the men he led. From this time forward, mistrust would run rampant while Custer was in command.

In January 1866 Custer reverted to the regular army rank of captain and began to consider his options, which included leaving the military altogether. In July, he was appointed a lieutenant colonel (second-in-command) of the Seventh Cavalry Regiment, stationed at Fort Riley, Kansas. Though he would never again rise above the rank of lieutenant colonel, because he had achieved the brevet rank of major general in the Civil War, custom dictated that his officers and troops refer to him as "General" Custer. He became in effect the commanding officer, a position he held for the rest of his life, because both the nominal commander and his successor served on detached duty and never with the regiment. Custer deeply appreciated the assignment and saw it as a great opportunity to achieve glory once again. He said, "I desired to link my name with acts & men, and in such a manner as to be a mark of honor—not only to the present, but to future generations." By this time some Americans—possibly even Custer himself—saw him as a potential future candidate for the presidency.

Among the officers in Custer's new unit was Captain Frederick Benteen, who had served with great distinction in the Civil War and been brevetted colonel for gallantry. He was like Custer in his physical courage, high intelligence, headstrong opinions, pride, and swagger. Benteen was born in 1834 into a staunchly secessionist Virginia family. When the Civil War commenced he opted to serve the North despite his father's threat that he would disown him, and Benteen's own apparent bias against blacks. Ironically, Benteen at the end of the Civil War and his military career (he retired from the army in 1888) was leading all-black units.

During his time in the west, Benteen fought skillfully in a number of battles and skirmishes, including at the Battle of the Little Bighorn, but military duty was hard on him. While he served on the frontier, four of his five children (each under age one) died of spinal meningitis. He was also fond of whisky and late in his career was court-martialed for drunkenness and the ridiculous behavior of disrobing in public to fight civilians.

To add to his troubles, from the moment they met, Frederick Benteen hated his new boss, George Custer. He saw Custer as a tactless braggart who was, as much as anything, the overrated creation of an adoring and misguided national press. Benteen initially worked to hide his true feelings, which almost certainly included a strong element of jealousy. Custer, always profoundly lacking in that sixth sense that today would be termed "emotional intelligence," apparently detected no animosity and at least initially thought highly of Benteen. Custer wrote about Benteen, "He is one of the superior officers of the regiment and one that I can rely upon."

Nevertheless, over time, two distinct camps emerged in Custer's Seventh Cavalry: those officers who were members of the Custer "family"—quite literally in the case of Custer's younger brother Tom and his brother-in-law James Calhoun—and those who were not (there were also a few officers who attempted to remain neutral in their allegiances). Two major incidents took place that exacerbated the split.

The first occurred in the spring of 1867 when the Seventh joined a large expedition that was led by General Winfield Scott Hancock (who had also played a prominent role at the Battle of Gettysburg). The mission was to find and punish marauding Indians, but the endeavor ended in failure. Now headquartered at Fort Wallace, Kansas, and having been away from Libbie for several months, Custer decided to leave his command in mid-summer and raced with an armed escort 150 miles back to Fort Riley to see his wife. The couple enjoyed an emotional and lustful reunion. Custer's excuse was that he was concerned for Libbie's safety, which was not sufficient to prevent formal charges being filed against him. Among other things, he was accused of being absent from his command without leave and conduct prejudicial to military order and discipline.

During the court-martial hearings, few officers of the Seventh testified on Custer's behalf. Many subordinates were resentful of his heavy-handed command style and probably reveled as his career teetered in the balance. The court found Custer guilty and punished him by suspending him from rank and command for a year without pay. Custer's sentence could have been much worse, including the possibility of dishonorable discharge. Nevertheless, he reacted to this outcome by charging one of the Seventh's officers with being drunk on duty. A subsequent trial on that matter caused a further division among Custer's leadership team. The wounds created would never completely heal.

Custer had served ten months of his yearlong suspension when he was called back to duty. His mentor General Phil Sheridan (newly installed as the commander of the Department of the Missouri) requested to higher authority that Custer be reinstated with the Seventh Cavalry. The move delighted Custer. When he rejoined the regiment in October 1868, he made at least a cursory effort to mend fences with some of the officers who had previously crossed him. He was still the same stalwart disciplinarian, but the entire command noticed a new energy and vigor in his behavior that they had not seen before. He installed a rigorous training regimen and made it apparent to all that he hankered to go on campaign again.

This desire to fight Indians aggressively led to the second major incident that split the command along pro and anti-Custer lines.

On a bitterly cold morning in late November 1868, Custer and his Seventh Cavalry (inspired by the faint strains of the regimental ditty "Garry Owen," played by the freezing band members who accompanied them) made an attack on a sleeping Cheyenne village on the Washita River, in what is today the state of Oklahoma. In short order, the unsuspecting Indian's feeble resistance was over. Chief Black Kettle—a leader who desired only peace for his people—and his wife were shot immediately as they attempted to escape. Custer reported that 105 Indians had been killed and fifty-three women and children captured. By implication, the Indian dead were warriors. But subsequent reports indicated that no more than thirty-eight warriors died in the fighting. Thus, most of the casualties at the Washita were women and children.

Before leaving, Custer burned Black Kettle's lodges, food stores, and implements. Custer had his troopers herd 900 Indian ponies into a draw and slaughtered them. When Custer returned to camp with his prisoners before him, General Philip Sheridan was delighted. Army commander William Tecumseh Sherman wired his congratulations from Washington, D.C., regarding the "great victory."

One aspect of the fight at the Washita was to have implications for Custer's later conduct of the Little Bighorn battle. When attacking the Cheyenne camp, he divided his forces, a high-stakes game that when successful worked well, but put his troops at risk of being surrounded and overrun. Further, Custer had not reconnoitered the area in advance, and he had no idea that Black Kettle's was only one of a number of Indian encampments nearby. As an estimated 1,000 warriors assembled to chase Custer down, he boldly moved in their direction—before they were fully organized—and caused them to scatter. Had those nearby villages been roused in a more timely manner, a version of the Little Bighorn battle may have taken place then and there. As darkness approached, the Seventh Cavalry made its withdrawal.

A further incident at the Washita complicated the situation and led directly to the second event that solidified the group that mistrusted Custer. After the main action, Major Joel Elliott of the Seventh led a group of nineteen troopers in pursuit of fleeing Cheyenne survivors. Elliott and all of his men were ambushed and killed. Custer mounted a search—some asserted it was only a token effort—but the badly mutilated soldier's bodies were not found until two weeks later. This perception of a callous abandonment of part of his force caused Custer to lose forever the loyalty of some officers. In particular, Frederick Benteen had been a friend of Elliott's. Further, Benteen believed that his own personal heroics were overlooked by Custer in the official report on the battle. Benteen was cemented as the informal leader of the anti-Custer faction and became open in his hatred of Custer. Benteen was heard to remark later, "I'm only too proud to say that I despised him."

One final person came into the picture to complete the circle of dysfunction, in the form of Major Marcus Reno. Reno joined the Seventh a month after the Washita battle. He was five years Custer's senior, a West Point grad and a career army officer. He had established a respectable record in the Civil War, but spent most of his time in staff jobs. Custer's initial impression was good: "Reno I know well, he is a finished gentleman and a most capable officer." That opinion would change over time.

Reno was a heavy drinker and most of his fellow officers, including Benteen, considered him stubborn, disagreeable, and barely competent as a cavalry leader. At one point Reno and Benteen, probably both drunk, disagreed over some trivial matter in an officer's club. Benteen later recounted, "I slapped his jaws for him till his ears must have rung; told him he was a dirty S.O.B., and if he wanted any other kind of satisfaction, I was only too ready to afford it."

In the spring of 1876, while Custer spent time causing problems for himself through impolitic congressional testimony in Washington, D. C., regarding corruption in the Grant administration, Reno applied for overall command of the Seventh. One soldier said, "A lot of the troopers didn't much care for Custer, but it looked as if Major Reno would command the regiment if Custer didn't arrive. And most of us didn't know or care a great deal about Reno.... He'd never fought Indians, and he didn't seem to be very popular with either the men or the officers." Later in his career, Reno was twice court-martialed.

Custer did return to command the Seventh, to spearhead an advance in the spring of 1876 against Plains Indians who were determined to hold onto their ancestral homelands. When it became clear that force would be required to bring the Indians to the reservation, U. S. military leadership devised a strategy involving a three-pronged attack. A column led by Colonel John Gibbon (also a Union hero of the Battle of Gettysburg) would embark from Fort Ellis in western Montana Territory and proceed east. From Fort Fetterman in Wyoming Territory, Brigadier General George Crook would march north. From Fort Lincoln in the Dakota Territory, the Seventh Cavalry would march west. This column would be supplemented with a battalion of infantry and some artillery, and General Alfred Terry would be the nominal commander. But the true military operator of the Dakota wing would be the Seventh's commander, George Custer. These three separate forces would converge on the non-treaty Indians, who were thought to reside in the Powder River country (see Little Bighorn Map Number Two, May–June 1876, Little Bighorn Campaign).

The team that Custer led could hardly have been more rife with mistrust and animosity. The Seventh's leadership was divided in its opinions of their commander. Custer did not fully trust his two primary subordinates, Reno and Benteen. Reno and Benteen detested Custer. Reno and Benteen detested each other. The enlisted men probably did not know what to think, but it can be safely said that at best they seriously questioned their entire top leadership group. With this as backdrop, the disaster that followed is not at all surprising.

* * CASE STUDY * *

CHAINSAW AL DUNLAP: MEAN BUSINESS

"I'm a superstar in my field, much like Michael Jordan in basketball and Bruce Springsteen in rock 'n' roll." In the opening pages of his 1996 autobiography *Mean Business: How I Save Bad Companies and Make Good Companies Great,* Albert J. Dunlap made clear his assessment of his own exalted status among turnaround artists in corporate America. Indeed, for much of the 1990s Dunlap was a darling of Wall Street. By the time he took over as chairman and CEO of the Sunbeam Corporation in 1996, he had firmly established his fearsome reputation as a leader who held top positions and fashioned dramatic turnarounds at such companies as American Can, Lily-Tulip, Diamond International, Crown-Zellerbach, Consolidated Press Holdings of Australia, and Scott Paper. He had created this amazing success story with a particularly zealous focus on cutting costs and, more specifically, by eliminating facilities and the thousands of jobs that went with them. He became known as "Rambo in Pinstripes" and "Chainsaw Al."

Yet by 1998 Dunlap's world had come crashing down around him. He was fired by his board of directors as CEO of Sunbeam. He became the target of a civil suit from the SEC and a class-action suit by shareholders. As part of the settlement of that litigation he was forever barred from serving as an officer or director of a public corporation. Al Dunlap became a poster child for the adage, "without trust the battle is lost."

While the list of Dunlap's bad behaviors and flagrant misdeeds is extensive, two executives who worked for him summed it up nicely. One said, "It was like a dog barking at you for hours. He just yelled, ranted, and raved. He was condescending, belligerent, and disrespectful." A second former minion said, "It was a very, very hostile environment. Everything was a confrontation and a put-down." Al Dunlap created a manic hit-the-numbers-to-boost-the-stock price-or-else culture based on deep, primal fear. He drove his team to undertake herculean efforts to achieve short-term results at the expense of long-term productivity. But in the end, for simple lack of fundamental trust, employees began to cut corners. Customers received deeply discounted prices to increase sales. Cover-up accounting gimmicks became routine. Financial results were grossly overstated. Wall Street finally took notice. And a great American company lay in ruins.

Dunlap was born in 1937 in Hoboken, New Jersey. He later claimed to have grown up impoverished, saying: "My success has everything to do with being a poor kid who was always being put down." He was just "a nothing kid from Hoboken." In fact, according to his only sibling, their upbringing was agreeably stable and middle-class. Al, said his sister Denise, was a pampered boy raised by doting parents. She remembered, "He was not only loved, he was adored, almost to the point of obsession. It was a very comfortable childhood."

Dunlap worked hard in school and excelled in athletics. He received an appointment to West Point, labored with great intensity to survive his four years there, and graduated near the bottom of his class (537 out of 550) in 1960. After serving his mandatory three-year army obligation at a nuclear missile base in Maryland, Dunlap embarked on his business career.

Money quickly became the sole measure by which Al Dunlap judged his professional success. He said, "I never met a dollar that I didn't love like a brother." His particular specialty became swooping from the outside into a leadership role with a company, then selling businesses, closing buildings, and cutting jobs. The result for Dunlap was a handsome personal profit from the increased stock value or from the outright sale of the company. He would walk away after just a short period, based on a compensation package tied to company stock price, millions of dollars richer.

At Lily-Tulip he cut the total salaried staff by 20 percent and headquarters personnel by half. He left with $8 million. At Crown-Zellerbach—a company he had been hired to run by his mentor Sir James Goldsmith—he decreased the number of distribution facilities from twenty-two to four. He cut 22 percent of the workforce. His personal financial gain in just one of the three years he worked there was $25 million. At Consolidated Press Holdings of Australia, he sold 300 of 413 total businesses. His personal take: $40 million.

Finally, in a precursor to his disastrous run at Sunbeam, Dunlap took the helm at the venerable but troubled Scott Paper in 1994. He spent a mere twenty months in his role as CEO. During that time, he fired 11,200 people, which represented 35 percent of the total employee base, 71 percent of headquarters, half of management, and 20 percent of hourly wage earners. He stated emphatically, "And guess what? It was all fat, blubber. We didn't even tickle a muscle and there we are."

Wall Street and Scott's shareholders loved him for it. Kimberly-Clark purchased Scott Paper for $9.4 billion. Dunlap had increased Scott's market capitalization by $6.3 billion. Investors realized a 225 percent increase in their share values. And Dunlap walked away with a cool $100 million.

But there was a dark side to this seemingly phenomenal Cinderella story. After Dunlap's arrival at Scott, it soon became apparent to insiders that his primary goal was to goose the company's numbers in the short term for the sole purpose of making Scott attractive to a buyer. One executive lamented, "At the employee meetings, he spoke about building the company. But by the end of 1994, it just became a volume-driven plan to pretty up the place for sale."

Volume reports became weekly rather than the standard monthly events. The research-and-development staff was cut by 60 percent and overall research and development budgets were axed by half. No plant or equipment maintenance occurred in 1995. Forty million dollars in bottom line benefits later, all Dunlap had really accomplished according to one despondent employee was to "….borrow a year, maybe two, from the future."

As always, Dunlap ruled by intimidation. One leader said, "Everyone talked about him. He put the fear of God into a lot of people. When he was in the building, people knew he was there. His presence was palpable."

Very few people paid much attention but, post-merger, Kimberly Clark's performance suffered badly. On top of an enormous $1.4 billion restructuring charge to cover the integration of Scott, actual profits were $160 million below what had been anticipated based on Scott's rosy projections for the fourth quarter of 1995. Leadership at Kimberly discovered mass accumulation of Scott paper and tissue products. This excess merchandise reflected Dunlap's policy of offering discounted prices to increase inventory, for purposes of maintaining unrealistically high sales and earnings numbers. Kimberly was forced to expend millions to provide basic maintenance—deliberately overlooked under the Dunlap regime—for plants and equipment. Kimberly lost significant market share in Scott Towels due to dumb strategic decisions—all designed to cut costs—by Dunlap. Kimberly was forced to take another restructuring charge, close plants, and, in the end, cut an additional 11,000 jobs after the merger with Scott. No matter. By that time Chainsaw Al was out the door, $100 million richer, and actively seeking his next gig.

Dunlap took over Sunbeam Corporation, the once iconic but now struggling appliance maker, in 1996. The stock price surged upon the news of his arrival. From the beginning, he made it clear that dramatic and painful changes would occur, and fast. He said, "I have a reputation to maintain. I don't want people to think I've lost my touch. I want big numbers."

The restructuring plan that Dunlap proposed to his board included firing half of Sunbeam's 12,000 people, eliminating almost 90 percent of existing product lines, closing or selling factories, warehouses, and regional offices en masse, and selling businesses. He also put forth an aggressive growth plan that included introduction of new product lines, joint ventures, and licensing agreements. Revenue would double by 1999, asserted Dunlap.

Dunlap's proposals were so draconian, however, and his growth scenarios so unrealistic, that Wall Street reacted with caution. He received criticism from skeptical management experts and incurred the ire of U. S. Labor Secretary Robert Reich who said, "There is no excuse for treating employees as if they were disposable pieces of equipment." All along, as had been true at Scott Paper and despite his protestations to the contrary, Dunlap's goal was to juice the numbers and prepare Sunbeam for sale. But no buyers came calling. In the end, Dunlap was forced to actually run the company, with disastrous results.

In an effort to perpetuate the perception of continued stellar earnings, Dunlap reverted to old (and some new) tricks. Invoices went unpaid. Retailers were encouraged through heavy discounts to purchase more product than they needed. Inventory piled up. Independent sales representatives did not receive their commissions. Numerous accounting changes were implemented that artificially boosted earnings. One of the most controversial techniques, called "bill-and-hold," involved selling product before it was needed, then holding the merchandise in a leased facility until the customer agreed to receive it in-store. Sunbeam immediately booked the sales and profits even though the customer might not accept the product for many months.

As always, Dunlap instilled terror in his team. One executive said, "There are tough people and then there are mean people. Tough people keep you up at night, worried about getting things done. Mean people make you piss in your pants. They scare the absolute shit out of you. They are violent. They beat on you. Al is a mean man." His intimidating style and his curious lack of interest in the details of the business made it impossible for anyone to tell him the truth. He became increasingly detached. Paranoia and mistrust ran rampant at every level of the company.

Wall Street finally took notice, as did his board, which unceremoniously fired Dunlap in 1998. His sacking brought great joy in many circles. Even his estranged family members were delighted. His son Troy said, "I laughed like hell. I'm glad he fell on his ass. I told him Sunbeam would be his Dunkirk." Dunlap's only sibling Denise said, "He got exactly what he deserved."

In the May 2009 issue of the business periodical *Conde Nast Portfolio*, Dunlap was rated the sixth worst CEO in all of American corporate history based on a poll of business school professors. The article stated, "You could call Chainsaw Al's story a fall from grace, but in his case, that's probably not the proper word." In his heyday, he symbolized "the middle finger of the free market's invisible hand," but Al Dunlap's downfall ultimately represents a tragic, cautionary tale of the dangers of a poisonous culture of mistrust.

Leadership Lesson Four:

WITHOUT TRUST THE BATTLE IS LOST

Early in my professional career, before I went to work for Target or Best Buy, I once observed a team whose leader was in many ways very capable. He was experienced and knowledgeable in the business, and a good operator. He had a commanding physical presence, was well-spoken, and could be charming and funny when he felt like it. He had strong ties to and the support of top management in his business unit. He was valued for his expertise.

But this leader tended to trust only a small band of sycophantic loyalists on his immediate team, and no one else. His functional team was highly insular. He led through fear and intimidation and loved to remind people of his powerful contacts among higher-ups. As it turned out, he was also pathologically dishonest and misbehaved in a number of ways that ultimately damaged individual people and the entire organization. It was only through the courageous actions of a small handful of folks, who put themselves at risk by stepping forward, that this individual was finally seen for who he was and forced to leave the organization.

This person, like George Custer and Al Dunlap, possessed many faults and committed many transgressions. Leaders like this are almost caricatures, and it is in some ways too easy to use them as examples. The simple and obvious lesson is: Don't do what these guys did.

To me, one of the really interesting and most consistent traits that these leaders have in common is that they all created a culture rife with mistrust. The very air about them was toxic with paranoia, intrigue, brown-nosing, back-stabbing, and ass-covering. Another notable similarity is how spectacularly they all failed when the end finally came. For each of them, without trust, the battle was completely lost.

But trust, even for leaders who are pure of heart and noble in intent, is still a very tricky and difficult thing. A leader cannot engender trust by simply saying, "Trust me." Trust is hard earned. Trust must be won. Trust takes time. Trust requires repeated demonstrations that the person who hopes to be trusted "walks the talk."

Do the members of your team trust each other? If so, isn't it amazing how smoothly things go and how much your team achieves? If not, why not? What is your position on the trust spectrum? Are you contributing to the mistrust, working to build better trust, or just waffling somewhere in the middle? The answers to these simple questions, in the end, can mean the difference between consistently outstanding business outcomes and abject, dismal, down-in-flames failure.

PART THREE

COMMUNICATE
CLEARLY & SHARE
INFORMATION

Chapter Five

GETTYSBURG

CEMETERY HILL: CONFIRM THAT THE AUDIENCE UNDERSTANDS YOUR MESSAGE

"Carry the hill occupied by the enemy, if practicable."

—General Robert E. Lee—

As late afternoon turned into early evening on the first day of the Battle of Gettysburg, one of the classic controversies of the Civil War played itself out. Confederate numbers and fighting skill had dislodged the Union First Corps from the ridges to the west, and the Eleventh Corps had been pushed from the north through town in a chaotic rout. What was left of these two disorganized units began to consolidate on the high ground of Cemetery Hill south of Gettysburg. The bedraggled men turned to face their Confederate enemies again and began to work furiously to fortify their position.

Rebel Second Corps commander Richard S. Ewell, flush from his success in knocking the Yankees back through town in disarray, pondered his next move. He was under orders from his superior, Robert E. Lee, to avoid a general engagement—orders Ewell had already technically violated by attacking the Federals north of town with great energy. Ewell now received a verbal order from Lee, through a staff officer, to take Cemetery Hill "if practicable," but also to continue to steer clear of a general engagement. The discretionary and confusing nature of this order, along with Ewell's ultimate decision that to take the hill was not "practicable," have engendered heated debate ever since.

From the standpoint of clarity of communication, Robert E. Lee failed to confirm that his intended audience—Richard Ewell—fully understood his message. The result of this failure to communicate clearly was that a golden, battle-winning opportunity may have been lost.

Richard Stoddert Ewell was born in 1817 in Washington, D. C., and raised in Virginia. He graduated thirteenth in a class of forty-two from West Point in 1840. He was almost entirely bald and therefore, not surprisingly, known as "Old Bald Head." He was quirky and eccentric, but also highly intelligent. Like so many of his fellow career officers, he fought courageously in the Mexican War and then battled Indians out west. He was wounded in a skirmish with Apache warriors in 1859. He started the Civil War as a lieutenant colonel in the state forces of Virginia, but was quickly promoted to brigadier general in the Confederate army. He led a brigade in the war's opening battle at Manassas.

Ewell first became well known as the second-in-command to the great Thomas J. "Stonewall" Jackson (the first commander of Lee's Second Corps) during Jackson's brilliant Shenandoah Valley campaign in the spring of 1862. This campaign—which involved deft trickery, hard marches, and sharp fighting as Jackson skillfully engaged Federal forces many times his size is still studied today in military academies and war colleges the world over. The campaign's architect, Stonewall Jackson, is arguably one of the great field generals of American military history.

Jackson, like Ewell, was also a quirky eccentric, but possessed the soul of a true warrior. As a soldier, Jackson was brilliant, bold, and aggressive. At first, Ewell thought Jackson was perhaps mentally unstable. But Ewell soon came to overlook Jackson's sometimes odd behavior and appreciate his formidable military abilities. Ewell transformed into Jackson's staunch supporter and disciple.

Jackson was a commander who gave precise orders. He did not want his subordinates to use their own discretion or judgment, but rather to carry out his directives to the letter. Jackson was a poor developer of talent. He held his cards close to his vest and did not consult with subordinates on matters of strategy and tactics. He spent no time teaching what he knew. He expected blind obedience to his orders and actively punished anything remotely resembling creativity on his team. In short, if one aspired to become the next Stonewall Jackson, the worst person in the world to work for was Stonewall Jackson. This style of leadership suited Ewell, who tended to see the world in black-and-white terms. Ewell appreciated clear direction and operated best when simply told what to do, rather than be required to make a critical decision on his own.

Jackson became by far the most trusted subordinate of Robert E. Lee. Lee—the master strategist—developed the plan and then turned matters over to Jackson—the daring tactician—who executed Lee's scheme. Lee said about his lieutenant, "I have but to show him my design, and I know that if it can be done it will be done." Lee came to rely heavily on Jackson. They formed a close bond, and their ability to communicate with each other bordered on telepathic. Lee knew with unfailing confidence that once he provided Jackson with broad guidelines and goals, Jackson would figure out a way to get the work done and almost invariably err on the side of vigorous action, in keeping with Lee's belief in the importance of the offensive.

The most dramatic example of the deft teamwork between Lee and Jackson occurred at the Battle of Chancellorsville near Spotsylvania, Virginia, in early May 1863. In the face of Joe Hooker's Union

Army of the Potomac, which outnumbered the Army of Northern Virginia by more than double, Lee and Jackson conferred and made a risky decision. While Lee held steady with a small force in the face of Hooker's army, Jackson would move with his entire 28,000-man corps in a stealthy twelve-mile march around the Yankee right flank. Once in position he would attack and roll up the Union line. Thanks mostly to the general timidity and indecisiveness on the part of "Mr. F. J. Hooker," Jackson moved undetected and struck the Yankee Eleventh Corps (the same unit that would be routed at Gettysburg two months later) on the right flank. Though Confederate casualties were heavy, the result was a disorderly retreat and complete defeat for the Union.

Tragically, at the very moment of his greatest triumph, Jackson was cut down. On the evening of May 2, after his successful attack, Jackson made a scouting ride with members of his staff. In the darkness, a unit of North Carolina troops, mistaking the dimly visible horsemen for Yankee cavalry, let loose a volley and Jackson was hit. At first it appeared he might recover, though his left arm had to be amputated. Unfortunately, he contracted pneumonia and died eight days later. His passing was deeply felt throughout the South. In particular, Robert E. Lee was despondent as he mourned Jackson's death. "It is a terrible loss," Lee wrote. "I do not know how to replace him."

Ewell was not a participant in any of this drama. At the Battle of Groveton, during the opening phase of the campaign of Second Manassas in August 1862, Ewell had been severely wounded. His left leg required amputation above the knee, and he spent nine months convalescing. He was eventually fitted with a wooden prosthesis. During his recovery, a widow named Lizinka Brown, who also happened to be Ewell's cousin, nursed him back to health. He had been fond of her for as long has he had known her and married her the day before he rejoined the army in late May of 1863. In his absent-minded eccentricity, even after their marriage, he sometimes referred to her as "Mrs. Brown." Ewell's critics have occasionally asserted that his status as a newlywed caused this formerly active commander to go soft at Gettysburg. We can only speculate as to exactly how his terrible injury, long recuperation, and the important new relationship in his life may have affected his subsequent behavior, but no doubt he was a changed man.

Robert E. Lee nevertheless had sufficient confidence in Ewell's professional abilities that he promoted him to command the Second Corps after Jackson's death. Lee did not regard Ewell as a particularly inspirational leader, but he wrote to President Jefferson Davis that Ewell was "an honest, brave soldier, who has always done his duty well." Lee also felt that the men of the Second Corps would welcome Ewell as their new commander, and in this Lee was correct.

But Ewell, though he had served under Stonewall Jackson and held the martyred hero in high regard, was nothing like Jackson. Lee soon came to find that Ewell, having become accustomed to Jackson's rigid leadership, would struggle with Lee's looser, more permissive, hands-off style of management and communication.

On June 3, 1863, the Confederate invasion of the North began. Longstreet's First Corps and Ewell's Second moved west from Fredericksburg, Virginia, to an assembly point at Culpepper. A. P. Hill's Third Corps remained in the original position opposite the Union pickets that occupied the north bank of the Rappahannock River, but the unit would follow in due time to join the rest of Lee's army.

On June 9, the largest cavalry engagement of the war took place at Brandy Station, northeast of Culpepper along the Orange and Alexandria Railroad. Union cavalry commander Alfred Pleasonton, during an effort to ascertain Lee's intentions, had surprised Jeb Stuart's cavalry division. The battle was essentially a tactical draw, but Stuart had been embarrassed by his own lack of vigilance and Union horsemen gained new confidence in their potential to fight successfully against their vaunted Southern counterparts.

The next afternoon, Ewell's infantry took the lead in marching due west to Sperryville, then north to Chester Gap and passage through the Blue Ridge Mountains to Front Royal in the Shenandoah Valley. The Allegheny Mountains to the west and the Blue Ridge to the east framed the Shenandoah Valley. Lee's idea was to use the Valley as a corridor to enemy territory and the Blue Ridge as a curtain to conceal his movements. Lee selected Ewell and his men to lead the way in recognition of their outstanding success in the Valley campaign of 1862.

On June 13 Joe Hooker and the Army of the Potomac backed away from the Rappahannock and began to track Lee on a line north to Manassas, cognizant of President Lincoln's orders to stay between Washington, D.C., and the Rebel forces.

On June 14 and 15 Ewell's Second Corps, proudly in the vanguard of the march, fought and won a tidy little victory at Winchester. Ewell caught a small Union force of 6,900 under Major General Robert Milroy by surprise. With great swiftness of maneuver, Ewell engineered a flanking attack that allowed him to inflict 443 casualties, take 4,000 prisoners, and capture 300 Yankee wagons, 300 horses, and twenty-three prized pieces of artillery. Ewell's men sustained only 269 casualties. At one point, as he observed the action through field glasses, a spent bullet struck Ewell in the chest. Though badly bruised, he continued to cheer his soldiers on. The engagement came to be known as the Second Battle of Winchester and would allow Lee to continue his invasion unhindered to crossing points over the Potomac River.

General Hill followed Ewell's lead by moving west from Fredericksburg on June 15. Longstreet moved from Culpepper north to Ashby's and Snicker's Gaps, then west into the Valley. By June 19, all three Confederate corps were now positioned to use the Blue Ridge as cover, and Hooker struggled mightily to determine their whereabouts. In a series of small but sharp cavalry skirmishes as the two armies traveled north, Hooker's horsemen failed to penetrate the mountain gaps to discover Lee's columns and where they were going.

Ewell's orders were to continue into Pennsylvania, collecting supplies for the army as he marched. His three divisions were to fan out with Robert Rodes's and Edward "Allegheny" Johnson's divisions to move northeast in the direction of the capital city of Harrisburg.

Ewell had permission to capture Harrisburg if the opportunity presented itself. Jubal Early's division would move east through the gaps in South Mountain (the extension of Virginia's Blue Ridge in Pennsylvania) through Gettysburg and on to York.

One tragic aspect of Lee's invasion involved the seizure by Rebel soldiers of African-Americans—many of whom had been born free and had lived on Northern soil all their lives—to be marched south and sold into slavery. As word of this dastardly practice spread, black families scattered in all directions to avoid the approach of Lee's army. There is no evidence of official sanction by the Confederate high command, but instances of such capture were widespread, so it is clear that Rebel officers implicitly condoned the activity. Estimates of how many blacks were subjected to this outrage through the course of the Gettysburg campaign number in the hundreds.

Jeb Stuart and three of his five cavalry brigades set off for Pennsylvania and his infamous ride around the Union army on June 25. Lee had directed Stuart to protect Ewell's right flank, but Lee also said: "You will, however, be able to judge whether you can pass around their army without hinderance [sic], doing them all the damage you can, and cross the [Potomac] river east of the mountains. In either case, after crossing the river, you must move on and feel the right of Ewell's troops, collecting information, provisions, &c [sic]." That Stuart might choose to pass completely around the Yankee army was therefore a possibility Lee accepted. But that Stuart would be mightily delayed in the process, lose touch with Ewell (and Lee) completely, and leave the army blind for eight days, Lee did not anticipate. While Stuart certainly bore significant responsibility, this episode served as another example of the potential pitfalls of Lee's highly discretionary and sometimes unclear style of communication.

By June 28, the divisions of Rodes and Johnson camped in proximity to Carlisle, preparing to move forward and capture Harrisburg. Early's division lay further south near York. Ewell's Second Corps was therefore widely spread out, and each of his units sat better than twenty miles away from Gettysburg. When Lee received information from Longstreet's spy that the Federal army was close at hand, he issued orders to Ewell to move east to meet the rest of the army at Chambersburg. However, the next morning on June 29, Lee changed his mind and sent word to Ewell to move directly south via Heidlersburg "in the direction of Gettysburg." Ewell felt frustration for the lost opportunity to take the capital city, but he quickly complied with Lee's orders.

At the same time, Lee and the First and Third Corps moved east from Chambersburg through the gap in South Mountain to rendezvous with Ewell. Harry Heth's division of A. P. Hill's corps, at the tip of the spear, reached Cashtown on June 30. Fighting with John Buford's Union cavalry commenced the next morning. Ewell proceeded with all due haste to the sound of the guns in time to arrive with his lead elements on the northern end of the battlefield early on the afternoon of July 1.

Ewell reached the field at a critical juncture. Despite Lee's admonition to avoid a general engagement, Ewell's men quickly became involved in an artillery duel with the enemy. Ewell made a decision to maintain momentum and continue the fight. Ewell said later, "It was too late to avoid an engagement without abandoning the position already taken up, and I determined to push the attack vigorously." His lead division, commanded by Rodes, deployed and moved forward to meet elements of the Union First Corps near Oak Hill. Jubal Early's division arrived from the northeast and immediately attacked the Union Eleventh Corps, which had rushed into positions directly north of town to meet the onslaught. After much hard combat and give and take, the weight of Ewell's assault from the north along with A. P. Hill's from the west broke the Yankee line and sent blue-clad troopers retreating through town to their rallying point on Cemetery Hill.

Just prior to the shattering of the Union line, Ewell, who had moved toward Early's position to assess the situation, was thrown to the ground when a projectile struck and killed his horse. Ewell was clearly shaken but unhurt, dusted himself off, found another mount, and resumed his duties. This near miss—coupled with the incident in which a spent bullet had hit and bruised his chest just two weeks earlier at Winchester—had to have been disconcerting for Ewell. How it may have affected his later conduct we cannot know, but the presence of constant peril during combat undoubtedly weighs on and distracts a soldier's mind (modern-day analysts should take pause when inclined to harshly judge historical battlefield decisions. Hindsight is always 20/20 and it is easy to negatively evaluate military leaders from the comfort and safety of one's study. No business leader today must make life and death decisions, with incomplete information, while in very real and sustained personal danger of being injured or killed).

The Federal line broke around 4:00 p.m. An hour later, Ewell rode into town behind his tired but energized soldiers. Ewell took stock of his forces: Rodes's division was in tough shape with 2,500 casualties, fatigued, and disorganized; Early was in somewhat better condition, and Allegheny Johnson's division was still en route, about an hour's march away to the east. Ewell wanted to follow up on his success. He scouted Cemetery Hill with his staff from Baltimore Street south of the town square, but they came under enemy fire. He found a safe spot from which he observed formidable defenses being put into place on the heights. Many cannon (eventually forty-three) along with solid lines of infantry facing north and west made any assault a daunting proposition, but Ewell was willing to try with help from A. P. Hill to the west.

Ewell sent a courier to find Lee, who established his headquarters near the Chambersburg Pike northwest of town, with a request for support. A moment later a staffer from Lee arrived with verbal instructions that Ewell was "to carry the hill occupied by the enemy, if he found it practicable, but to avoid a general engagement until the arrival of the other divisions of the army...." In other words, Ewell had authority to use his discretion in making a decision. In Lee's defense, he was obviously not on the scene to make his own assessment. A commander sometimes needs to rely on his subordinates to use their judgment.

On the other hand, the challenge of how to carry a hill bristling with defensive works without bringing on a "general engagement" seems difficult and perhaps impossible. As historian Stephen Sears noted, Ewell "was urged to start a fight but not to start a battle." At the very least, Lee's verbiage was perplexing and open to more than one interpretation.

Further, by this time in the course of their relationship, Lee should have been well aware of Ewell's need for clarity. Lee should have known his audience better and adapted his communication style to fit the individual. Had Lee delivered such an order to Jackson, he might well have expected Jackson to immediately launch an attack with all available resources. But Ewell was not Jackson, and Lee missed an opportunity to tailor his approach in a way that might have been more helpful to his subordinate and achieved a better result.

Finally, the situation was complicated by the fact that Lee's directive was delivered verbally via an intermediary, rather than in writing. Again, as overall commander, Lee could only be in one place at a time, and it was standard battlefield procedure to deliver communication by messenger. Lee was somewhat paranoid about delivering written messages for fear they might fall into the hands of the enemy. Nevertheless, Lee and Ewell were probably never physically more than a mile apart as this drama unfolded. Had Lee taken the opportunity to consult in person with Ewell at this critical moment, had he been able to look Ewell in the eye and ensure that his intent was clearly understood, they might have arrived at a better decision. We will never know.

In any event, Ewell had multiple issues at this point. He was alerted to the possibility that Union troops in force might be approaching his position from the northeast. This report turned out to be false, but it wasted time and energy for Ewell and reduced his available force for attack when he posted two brigades to guard his rear as a precautionary measure. Ewell's messenger, who had crossed paths with Lee's, was inquiring with the commanding officer as to the possibility of support from A. P. Hill in Ewell's effort—which he and his subordinates Rodes and Early were willing to undertake—to capture Cemetery Hill.

When Ewell's messenger reached Lee with the request for help, Lee turned to his trusted advisor Longstreet. The closest First Corps division was still six miles away and Longstreet was lukewarm to the idea of committing troops to assist Ewell. Disregarding the fact that A. P. Hill's corps was at hand—though relatively bloodied from the day's fighting, Hill did have at least one fresh division and artillery that could have been thrown into the fray—Lee told the messenger to apologize to Ewell because support was not available. Lee also asked that Ewell be reminded to take the hill if possible. Perhaps Lee was still adamant that his entire army should be together before undertaking a major fight, or he may still have been uncertain that Gettysburg was the suitable place for battle. The practical result was that Ewell was on his own.

Before receiving Lee's refusal of his request, Ewell had begun to consider instead the option of an assault on Culp's Hill. This objective sat a little less than a thousand yards east of Cemetery Hill. Due to its greater elevation, Culp's Hill could potentially command Cemetery Hill in a way that would negate the need to make the difficult and bloody attack on the latter. Ewell could potentially capture a more valuable piece of real estate, and do it in such a way as to avoid the full-blown battle that his superior was not yet ready to bring about.

Ewell ordered a reconnaissance of Culp's Hill, and his scouts reported back that the hill was unoccupied and offered a chance to dominate and potentially clear Cemetery Hill. Unbeknownst to the Confederates, Yankee defenders were in fact quickly accumulating on Culp's Hill, their own commanders—General Hancock in particular—having recognized its tactical significance. But the Union presence was still small, and Ewell had a prime opportunity to act. He failed to do so, again.

Allegheny Johnson's fresh division, whose arrival had appeared to be imminent, was delayed in its route to the battlefield by a ponderous supply train. Ewell turned to Jubal Early, who had two brigades on hand, but who now complained that his troops were spent and had already been asked to do too much marching and fighting on this day. Instead of taking charge of the situation and ordering Early to move into action, Ewell decided to wait for Johnson's men, whenever they might arrive. This was a deeply unfortunate turn of events for the Confederate cause, as there were still a couple of hours of daylight left and Early's force would in all likelihood have been able to carry and occupy Culp's Hill.

When Johnson finally arrived, Ewell instructed him to assault Culp's Hill, but only if he found it unoccupied. Why Ewell wouldn't have ordered Johnson to attack as soon as possible regardless of whether the hill was occupied or not is open to question. Ewell then finally received a visit from General Lee, and matters of larger strategic importance came to occupy his attention. During this conference the generals discussed Ewell's decision not to assault Cemetery Hill, but Lee pressed Ewell on the possibility of an attack in the morning. Ewell and his subordinates argued against the idea, for Cemetery Hill would be no less formidable (and probably more so) in the morning than it was at this time. Lee then inquired whether Second Corps should abandon its position entirely and move around to the right to join the rest of the army. Lee's audience did not like that idea either. The meeting ended with agreement that Ewell would stay where he was and conduct diversionary operations the next day, as Lee decided the main assault would go against the Union left flank to the south (see Gettysburg Map Number Three, July 1, 1863, Late Evening).

Lee returned to his headquarters, but then exercised the commander's prerogative to change his mind. He sent another messenger to Ewell telling him he wanted Second Corps to move to the right after all. Ewell was sufficiently alarmed by this proposition that he rode to see Lee personally and debate the issue all over again. At this time, over the course of an hour, Ewell argued that the capture of Culp's Hill would present an opportunity to knock the Yanks off Cemetery Hill. Lee finally acquiesced, but precious time had been lost in talk rather than action. For when Ewell returned to his headquarters near midnight, he found that Allegheny Johnson had made no effort against Culp's Hill. Johnson had instead remained essentially idle for five hours, and Ewell had been guilty of not "inspecting what he expected." The tardy Johnson finally conducted a probing movement against the position in the pitch-black darkness, which resulted in a quick and violent repulse of Confederate scouts. Many historians would assert that Culp's Hill, rather than Cemetery Hill, had it been attacked in a timely matter, may have been the better tactical option. Perhaps the most important opportunity of the day had been irretrievably lost.

While Confederate forces no doubt carried the day on July 1 at Gettysburg, serious lapses in communication prevented what could have been a battle-winning setup for the next day. Yankee forces occupied the critical high ground and would never be knocked from their perch. If Lee had been crystal clear in his messaging directing Ewell to take Cemetery Hill, and if an assault had commenced immediately or been supported with additional troops and firepower, there was at least the possibility of success. Military historians and analysts mostly agree now that taking the hill at any point, even early on, would have been an extremely tough proposition; but what is never attempted will never be accomplished.

Similarly, Ewell himself was guilty of both waffling in his orders and lax oversight of his subordinates. After passing on the idea of assaulting Cemetery Hill, he missed another opportunity to take a prized piece of real estate in Culp's Hill. All in all, not the best performance by this command team from a communication standpoint. As a result of overall failure to check that the audience understood the message, Robert E. Lee and his subordinates failed to capitalize on their dramatic initial success and would live to regret the consequences.

★ ★ CASE STUDY ★ ★

JOHNSON & JOHNSON
AND THE TYLENOL TRAGEDY:
COMMUNICATIONS MASTERPIECE

In 1982 the highly respected health care and pharmaceutical company Johnson & Johnson confronted a tragic public relations and communications challenge the likes of which have rarely been experienced in corporate America. The company's handling of the situation has come to be seen as the quintessential model for crisis communication strategies. The leadership team performed brilliantly in making sure that critical communication was completely clear and perfectly understood. By skillfully using myriad channels, Johnson & Johnson not only succeeded in ensuring that its messaging around public safety reached the intended audience, but also enhanced its reputation with that same audience and laid the foundation for a full recovery from the disaster.

Over time, the pain medication Tylenol had become the most important product in Johnson & Johnson's line of offerings. By 1982, Tylenol was used by 100 million Americans and owned 37 percent of the market for painkillers, outselling its next four leading competitors combined. For the first three quarters of 1982, Tylenol would account for nearly 20 percent of Johnson & Johnson's profits. Revenues from Tylenol alone would have placed Johnson & Johnson in the top half of the *Fortune* 500.

In October 1982, seven people died suddenly and mysteriously on the west side of Chicago. An investigation quickly determined that each of these individuals had ingested an Extra-Strength Tylenol capsule laced with sixty-five milligrams of the deadly poison cyanide (more than 10,000 times the dosage required to kill a human being). A treacherous person or persons had replaced Tylenol capsules with the cyanide-laced substitutes, resealed the packaging, and then placed the product on the shelves of several area pharmacies and food stores. When innocent and unsuspecting people began to die agonizing deaths, media reaction was swift and sensational. A near national panic ensued.

Johnson & Johnson officials first learned of the situation from a Chicago-area reporter who called the public relations department and asked for their comment about a press conference from a medical examiner who stated people were dying from ingesting Tylenol. One of the company's public relations directors said, "In that first call, we learned more from the reporter than he did from us." Nevertheless, despite being caught flatfooted, the company reacted immediately.

The chairman of Johnson & Johnson, James Burke, quickly assembled a seven-member strategy group. His first and foremost challenge to the team was to protect the public. This was their primary mission. Second, and less important, was to save the product if possible. Consumer safety came first, before any consideration of financial impacts. In arriving at this critical decision, Burke and team had to look no further than the company Credo, written by Robert Johnson in 1943: "We believe our first responsibility is to doctors, nurses and patients, to mothers and fathers and all others who use our products and services." The Johnson & Johnson team was about to live out the true meaning of that mission.

The company jumped into action by using the media to alert consumers not to take Tylenol in any form, until the extent of the problem became better understood. Production of and advertising for Tylenol ceased. All Tylenol capsules were withdrawn from store shelves in Chicago and surrounding areas. The local action was followed by a nationwide recall of 31 million bottles of Tylenol at a cost to the company of $100 million.

The company initiated relationships with the Chicago Police Department, the FBI, and the Food and Drug Administration, so as to participate in the effort to solve the crime. Johnson & Johnson offered a $100,000 reward for information leading to apprehension of the murderer(s) and provided counseling and financial assistance to the families of victims.

The company established a toll-free number for inquiries from the public concerning Tylenol and a toll-free line to provide daily updates to news organizations. National level press conferences were followed with appearances on *60 Minutes* and *The Phil Donahue Show* by Chairman James Burke to continue to hammer home the message that Johnson & Johnson took full responsibility for fixing the situation and ensuring public safety.

The second phase of Johnson & Johnson's communications strategy, after the immediate situation had been dealt with involved restoring trust in the company and its flagship product, Tylenol. Immediately after the incident, the company's stock price dropped seven points and market share for painkillers dipped to a meager 8 percent. Within thirty days, the company took several key affirmative steps to regain public confidence. First, Tylenol products were reintroduced in triple-seal tamper-resistant packaging, making Johnson & Johnson the first company to comply with the Food and Drug Administration's new regulations and mandate for such packaging. Also, Johnson & Johnson promoted the use of caplets, which are less susceptible to tampering.

Next, the company provided $2.50-off coupons for Tylenol, which people could clip from newspapers or receive by calling a toll-free number. A revised pricing program went into effect that provided consumer discounts as high as 25 percent, and a new advertising campaign was launched in 1983. Finally, the company deployed more than 2,250 sales specialists from domestic affiliates to make presentations to the medical community to restore confidence in Tylenol. In the end, the comeback of Johnson & Johnson and Tylenol was a resounding success, helped in no small part by the intelligent, compassionate manner in which the company handled the initial crisis.

Accolades for Johnson & Johnson's response to this tragic act of a depraved mind came in both immediately and after the fact. On October 11, 1982, the *Washington Post* stated, "Johnson & Johnson has effectively demonstrated how a major business ought to handle a disaster.... This is no Three Mile Island accident in which the company's response did more damage than the original incident.... [W]hat Johnson & Johnson executives have done is communicate the message that the company is candid, contrite, and compassionate, committed to solving the murders and protecting the public." Eight years later in a scholarly journal, an analyst summarized, "The Tylenol crisis is without a doubt the most exemplary case ever known in the history of crisis communications. Any business executive who has ever stumbled into a public relations ambush ought to appreciate the way Johnson & Johnson responded to the Tylenol poisonings. They have effectively demonstrated how major business has to handle a disaster."

Within very short order after the initial event, Tylenol's prominent place within the marketplace for painkillers had been re-established. If anything, the overall reputation of Johnson & Johnson as a great American company who sincerely looked after its customers was enhanced. Clear communication, repeated over and over using multiple channels, with a deft feel for the audience, had enabled Johnson & Johnson to recover from the precipice of disaster and move confidently into the future.

Leadership Lesson Five:

CONFIRM THAT THE AUDIENCE UNDERSTANDS YOUR MESSAGE

As a human resources professional, I was involved on several occasions over the years in the administration of reductions in force. In other words, we had to go through the very painful exercise of firing people en masse. Through a process of trial and error, what we discovered over time was perhaps surprising: Even if the truth was incredibly distressing, people wanted to know as much as we could tell them, as soon as we could tell them. They wanted management to look them in the eye and tell them the unvarnished truth, or to at least share as much information as possible. They also appreciated communication through as many channels as were available.

They wanted to make sure, in turn, that their concerns were heard and understood. Because of this imperative for abundant two-way communication in those trying and sensitive situations, it was critical that leadership crafted messaging carefully and confirmed, again and again, that the intended audience comprehended the message.

Our communication strategies took many forms. We assembled cross-functional working teams to manage the process around the clock. We provided written updates for the larger team via e-mail. We shared information through Q & A, which was continually updated as we received new questions and fresh data. We provided call-in numbers for people to get their queries answered and made HR representatives available for consultation.

Perhaps most important, we held team-by-team meetings in which business leaders, with HR support, were responsible for talking to their people face-to-face to address questions and concerns. We held larger town hall meetings in which top management appeared and interacted with employees. We provided outplacement counseling for individuals who were laid off.

No process like this ever goes perfectly, but we found that more communication rather than less, with an emphasis on making sure people understood the message, not only worked effectively but also was the right thing to do.

Johnson & Johnson provided a superb example of just such a communication process in the early '80s. In the face of tragedy, the company focused primarily on the right thing to do, based on a decades-old values statement that turned out to be very real, not just words, and only secondarily on the costs to the company. In so doing, Johnson & Johnson provided a model for the ages for how to craft a compassionate, responsible message, using multiple channels of communication, and to ensure a positive impact on the intended audience.

Conversely, Robert E. Lee realized the very real dangers in not confirming understanding. Had Lee shown more dexterity in understanding the individual quirks of his command team, had he been more clear in his choice of words, had he communicated in writing rather than verbally, or had he bothered to take the time to talk with his subordinate Richard Ewell face-to-face instead of via messenger, the Battle of Gettysburg and the Civil War might have turned out very differently.

Chapter Six

LITTLE BIGHORN

MEDICINE TAIL COULEE: HOLD INFORMATION CLOSE AT YOUR PERIL

"… you and I are going home today,
and by a trail that is strange to us both."

—Half Yellow Face—

To the Lakota Indians, the vast region in western Dakota Territory that they called Paha Sapa, or "Hills That Are Black," was a sacred place. It was part of the Great Sioux Reservation and, though theirs by birthright, these ancestral hunting grounds had also been ceded to the Sioux by treaty. Within these Black Hills, it had been rumored for years, lay gold.

In the summer of 1874, George Custer led a 1,000-man expedition from Fort Abraham Lincoln west to the Black Hills. In addition to his mighty military host, Custer brought with him a geologist, two miners, and some newspaper reporters. Their mission was to find gold, which indeed, in short order, they succeeded in doing. News of Custer's discovery spread far and wide, causing a gold rush the likes of which had not been seen since prospectors headed to California en masse in 1849. This influx of white intruders into their territory greatly angered the Sioux and precipitated the series of events that led to the showdown at the Little Bighorn in 1876.

Ironically, though Custer was always swift to ensure that information that made him look good was distributed as widely as possible, he was much more circumspect in sharing critical strategic and tactical data at the level of his own leadership team. Throughout the campaign that led to his last battle, his multiple failures to keep his team informed and to clearly communicate his intentions and desires were directly responsible for his downfall. Custer provides a classic example of a leader who held information too closely. The result of this breakdown of communication was extremely detrimental to him and to his team.

After Custer's 1874 expedition, the white public demanded that governmental policy makers open the Black Hills to gold-seekers. When unwilling Indians refused to sell their land back to the U. S. government, the Grant administration simply trumped up charges that the Indians were in violation of the treaty of 1868, which had given them the Black Hills in the first place.

In November 1875 the government ordered all non-treaty Indians (those who roamed free outside of the reservation) to come in to reservations by January 31, 1876, or face the wrath of the U. S. army. Very few Indians complied. One warrior said, "We were in our own country and doing no harm." Even General Philip Sheridan stated that the government's order "will in all probability be regarded as a good joke by the Indians." Sitting Bull and Crazy Horse in particular were adamant that they would defend the Black Hills to the death from white incursion.

The government therefore unleashed its strategy of converging three columns—Colonel Gibbon from Montana Territory moving east, General Crook from Wyoming Territory moving north, and General Terry and Custer from Dakota Territory moving west—to trap the recalcitrant Indians. The Seventh began its journey on May 17. General Terry boasted with supreme confidence he had "no doubt of the ability of my column to whip all the Sioux we can find." It soon became apparent, however, that it would take many weeks on the march before those Sioux would be discovered.

Unbeknownst to Terry, Custer, and Gibbon, on June 17 General Crook and his Wyoming column of 1,300 men met a force of about 700 Sioux and Cheyenne warriors, led by Crazy Horse as their war chief and Sitting Bull (who did not participate in the fighting). The Indians surprised Crook and his men as they camped along Rosebud Creek, about twenty-five miles southeast of the Indian village near the Little Bighorn River. Though outnumbered, the Sioux and Cheyenne fought aggressively in a day-long battle that was a tactical draw. Crook ended the fight still in possession of the field, claiming victory.

But the effect of the Battle of the Rosebud was to take the Wyoming force out of the strategic equation, because Crook returned south to his base at Goose Creek where he waited six weeks for resupply. Crook also failed to inform Terry and Custer of what had transpired with his force. The battle served as a huge confidence boost for Sitting Bull, Crazy Horse, and their warriors, who had attacked furiously and held their own against the superior numbers of the hated wasichu.

On June 21, in a strategy session attended by Custer and Colonel Gibbon aboard the steamship *Far West,* at the confluence of the Powder and Yellowstone Rivers, General Terry outlined his plans. Gibbon's Montana column, with its supplement of infantry, would serve as a blocking force. Terry and Gibbon would head to the mouth of the Bighorn River, and then proceed south to its tributary the Little Bighorn, thus preventing any escape of Indians to the north. Meanwhile, Custer and his larger but more mobile striking force would move to the headwaters of the Rosebud. If the Indian trail diverged west Custer was to delay in order to give Terry and Gibbon time to position themselves on the Little Bighorn, then proceed north through the valley of the Little Bighorn to drive the enemy into Gibbon's waiting soldiers. Terry estimated he and Gibbon could reach the Little Big-horn by June 26.

Terry offered Custer rapid-fire Gatling guns to take with him, and much has been made subsequently of his decline of that option. Custer was not ordered to take the guns, but given a choice. In fact, the Gatlings were cumbersome and highly prone to misfire. Custer felt these weapons gave him no particular tactical advantage, and he wanted nothing to hinder his ability to move rapidly.

Much has also been made of Custer's "disobedience" of Terry's orders as the disastrous series of missteps leading to the Little Big-horn unfolded. But Terry's written orders were highly discretionary. Deferring to Custer's superior military experience, Terry in effect gave him carte blanche to use his judgment in assessing the situation. Terry said, "It is of course impossible to give you any definite instructions in regard to this movement, and, were it not impossible to do so, the Department Commander places too much confidence in your zeal, energy and ability to impose on you precise orders which might hamper your action when nearly in contact with the enemy." Within very broad strategic guidelines, therefore, Custer's mission essentially became to seek out and capture or destroy his opponent, in the best way he knew how.

As Custer and the Seventh Cavalry rode off to their destiny on June 22 , Gibbon shouted to Custer, "Now Custer, don't be greedy, but wait for us." "No, I will not," replied Custer, as he laughed and gave a final wave good-bye. Custer, wearing a buckskin jacket and pants, a red scarf about his throat, and a gray, broad-brimmed hat, traveled at the head of about 660 officers, enlisted men, Indian scouts, and a handful of civilians. Each enlisted man was armed with a breechloading, single-shot 1873 Springfield carbine. These weapons were heavy and reliable at long range but, unfortunately for the Seventh, many of their Indian opponents in the upcoming battle would be armed with repeating rifles, which were less effective from a distance but deadly at close quarters. The standard army sidearm, carried by both officers and enlisted men, was the Colt 45 pistol. The men were energetic and optimistic about their situation and happy to be underway again on the trail of the Lakota and Cheyenne enemy. But their well-being on this campaign, the last for many of them, would be seriously compromised by a dysfunctional leadership team that, among other faults, communicated poorly.

At the end of the opening day's march, the first of several critical breakdowns in communication occurred when Custer called his officers together for a briefing. They gathered near his tent, and he began by discussing various details connected with the march. With great prescience, he predicted they would meet an Indian force of as many as 1,500 warriors. The pervasive idea that Custer must have been shocked by the number of Indians that ultimately confronted him is untrue. He believed the Seventh could defeat whatever number foe they might face and stated they would follow the trail until they found the enemy. Custer's primary concern was that the Indians would disperse before they could be engaged.

Astoundingly, he made no mention of the strategic concept of the campaign involving Terry and Gibbon as a blocking force and Custer's Seventh as a strike force, or that the regiment had been specifically directed to link up with Terry and Gibbon at the Little Bighorn on June 26. In effect, unless they had somehow heard the news through the grapevine, Custer's officers had no clue with respect to the overall plan for the campaign. Such information, at the very least, might have given them confidence that there was an overarching thought process beyond simply riding until the enemy came into view. In addition, if Custer became incapacitated—which in fact he did, permanently so, on Last Stand Hill on June 25—his subordinates would have known that a link-up with Terry and Gibbon was anticipated, where and when. But Custer chose to hold on to this essential information.

By June 24, the Seventh had completed much hard riding. Custer's scouts knew that a gigantic convergence of trails indicated a large gathering of Indians coming together and moving west, past the Rosebud to the valley of the Little Bighorn. In the early morning light of June 25, these same scouts pointed west from the elevated spot known as the Crow's Nest to the enormous camp fifteen miles distant. Though he struggled to see what his scouts assured him was there, when he received information that his regiment had been discovered, Custer made the momentous decision to forego rest and careful reconnaissance and instead to attack immediately.

At this point, in another critical decision that would further hamper his communications capability, Custer determined to reorganize and subsequently split his forces into four separate units. The entire command moved west, through the divide and past the Crow's Nest, into a narrow valley. The regiment attained the headwaters of a little creek, later to become known as Reno Creek, which meandered in the direction of the Little Bighorn. During a halt, Custer made his organizational assignments.

Custer retained control of five companies, C, E, F, I, and L. Two of Custer's favorite subordinates, Myles Keogh and George Yates, would each command a wing of this battalion, about 220 men in total, under Custer's overall direction. Custer put Major Reno in charge of another battalion, consisting of companies A, G, and M, with about 150 officers and troopers. Captain Benteen would command companies D, H, and K, approximately 130 strong. Finally, Captain Thomas McDougall and his B company, with attachments from other units, would lead 135 men assigned to guard the mule-drawn pack train.

One of Custer's Crow scouts, Half Yellow Face, hearing of the plan, offered tactical advice through an interpreter, saying, "Do not divide your men. There are too many of the enemy for us, even if we stay together. If you must fight, keep us all together." Custer replied testily, "You do the scouting, and I will attend to the fighting." Half Yellow Face, along with several of the other scouts, began to strip out of his army dress and into Crow war regalia. The men painted their faces. Custer, his curiosity piqued, inquired through the interpreter why they were taking such action. Half Yellow Face responded with foreboding, "Because you and I are going home today, and by a trail that is strange to us both."

While the Seventh halted, Custer also directed Captain Benteen to take his three companies and scout some bluffs Custer had observed to the southwest. Benteen was instructed to "pitch into" any Indians he might encounter. If he found nothing, he was to countermarch and rejoin the main body. Benteen, ever mistrustful of Custer's motives, saw this assignment as a direct attempt to remove any possibility that Benteen might win glory in the upcoming battle. It appears, however, that Custer truly intended that Benteen only be gone a short while to check out the situation, and then return. But clearly this was not how Benteen interpreted his orders.

Custer failed to communicate Benteen's orders to Reno. As Benteen turned to ride south, Reno asked him where he was going. Benteen replied vaguely that he was simply to drive everything before him. Thus continued the breakdown of communication and unraveling of order that would plague the Seventh for the remainder of the day. As Libbie Custer (who in the past had often accompanied her husband on campaign) once commented, "The general planned every military action with so much secrecy that we were left to divine as best we could what certain preliminary movements meant."

Custer, Reno, and their eight companies now proceeded to follow the course of the stream for several more miles. The slow-moving pack train fell far to the rear. The scouts, who had ranged ahead, came across an abandoned campsite and two tipis about five miles from the main encampment on the Little Bighorn. They also saw a war party of about fifty Indians ride away in the distance, and could only assume these men were headed off to warn the village of the approaching soldiers.

When Custer arrived on the scene, he immediately dispatched his adjutant, Lieutenant William Cooke, to instruct Reno to follow the fleeing Indians and begin the attack. Cooke told Reno, "The Indians are about two and a half miles ahead—they are on the jump. Go forward as fast as you think proper and charge them wherever you find them and we will support you."

As Reno moved out with his troops, Custer shouted "Take your battalion and try and overtake and bring them to battle and I will support you. And take the scouts with you." Reno later stated that, based on these assurances, he fully believed Custer intended to directly follow Reno's command into the valley toward the village.

It was around two o'clock on a stifling hot afternoon. Benteen had been gone two hours on what was supposed to be a short scout. Custer had heard nothing from Benteen. Custer had still not fully viewed the village that lay ahead and, again, had not relayed any concept of an overall plan to Reno or Benteen. The breakdown of communication continued.

Reno's command moved three miles forward and crossed the Little Bighorn to the western side. The Indians in their encampment were now in view farther ahead on the plain. For all of the commotion and concern about the village being alerted to the coming of the wasi-chu, in fact, the Sioux and Cheyenne were genuinely surprised to see soldiers. But they quickly got over their shock and assembled to fight.

One of the scouts, Frederic Gerard, informed Reno, "Major, the Indians are coming up the valley to meet us." With that, Reno delivered the order, "Forward." Gerard rode away to inform Custer that Reno was about to engage the enemy. As Reno's men formed up in column of fours, they saw Custer and his five companies on the hills to the right moving rapidly north. Reno must have wondered whether Custer would truly "support" him, as promised.

When Custer received the news from Gerard a short while later that the Indians in front of Reno were not scattering but advancing to fight, instead of going to Reno's aid, Custer made a wholly different decision. He chose to use the age-old tactic of the pincer movement. He would count on Reno's force to hold the enemy in place, while Custer and his battalion rode to the north around the flank to prevent the Indians from escaping. This was the method Custer had successfully employed at the Washita River in 1868.

Not surprisingly, though Reno made a concerted effort to communicate his situation to Custer (Reno sent a second messenger a short while after Gerard's departure to again inform his commander he was about to engage with the Indians), Custer did not return the favor. Whether Custer thought that Reno would divine his intentions or otherwise, there was no message telling Reno that he was on his own and that Custer was moving ahead with his battalion (see Little Bighorn Map Number Three, Custer's Approach to Medicine Tail Coulee and Reno's Retreat, Mid-Afternoon).

As Reno's men advanced, they could now see hundreds of tipis in a series of large circles. More important, a horde of warriors, angry and mobilized for battle, were moving in their direction. It was now about 3:30 p.m. An aggressive commander—such as Custer, for example—might have moved as swiftly as possible to meet the enemy head on in hopes of causing him to fall back and become disorganized. But rather than proceed with his attack on horseback into the village, Reno began to lose his nerve and ordered his men to dismount and form a skirmish line. They were still half a mile from the camp.

Undoubtedly Reno had not anticipated such stiff resistance, and he now also surmised that Custer would not come to his assistance. There are many eyewitness reports that Reno repeatedly drank out of a whisky flask during this time frame. He began to act erratically and, in keeping with the general pattern for officers in the Seventh, communicated poorly with his men.

The excited troopers exercised little fire discipline as they discharged their breech-loading Springfield carbines toward the Indians in the distance. After about fifteen minutes, the skirmish line they had formed began to be outflanked on the left by the rapidly massing Sioux and Cheyenne. Reno ordered his men to move into a stand of timber next to the river, where some of the troops had already been dispatched to hold the horses. The soldiers retreated but continued to pour fire into the enemy from the position in the woods. All was noise and confusion and, one man recalled, "It was one long continuous roar."

Now Indians began to infiltrate the wooded position. Ammunition was running low. Reno made a determination that this spot was untenable and that the battalion had to move. He decided to retreat to some high bluffs across the river to the southeast. Reno delivered his order to mount up through subordinates, but in the chaos of the moment, many of the men did not get the message. Great anxiety and increasing confusion set in while the soldiers scrambled to find their horses.

As he struggled in the din to talk with the scout Bloody Knife (Custer's personal favorite), Reno received an unbelievable shock when a bullet hit Bloody Knife in the head, splattering bone splinters and brain matter all over Reno. Dazed by this horrifying surprise, Reno now gave an order to dismount. Again, some troopers heard him and some did not. He followed quickly with another order to mount up.

Finally, and unforgivably, Reno shouted, "Any of you men who wish to make your escape, draw your revolvers and follow me." He raced away on his horse, without regard to the state of the unit he left behind, with no plan for a rearguard action, and with no apparent intent to retrieve his dead and wounded.

Panic now ran rampant. Not surprisingly, someone called out, "Every man for himself." Any soldier who could do so followed Major Reno, who was hell-bent to save himself, out of the woods, onto the plain, across the river, and toward the 200-foot-high bluffs. In the process, the emboldened Indians fired into the retreating mass, chased men down in the river, and generally caused heavy casualties among Reno's beleaguered troopers, both those abandoned in the woods and those attempting their escape to the hills. The Indians later likened the experience of the race to the high ground to a buffalo hunt.

By the time the frightened and exhausted remnants of Reno's command—only about half the number who started the fight were unhurt—made the summit of the bluffs, it was around 4 p.m. Forty percent of their comrades were still in the valley beneath them, dead, wounded, or unaccounted for. The men endured the horror of watching Indians below (including women and elderly people from the village) mutilate the bodies of the fallen soldiers (the Indians believed that mutilating an enemy's dead body would leave the victim permanently disfigured in the afterlife).

But there was also a glimmer of hope. For whatever reason, the Indians did not press the attack. Their attention suddenly appeared to be diverted elsewhere, and the soldiers watched them gallop off to the north. In addition, very soon after their arrival at the hilltop, the weary troopers were heartened to see Benteen's battalion ride toward them from the south.

Earlier in the afternoon, simultaneously with the approach of Reno's command to the lower end of the Indian village, Custer had finally reached a piece of high ground from which he could take in at least a partial view of the immense encampment below. Though it was difficult to see because many of the Indians were working to deliberately kick up dust to hide their movements, the village was perhaps two miles in length and contained something like one thousand lodges, in six great circles. Custer's officers and scouts also reported that another party of Indians had been seen riding away to the north.

The excitement of seeing the enemy at last, coupled with the view of their comrades galloping forward in the valley below caused some of Custer's men to shout with exhilaration. Custer called out, "Boys, hold your horses—there are plenty of them down there for us all."

Through his brother Tom, Custer now issued an order to Sergeant Daniel Kanipe to act as a courier and rush a message to Captain McDougall to bring the pack train ahead as quickly as possible. Tom Custer also told Kanipe, "And if you see Benteen, tell him to come on quick—a big Indian village." From this position Custer could see dust rising to the southeast. Benteen and his battalion were within a few miles, with the pack train trailing not far behind.

Custer's men moved on, traveling another half mile. Custer waved at Reno's command in the valley below, then encouraged his men, "Courage, boys, we've got them! We'll finish them up and then go home to our station." As Kanipe rode away to deliver his message, he heard Custer's troopers cheer in response.

Custer finally reached a large ravine called Medicine Tail Coulee. He halted his battalion and allowed the men and horses to rest for a brief moment. The hot and tired soldiers adjusted their equipment and prepared to continue on the move. As they did so, Custer instructed his adjutant, Cooke, to write a message for Benteen. The now famous note—hastily scribbled in pencil—read, "Benteen—Come on. Big Village. Be quick. Bring packs. W. W. Cooke P. S. Bring pacs [sic]."

Cooke dispatched orderly John Martin as a courier and told him to find Benteen and deliver the message as soon as possible. The leadership team now surmised that Benteen was about four miles away and if he hurried, could arrive to help within half an hour. But there was also the question of the "packs," i.e., ammunition packs. They were with the slower moving supply train.

Once Benteen had received Custer's directive earlier in the day to scout the bluffs to the southwest, he moved out with his three companies at a walk. Benteen did not agree with Custer's orders, but he followed them. Benteen's battalion meandered from ridge to ridge for five miles, but saw no Indians. Finally, after two hours of fruitless effort, Benteen ordered his men to turn back in the direction of Custer and the main body. Benteen's own scouts had informed him that there were many Sioux to the north. About five miles later, Benteen saw the Indian trail and now knew he was but a few miles behind Custer and less than a mile ahead of the pack train.

Inexplicably, Benteen stopped to rest and water his horses for twenty precious minutes. When the battalion finally began to move again, Custer's messenger Sergeant Kanipe reached Benteen. Kanipe said, "They want you up there as quick as you can get there—they have struck a big Indian camp." Kanipe then moved to the rear toward the pack train and down the length of Benteen's column saying, "We've got 'em boys!" As far as Kanipe knew, this was true. When he had left Custer, the men of the Seventh and their commander were still confident of victory.

Benteen's battalion now had the distinct impression that the primary work was done and that Custer and his detachment would receive all the accolades. Perhaps now in a funk, and despite orders to the contrary and audible gunfire in the distance, Benteen continued to move his unit forward at nothing more than a brisk walk.

About a mile further along the trail, Sergeant John Martin arrived with Cooke's hastily scribbled note. Benteen later described his interpretation of Custer's orders as vague and making no sense. In Benteen's defense, Custer's orders were open to more than one conclusion. How could Benteen both "be quick" and "bring packs"? And by "packs," did Custer specifically mean ammunition or some other kind of packs from the supply train? Why not simply say, "Bring bullets."?

Benteen declared, "Well. If he wants me to hurry, how does he expect that I can bring the packs? If I am going to be of service to him I think I had better not wait for the packs." So the battalion moved forward at a trot to see what lay ahead.

At about twenty minutes after four o'clock Benteen reached Reno and the other beleaguered survivors on the bluffs. Reno begged, "For God's sake, Benteen, halt your command and help me. I've lost half my men. We are whipped." Benteen showed Reno, his superior officer, Custer's written order, but Reno insisted they wait for more ammunition before taking any additional action. Reno had no idea where Custer might be at this point. The last time he had seen Custer, he waved to Reno from atop the high ridge across the river and had ridden away.

As they evaluated the situation, Reno and Benteen together gave up any thought of working to make a juncture with Custer. They no doubt had their own chaotic situation to deal with, but the practical result of their mutual decision became that Custer's orders to advance quickly, unclear though they may have been, were disobeyed. Catastrophe resulted.

Perhaps if Reno and Benteen had better knowledge of both the overall strategic plan and the immediate tactical objectives, they may have acted differently. Custer had a great propensity for secrecy and was a terse communicator on his best day. His failure to share important information up front and the lack of absolute clarity in his orders on the battlefield caused uncertainty and confusion for his subordinates. Custer's failure to communicate provides a dramatic cautionary tale for all leaders and proves that the adage is true: hold information close at your peril.

★ ★ CASE STUDY ★ ★

PIXAR ANIMATION STUDIOS: ALIENUS NON DIUTIUS (ALONE NO LONGER)

Pixar Animation Studios, based in Emeryville, California, is one of the most successful film production companies of all time. The source of Pixar's magic centers on a revolutionary technical innovation that changed animation forever. The "fraternity of geeks" who work at Pixar succeeded in transforming hand-drawn cel animation to computer-generated 3-D graphics. The string of movies they have created, starting with *Toy Story* in 1995, have been hugely popular and critically acclaimed. Through it all, a corporate culture that highly values information-sharing at every level within the organization has enabled Pixar to continue to produce one hit after another.

Pixar was founded in 1979 as the Graphics Group, part of the Computer Division of Lucasfilm. Dr. Ed Catmull, who was brought in to lead the team, had been head of the Computer Graphics Lab at the New York Institute of Technology. As a kid, Catmull dreamed of becoming an animator, with Disney's *Peter Pan* and *Pinocchio* serving as his inspiration. He soon realized that he possessed no particular artistic talent, so opted instead to study the burgeoning field of computer science at the University of Utah. At the New York Institute of Technology, Catmull's group pioneered computer graphics techniques that they then brought with them to Lucasfilm. Using these methodologies, and after years of research and experimentation, computer generated 3-D capabilities came alive under Catmull's leadership.

Steve Jobs, after his ignominious exit from Apple, purchased Catmull's group from George Lucas in 1986 for $5 million. The newly independent Pixar was basically a computer hardware company that sold a primary product called the Pixar Image Computer to the government, the medical community, and corporations such as the Walt Disney Company. The Pixar Image Computer provided amazing capability for analyzing and enhancing images, but after an initial spurt of sales, purchases dropped off. Pixar hemorrhaged money, specifically Steve Jobs' money, for years.

But during the lean times, Pixar employee John Lasseter and his team worked hard to develop a series of short computer animations using the new technology (including some television commercials) that were well received. Pixar entered into a deal with Disney in 1991 to produce three animated feature films, the first of which was *Toy Story*. *Toy Story* premiered in 1995 and went on to gross in excess of $350 million around the world. Every film that Pixar has produced since that time has also been a resounding commercial success. Despite many rough spots in the business relationship, Disney purchased Pixar in 2006 for $7.4 billion.

From the very beginning, Pixar's culture reflected a deep desire to avoid bureaucracy and focus on the creative process. Pixar employees worked hard, but more or less on their own schedules. If someone chose to arrive at noon and work late into the evening, that was just fine. People brought their pets to work. People walked around the office with no shoes on. The atmosphere was "anti-corporate" in feel. The atmosphere was laid-back. The atmosphere was fun. And the workforce was incredibly productive. One leader of an animation workshop from the UCLA film school said, "For us now, the high-water mark is Pixar. I remember just a few years ago when students wanted to go to Disney. Now they want to go to Pixar."

The September 2008 issue of *Harvard Business Review* cited several reasons for Pixar's sustained creative success. Among other things, the company espouses a philosophy that "we are smarter than me." The company believes that everyone needs to be involved in the creative process and, to that end, communication sharing at all levels within the organization is imperative. Next, Pixar works to hire good people, to support them, and to foster an environment where trust and respect are a given. More specifically, those good people are encouraged to take risks knowing that they will inevitably make mistakes. Talented people will learn from their mistakes and use the hard-won lessons to move forward to the next project. Finally, Pixar's culture is flat, collegial, and extremely peer-oriented. Hierarchies are out, everyone is treated with respect, and both honest feedback and careful listening are encouraged.

One very specific and practical example of the way information-sharing plays itself out is Pixar University. Every employee is encouraged to spend as many as four hours a week furthering his/her education. Pixar University offers more than a hundred courses, from filmmaking to writing to sculpture, painting, and drawing. Randy Nelson, dean of Pixar University, says, "We offer the equivalent of an undergraduate education in fine arts and the art of filmmaking." And this is not just fun time or a way to avoid work, but rather a critical job expectation. Nelson says, "This is part of everyone's work. We're all filmmakers here. We all have access to the same curriculum. In class, people from every level sit right next to our directors and the president of the company."

Pixar University epitomizes the concept of broad knowledge-sharing. Nelson asserted, "The skills we develop are skills we need everywhere in the organization. Why teach drawing to accountants? Because drawing class doesn't just teach people to draw. It teaches them to be more observant. There's no company on earth that wouldn't benefit from having people become more observant." At Pixar University, employees are also encouraged to try new things, take risks, and learn from mistakes. The University crest says in Latin: "Alienus Non Diutius," which translates to "alone no longer." As Nelson says, "It's the heart of our model, giving people opportunities to fail together and to recover from mistakes together."

Pixar's creative gurus have a thirst for knowledge from outside the organization as well. In the effort to bring authenticity to Pixar movies, the production teams often carefully research a topic. During the making of Pixar's all-time hit, *Finding Nemo* (released in 2003), leadership realized there was no precedent in their experience for a film set mostly underwater. So the team screened underwater sequences from previous Disney films like *Pinocchio* and *The Little Mermaid*. They also viewed Jacques Cousteau documentaries and live-action films such as *Jaws* and *The Abyss*. They brought in a massive fish tank and stocked it with exotic saltwater species. Lasseter funded a team excursion to Hawaii to go scuba diving in an effort to see and experience the underwater world firsthand.

Pixar University brought in world-class lecturers from the world of academe to discourse on fish species, waves, whales, jellyfish propulsion, the movement of algae and sea grass, and underwater translucence. One scholar who served as Pixar's lead aquatic consultant marveled, "It felt like people genuinely wanted to hear my complaints and my poking holes in what they were doing. If a fish was doing the wrong thing, they actually wanted to know." This desperate pursuit of detailed knowledge and precise accuracy resulted in a film that grossed more than $800 million worldwide.

In addition to stellar financial results, Pixar has earned countless industry accolades for its work, including twenty-two Academy Awards, four Golden Globes, and three Grammys. Every Pixar film produced since 2001 was nominated for a Best Animated Feature Oscar and four of those movies, *Finding Nemo, The Incredibles, Ratatouille*, and *WALL-E*, came home with the little golden trophy.

Pixar Animation Studios provides an incredibly compelling example of an organization that sees the critical value in gathering information from a diverse variety of sources and then sharing it openly up, down, and across the company. Those individuals who would hold information closely would not survive in such a culture. Pixar's reputation as a place where creative genius thrives is indeed well-earned.

Leadership Lesson Six:
HOLD INFORMATION CLOSE
AT YOUR PERIL

Early in my career, I earned a law degree and practiced litigation for about four-and-a-half years with a couple of private law firms. Over time, for a variety of reasons, I decided the legal profession was not for me. Mostly, I just got tired of fighting with other attorneys about money—someone else's money, never mine—all day long. But as I look back, I now realize that one of the frustrations for me in the law firm setting revolved around a lack of information and knowledge sharing.

While the firms I worked for were collegial enough places, they were also extremely busy places. Each lawyer, from the most senior name partner to the newest associate, was expected to bill an immense number of hours each year. This effort to bill time and make money put a premium on using every minute efficiently—to bill time and make money. Therefore, the opportunities for seasoned people to spend time with inexperienced associates in the spirit of mentoring and sharing knowledge were few and far between. I remember having complex litigation files dropped on my desk with not much more than a "good luck" by way of guidance. It was truly a sink or swim environment.

One funny story I have enjoyed telling through the years illustrates the point. I had a hearing coming up over at the local courthouse. I stepped inside the office of one of the gray-haired senior partners—a man who was an extremely skilled and experienced trial lawyer—to ask his advice. I briefly related the facts of the case and the subject of the hearing. I asked if he had any counsel for me. He pondered the question for a moment. "Yes," he replied, "don't fuck it up." With that for inspiration, I was on my way. I don't honestly remember how the hearing came out, but I do know that I soon decided to pursue a career in business.

No organization achieves perfection with regard to sharing information, because human judgment is involved. To be sure, some information is not appropriate for wide distribution. Sometimes, confidentiality is a necessity. To communicate well requires time, focus, and effort, which are often in short supply.

Nevertheless, companies like Pixar that set themselves up as learning organizations and follow through on that commitment tend to be successful. And organizations like the George Custer-led Seventh Cavalry—where secrecy, lack of clarity, and generally poor communication all around are the rule—suffer in the end.

Where does your organization or team sit on the communication spectrum? Do you openly share important information and knowledge up, down, and across? Does your culture foster honest feedback and careful listening? Or have you failed to open up and are now desperately calling for support from your teammates, only to have them abandon you to your fate?

PART FOUR

SEEK
SELF-KNOWLEDGE
& LEARNING

Chapter Seven

GETTYSBURG

THE PEACH ORCHARD:
LOOK IN THE MIRROR AND BE HONEST
ABOUT WHAT YOU SEE

"The entire battlefield is a memorial to Dan Sickles."

—General Dan Sickles—

Major General Daniel Edgar Sickles was George Meade's Third Corps commander at the Battle of Gettysburg. Sickles was also a notorious rogue and what might be called in modern business parlance a "maverick." On the second day of the battle, Sickles took it upon himself, without orders, to move his entire corps forward of the position he had been directed to occupy. In so doing, Sickles placed his own needs and desires first, imperiling the entire Union army in the process. That afternoon, despite Sickles's egregious miscue and after some of the most ferocious fighting in all of American military history, the Union line was tenuously held. To his dying day many years later, Sickles maintained not only that he had done the right thing but that, thanks primarily to him, the Union had won the battle. Dan Sickles presents

141

a prime example of a leader—intelligent, energetic, and charming though he may have been—with extraordinarily low self-knowledge, who never acknowledged his own faults and mistakes. Dan Sickles selfishly refused ever to look in the mirror and be honest about what he saw.

Sickles was born in 1819 in New York City. He trained as a lawyer and then entered New York politics under the support of the infamous Tammany Hall machine. He was elected as a Democrat to the New York State Assembly in 1847, where he proved adept at the scheming, maneuvering, and manipulation inherent in politics. He was allegedly involved in fixing elections, theft of funds, and the occasional brawl. Sickles was a flagrant womanizer who was censured by his peers for casually bringing a known prostitute onto the floor of the Assembly. He created further scandal when—to the chagrin of both families—he married Teresa Bagioli in 1852, when he was 33 and she was a mere 16 years old. Teresa gave birth shortly after their marriage. Sickles did not let wedded life constrain him from continuing to cavort with prostitutes.

Through his powerful political connections, Sickles became a member of the U. S. diplomatic legation in London in 1853, under the American Minister to London and future president James Buchanan. Sickles returned to America to be elected in 1855 as a State Senator in New York and, in 1857, to the U. S. House of Representatives.

Despite his own numerous indiscretions, Sickles became enraged when he learned that his young wife was having an affair with the U. S. Attorney for the District of Columbia, Philip Barton Key (son of Francis Scott Key, who composed "The Star Spangled Banner"). In 1859, the jealous husband spotted Key near the Sickles's home on Lafayette Square in Washington, D. C.—right across the street from the White House—attempting to signal Teresa by waving a white handkerchief. Livid with anger, Sickles rushed outside in broad daylight and shot the unarmed Key multiple times with a pistol. Key died a short while later.

A terrifically high-profile courtroom drama followed—the nineteenth century equivalent of the O.J. Simpson murder trial—before which Sickles was able to produce a confession of infidelity that he had coerced from his wife. Teresa's disclosure of guilt was not admissible in court but was leaked to the press, generating significant public sympathy for the defendant. Also much like O.J. Simpson, Sickles was ably defended by a "dream team" of several prominent lawyers that included Edwin Stanton, who would later become Lincoln's Secretary of War. Sickles's attorneys devised the legal strategy of a temporary insanity defense, arguing that Sickles was so distraught at catching his wife's lover in the act of beckoning her to be seduced that he momentarily lost his mind and, therefore, could not be held responsible for his actions. In the first instance of an American court ever accepting such a defense, Sickles was acquitted. He then set tongues wagging further—and significantly damaged his own rising political career—by reconciling with his wife and continuing their married life together, which was seen as disgraceful by the moral standards of the day. Clearly, Dan Sickles was colorful, outrageous, and produced good copy.

When the Civil War began, Sickles set out to do his part and restore his reputation by raising a brigade of volunteers. Though he was a complete amateur, he assumed technical command at the rank of colonel of one of the regiments he recruited, and in effect was the brigade's commanding officer. He became a brigadier general of volunteers in September 1861 and proceeded to demonstrate some competence as a soldier. He participated effectively and with energy in the Seven Days Battles in the spring of 1862. He was promoted to major general just prior to the Battle of Fredericksburg in the winter of 1862.

When his close friend General Hooker took command of the Army of the Potomac, "Fighting Joe" promoted Sickles to command the Third Corps. Hooker and Sickles were two peas in a pod who both enjoyed drinking, womanizing, and generally conducting themselves in a bawdy manner. One young captain stated, "... the headquarters of the Army of the Potomac was a place to which no self-respecting man liked to go, and no decent woman would go. It was a combination of bar-room and brothel."

Unfortunately for the Union cause, Dan Sickles had now officially been elevated to his level of incompetence. He performed with mixed reviews in his new role as corps commander at the Battle of Chancellorsville in May 1863. As historian Stephen Sears noted, "As a corps commander Dan Sickles was operating at a level far beyond his talents, and most everyone recognized it but Dan Sickles."

Hooker was toppled as army commander just prior to Gettysburg, and the new leader was the West Point-trained, no nonsense disciplinarian George Gordon Meade. As a "political general," Sickles had always looked down his nose at the professional soldiers. At Gettysburg, Sickles was the only corps commander on either side who had not been educated at the U.S. Military Academy or served in the pre-war army. As far as Sickles was concerned, Meade—with whom he enjoyed a decidedly chilly relationship—represented the very epitome of the cliquish, insular brotherhood of "Old Army" officers that Sickles detested.

Indeed, new leader and subordinate got off to a rocky start when Meade sent Sickles a note on June 30 chastising him for "the very slow movement of your corps yesterday." But Meade also bore some responsibility for confusion, as in his first days of command—not knowing the exact disposition of the enemy—he issued a series of contradictory orders. On July 1, Sickles received multiple directives, including a message from John Reynolds (his immediate superior as wing commander) telling him to move quickly to Gettysburg, and two messages from Meade telling him to stay put and guard the army's western flank at Emmitsburg. Not for the last time, Sickles chose to disregard Meade's order in the conviction that events now dictated that he move quickly to the scene of the combat. In making this judgment to head straight to the battlefield, it soon became apparent, Sickles did the right thing. His confidence in his own military intuition no doubt bolstered, Sickles arrived with the first elements of his Third Corps too late to influence the outcome on the first day of battle. His part in the story would dramatically play itself out on Day Two of the battle.

Early on July 2, General Meade assigned Sickles and his Third Corps responsibility for the southern portion of Cemetery Ridge. Sickles was to occupy positions that had been held by elements of Twelfth Corps, who moved north to join their comrades on Culp's Hill. He was expected to tie in with General Hancock and the Second Corps on his right and anchor at the hill to the south variously called Sugar Loaf or Signal Hill, but that would soon go down in history as Little Round Top. Instead of working diligently to set up a defensive line, linking up with Hancock, and taking the obvious step of occupying the high ground of Little Round Top, Sickles ended up putting his troops into bivouac. Essentially, he was peeved with his assignment.

The reason for Sickles's consternation with what Meade had instructed him to do lay in his analysis of the ground. While Hancock's men to his right enjoyed the benefit of at least somewhat elevated terrain, the Third Corps occupied a flat area with trees in front that limited vision and fields of fire. That ground rose gradually upward to the west to a commanding piece of earth about three-quarters of a mile away. This area was farmer Joseph Sherfy's soon-to-be famous peach orchard that butted against the Emmitsburg Road. In Sickles's judgment, an alert enemy could set up artillery batteries there that would wreak havoc on his corps. At some point in his review of options, he formulated an alternate plan to occupy this critical piece of ground himself, before the Rebels arrived.

Captain George Meade (the commanding general's son and aide who had been recently expelled from West Point for too many demerits) was dispatched around 8 a.m. to confer with Sickles. Sickles's staff told the young man that the general was resting in his tent after a long night and therefore would not see him, and that Sickles was unhappy with the position he had been assigned to defend. Meade dutifully rode back to headquarters to inform his father of Sickles's dissatisfaction. The commander, annoyed and without time for such foolishness, reiterated his instructions that Sickles was "to go into position on the left of Second Corps; that his right was to connect with the left of Second Corps; that he was to prolong with his line the line of [Second] Corps, occupying the position that [Twelfth Corps] had held the night before." Meade further directed that is was of the utmost importance that Sickles's troops should be in position as soon as possible.

General Meade's instructions—which in his mind were eminently understandable—were relayed once more to Sickles. Again, Sickles objected to the assignment. Around 11 a.m. he personally rode north to the tiny homestead of the widow Lydia Leister, which served as Meade's headquarters. There, Sickles consulted with his commanding officer directly. Though he succeeded in holding his temper, one can imagine Meade's impatience as he repeated his orders yet again. Meade told Sickles to connect with Hancock on his right, and then he gestured in the direction of Little Round Top as the obvious anchor for Sickles' left flank. Without revealing precisely what he had in mind, Sickles described to Meade some ground in the vicinity which was ideal for artillery. Sickles requested that he be given leeway to post his corps in the most advantageous way. Meade told him, "Certainly, within the limits of the general instructions I have given to you; any ground within those limits you choose to occupy I leave to you." A more forthright officer would have directly requested permission to make the specific movement that Sickles contemplated, but Dan Sickles was far from a forthright officer.

Sickles requested guidance in posting his guns, and Meade dispatched head of artillery General Henry Hunt to assist him. Sickles brought Hunt to the ground of the Peach Orchard and the two men discussed the relative merits of the position. Hunt pointed out the obvious facts that in moving his corps forward Sickles would not only create a dangerous salient, but because he would be stretching his lines thin, would be unable to both connect with Hancock on the right and anchor on Little Round Top on his left. Sickles, oblivious to the sound military advice he had just received, asked Hunt for permission to

move his men. "Not on my authority," Hunt replied. Hunt then recommended that at the very least, as a precautionary measure, Sickles
send a force to reconnoiter the forested area west of the Emmitsburg
Road, called Pitzer's Woods.

Sickles deployed elements of the First U.S. Sharpshooters (an
elite group of superb marksmen let by Colonel Hiram Berdan) across
the Emmitsburg Road to see what they could find. After initial contact
with Confederate pickets who fell back, Berdan's men soon became
engaged in a brief but fierce firefight with a large body of Rebel infantry. These men were elements of James Longstreet's First Corps. The
Yankee sharpshooters withdrew and dutifully reported to Sickles that
the woods to the west were crawling with the enemy. For Sickles, this
was all the information he needed. In his mind the Peach Orchard was
soon to be occupied by Rebel batteries, to his profound disadvantage—
unless he got there first.

Sickles gave the fateful order at around 2:00 p.m., directing his
two divisions to march three-quarters of a mile forward to occupy the
Peach Orchard and the ground to the south of it. They moved out in
grand fashion, as if on parade. Sickles had not received authoriza-
tion to advance, nor did he inform his commander of his decision.
He certainly had not communicated with his comrades to the right,
who were entirely depending on him to protect the southern flank.
Generals Hancock and Gibbon of the Second Corps watched in per-
plexed wonder as Third Corps marched away. An eyewitness said they
"… both exclaimed what in hell can that man Sickles be doing!"

On the Confederate side, all had been busyness from early in the
morning (with a good bit of poor communication and confusion as
well) in preparation for the day's battle. Early in the morning Lee had
ordered a reconnaissance of the Union left, or southern, flank. For
whatever reasons, his scouting party fed Lee utterly false information
about the Union position, giving the commanding general the impression the enemy's southern flank was lightly defended, if at all. In fact,
two Union infantry corps and a couple of brigades of cavalry were

bustling about in the vicinity all morning and would have been impossible to miss by a competent team of scouts.

Lee envisioned a simultaneous attack on both Union flanks on this day, with General Longstreet leading the main assault against the enemy left. With the Union flank "in the air," that is, unprotected, Lee no doubt hoped for a rolling up and disintegration of the enemy line much in the fashion of Chancellorsville. Lee informed Ewell via courier that he should commence his attack against the Union right flank in coordination with Longstreet on the left. Ewell was to listen for the sound of Longstreet's guns before beginning his advance against Cemetery and Culp's hills.

Not surprisingly Longstreet opposed this plan, advocating again for a flanking maneuver that would place the Confederate army between Meade and the Federal capital. Longstreet was also reluctant to attack because he was still missing Pickett's division of Virginians. "I never like to go into battle with one boot off," said Longstreet. Lee would have none of it. Longstreet lamented later, "He seemed resolved, however, and we discussed the probable results." When Lee received the inaccurate report regarding the lack of preparation on the Union left, he told Longstreet, "I think you had better move on."

Lee directed that Longstreet's two divisions, along with a reinforcing division from A. P. Hill's Third Corps, should form on a line perpendicular to the Emmitsburg Road and drive north in an oblique attack against the Union positions on Cemetery Ridge. By 1:00 p.m. Longstreet's columns were moving, but this was much later than Lee would have preferred. Critics would later assert that Longstreet dallied in a pout over Lee's lack of support for his alternate plan. But it should also be noted that along the initial route to the line of departure—through no fault of Longstreet's—it soon became apparent that the moving mass of gray-clad soldiers would be seen by the enemy if the march continued on the same path. A tedious process of countermarching to find an alternate route ate up more precious time. Finally, almost two hours later, Longstreet's men reached the designated ground, only to find it now occupied by a substantial force of Yankee infantry. One Rebel division commander wrote later, "The view presented astonished me, as the enemy was massed in my front, and extended to my right and left as far as I could see."

The massed enemy was of course none other than the Third Corps of Dan Sickles. A new plan was in order and General Lee now directed a shuffling of his forces, moving John Bell Hood's division of Texans to the extreme right of the formation. Hood conducted a brief reconnaissance, and saw that Round Top was undefended and that the ground east of Round Top was also in the air. Hood pleaded with Longstreet to allow a flanking maneuver to exploit this weakness. But Longstreet, frustrated, angry, and resigned to his fate, denied Hood's multiple requests and forcefully ordered him forward, pursuant to direction from General Lee.

As Longstreet's units maneuvered into their places to commence the assault, General Meade finally found time to ride south and inspect his lines. When he reached the end of Hancock's Second Corps positions, he found an enormous and dangerous gap. His fury rising, he enquired of Sickles as to where the devil his Third Corps might be. Sickles pointed to his postings in and near the Peach Orchard well forward of the rest of the Union forces, stating that he felt this ground was most advantageous to defend Round Top. Meade replied, "General Sickles, this is neutral ground, our guns command it, as well as the enemy's. The very reason you cannot hold it applies to them." Sickles sheepishly asked whether he should move back to his original spot, just as preliminary Rebel shellfire began to rain down on his men. Meade responded, "I wish to God you could, but the enemy won't let you!"

The fighting that followed for the remainder of that day was some of the most horrific in the annals of war, and will be outlined in detail in Chapter Nine. Suffice it to say, the Third Corps was decimated and Dan Sickles, the maverick, nearly cost the Union the battle.

Sickles had gravely feared the effect of Rebel artillery on his forces. Ironically, in the early evening, as he worked to manage the chaotic combat that swirled around him from his headquarters near the Trostle farm, an enemy cannonball tore into his right leg, nearly severing the limb just below the knee. As he lay seriously wounded and his staff rushed to apply a tourniquet, Sickles groaned that they must not allow him to be captured. As always, his first thought was for himself—though one could sympathize with the undoubted shock of the injury and his physical pain. Legend has it that as he was carried away on a stretcher he composed himself sufficiently to puff a cigar, though some historians believe that story is apocryphal. One officer in Second Corps commented, "The loss of his leg is a great gain to us, whatever it may be to him."

Sickles leg was amputated, and he was transported to Washington, D.C., to recover. In effect, the war was over for him. He spent a great deal of time and energy for the duration of the conflict and afterward chastising his nemesis General Meade and defending his own actions at Gettysburg. In February 1864 Sickles testified before the joint Congressional Committee on the Conduct of the War (a group of elected representatives brought together to investigate the army's conduct of the war). Outrageously, Sickles asserted in his testimony that it had been Meade's intention to withdraw on July 2 to a defensive position some distance south of Gettysburg. Only Sickles's own initiative in moving his corps forward and the resulting surprise to the Confederates and blunting of their attack, he argued, had kept Meade from retreating.

In March 1864, an extended account of the battle appeared in the *New York Herald*. The anonymous author was called "Historicus," and it is possible that he was none other than Dan Sickles. At the very least it was someone who favored Sickles and hated Meade, for the *Herald* story contained an extremely positive evaluation of Sickles's conduct at Gettysburg. Among other lies, the article stated, "General Sickles saw at once how necessary it was to occupy the elevated ground in his front toward the Emmitsburg road and to extend his lines to the commanding eminence known as the Round Top, or Sugar Loaf

Hill. Unless this were done, the left and rear of our army would be in the greatest danger. Sickles concluded that no time was to be lost.... Receiving no orders, and filled with anxiety, he reported in person to General Meade and urged the advance he deemed so essential. 'O,' said Meade, 'generals are all apt to look for the attack to be made where they are.' Whether this was a jest or a sneer Sickles did not stop to consider...."

After he was wounded, Sickles saved and then donated his shattered right tibia and fibula to the Army Medical Museum (now the National Museum of Health and Medicine) in Washington, D. C. Periodically over the years, Sickles would stop by to visit his leg, even occasionally bringing guests with him, and the pulverized bones remain on display to this day. More than three decades after the war, Sickles arranged through his political connections to receive a Medal of Honor for his "gallantry" at Gettysburg. He was the only Union corps commander who was so recognized.

Sickles lived a long, varied, and controversial post-war life. He remained in the army until 1869, at which time he became U. S. Minister to Spain. Ever the roguish womanizer, he is said to have had an affair with the deposed Queen of Spain, Isabella II. He served in various public sector jobs in New York and was elected to the U. S. House again, sitting for one term from 1893–95. He was chair for many years of the New York State Monuments Commission, but left that role due to financial scandal. Sickles was instrumental in the development of the Gettysburg National Military Park but even there, allegations of financial improprieties continued to attach to him. Of all the major figures who played a prominent role at Gettysburg, Sickles is the only one without a monument. When asked about this omission, true to form, Sickles supposedly replied, "The entire battlefield is a memorial to Dan Sickles." He died in New York City, an old man at the age of 94, in 1914.

Sickles maintained to his dying day that he was the true hero of Gettysburg. Over the post-war decades, he shamelessly played on his status as a wounded amputee to garner sympathy. Dan Sickles represents that kind of leader who may be highly talented in some respects, but who is also so profoundly out of touch with his own deficiencies as to be deluded. Sickles's actions at Gettysburg were not heroic but reckless, jeopardizing the entire war effort for the Union. Such leaders are particularly dangerous in wartime because they needlessly waste blood and treasure, but they are always problematic no matter the context. The best leaders are truthful about who they are, admit their own opportunity areas, and try to play to their strengths. The best leaders are their own toughest critics. In short, the best leaders are willing to look in the mirror and be honest about what they see.

★ ★ CASE STUDY ★ ★

OPRAH WINFREY:
SEEK TRUTH IN YOUR LIFE

"I think the most important thing to get ahead falls back to what I truly believe in, and that is the ability to seek truth in your life. That's in all forms. You have to be honest with yourself. You can be pursuing a profession because your parents say it's the best thing. You can be pursuing a profession because you think you will make a lot of money. You can be pursuing a profession because you think you are going to get a lot of attention. None of that will do you any good if you are not being honest with yourself."

Oprah Winfrey spoke these words in an interview in the early 1990s. That philosophy of life has carried her from a hardscrabble upbringing with many trials and tribulations along the way to the pinnacle of success in the worlds of entertainment and business. Today she enjoys status as a beloved American icon and one of the most influential people in the world.

Oprah Winfrey was born in 1954 to unwed teenage parents, and she began her life in poverty on her grandmother's farm in Mississippi. In early childhood, Oprah moved back and forth several times, first to be with her mother, Vernita Lee, in Milwaukee and then with her father, Vernon Winfrey, in Nashville, Tennessee. In 1963, at the age of nine, while living with her mother, Oprah was raped. She became sexually promiscuous and at age fourteen, secretly pregnant. She was sent again to live with her father. She lost her infant son, but throughout her time with her father he gave her discipline and support, emphasizing the importance of education.

In 1971 Oprah won the Miss Fire Prevention contest in Nashville. The contest sponsor was a radio station that invited Oprah to read the news on air. She became Miss Black Tennessee in 1972, and subsequently competed in the Miss Black America contest. From there, at age nineteen, she became a reporter for the Nashville radio station WVOL. She also enrolled at Tennessee State University to learn performing arts. She became the first African-American news anchor in Nashville at WTFV-TV, and it soon became apparent that she and her radiant personality were meant to be on screen.

Oprah took a job as a news co-anchor at station WJZ-TV in Baltimore, but management decided it did not like her appearance and moved her out of prime time to a morning slot. Phil Baker, an executive with WLZ, offered Oprah the chance to host a talk show called *People Are Talking*. The show quickly became popular, and ratings were good. People liked Oprah's friendly, approachable style. Her career continued to ascend when in 1984 she relocated to Chicago to become the host of *AM Chicago*, a morning talk show at WLS-TV. She competed directly in the same time slot with Phil Donahue, who had the most popular talk show in America. Within a month, the 30-year-old Oprah Winfrey passed Phil Donahue in the ratings.

Oprah's multiple talents became even more apparent in 1985 when she played the part of Sofia in the movie adaptation of Alice Walker's novel *The Color Purple,* directed by Steven Spielberg. Oprah was nominated for an Academy Award for her critically acclaimed performance. In 1986, she went national with the *Oprah Winfrey Show.* She soon had an audience of 14 million viewers per day and won her first daytime Emmy (her program would eventually earn more than forty Emmy awards) in 1987. She continued to appeal to her fans by simply being herself. In 1988 she launched Harpo (her name spelled backward) Productions, securing the rights to her show from Capital Cities/ABC and opening a $20 million Chicago studio facility.

Her audiences appreciated Oprah's open and honest style. She made no excuses for her own difficult past and showed her emotions openly. She discussed her struggles with her weight. She touched and connected with regular people in a very real way. In 1998 *Time* magazine honored Oprah as one of "The Time 100" most influential people. Noted author and linguistics professor Deborah Tannen stated in that article, "Women, especially, listen to Oprah because they feel as if she's a friend…. Winfrey transformed the [talk show] format into what I call 'rapport-talk,' the back-and-forth conversation that is the basis of female friendship, with its emphasis on self-revealing intimacies. She turned the focus from experts to ordinary people talking about personal issues. Girls' and women's friendships are often built on trading secrets. Winfrey's power is that she tells her own, divulging that she once ate a package of hot dog buns drenched in maple syrup, that she had smoked cocaine, even that she had been raped as a child. With Winfrey, the talk show became more immediate, more confessional, more personal. When a guest's story moves her, she cries and spreads her arms for a hug."

Many talk shows sprang up over time imitating Oprah, and the trend for a number of these programs became a focus on the sordid, sleazy side of life. In 1994, Oprah made a conscious decision to differentiate herself from the competition by presenting more positive, upbeat content. She called her new principle "change your life television." *New York Times* media analyst David Carr said, "...just when tabloid television was beginning to crest and threatened to tip over in a sea of cross-dressing Nazis, [Oprah] pulled back, saying that she could build a bigger audience on uplift than on baser instincts—and the critics scoffed. So she began proselytizing good books, nagging herself about her own weight and, most of all, listening to her audience. And the money kept rolling in bigger and bigger waves."

Deborah Tannen said, "Winfrey saw television's power to blend public and private; while it links strangers and conveys information over public airwaves, TV is most often viewed in the privacy of our homes. Like a family member, it sits down to meals with us and talks to us in the lonely afternoons. Grasping this paradox, Oprah exhorts viewers to improve their lives and the world. She makes people care because she cares. That is Winfrey's genius, and will be her legacy, as the changes she has wrought in the talk show continue to permeate our culture and shape our lives." Author and columnist Arianna Huffington observed, "She was transparent and authentic before those things were cool. When she went through her battles with weight, with her battles to come to grip with her past, we went through those things with her. Now with social media and the Internet, those things are coin of the realm, but she got there before the rest of us did."

In 1996 Oprah established "Oprah's Book Club," which through its recommendations has launched many a book to best-seller status. Two years later Oprah was named the second most admired woman in America (behind Hillary Clinton) and received an Emmy award for lifetime achievement. In 1999 Oprah promoted and invested in the Oxygen cable TV network, but has more recently launched her own cable venture called OWN, the Oprah Winfrey Network, which will debut in January 2011. She began publication in 2000 of a new magazine called *O*, which became the most successful startup ever in magazine publishing. In 2003, she became the world's first female African-American billionaire (her wealth has been estimated at more than $2.3 billion), who is also a profoundly generous philanthropist; among other endeavors, she established the Oprah Winfrey Academy for Girls in South Africa to provide educational opportunities for underprivileged girls. In 2005, Oprah Winfrey was named by *Forbes* magazine as the world's most powerful celebrity. In a move that will have a profound impact on the world of broadcast television, in November 2009, Oprah announced that after twenty-five years on the air, "The Oprah Winfrey Show" would cease production in September 2011, and that she would move her amazing act to cable TV and OWN.

Despite her many achievements, Oprah is not without her critics. Detractors point out that the average audience numbers for *The Oprah Winfrey Show* and circulation of *O* magazine have both fallen in recent years. On one of her shows, when the discussion turned to mad cow disease, she said the threat, "just stopped me cold from eating another burger." The perceived damage to the beef industry was such that cattlemen sued her in a multi million-dollar legal action—which she won. Some of her recent "Oprah Book Club" choices have delved into new-age spiritualism in a way that has drawn disapproval even from long-time fans. Her early, enthusiastic endorsement of Illinois Senator Barack Obama for president angered some of her female supporters who are either not Democrats or were staunch backers of Hillary Clinton in her bid for the White House.

Criticisms aside, Oprah Winfrey's is an inspiring American story of rising from humble and troubled beginnings to achieve wealth and fame, but not at the expense of her authenticity and integrity as a person. She has risen to the top through talent, hard work, some measure of luck, and by being her true self in a way that resonates deeply with ordinary people. Oprah said it well herself, "Honesty comes from your natural instinct telling you when you are doing something, whether or not this feels right. You feel a sense of accomplishment and fulfillment and worthiness to the world, in such a way that you know that you are doing the right thing. You don't have to ask anybody. When you are doing the right thing you don't have to say, 'Do you think this is OK?'

It works on every level." Oprah Winfrey presents a stellar example of a leader who is willing to honestly examine her own life and actions (both the good and the not so good) and to move forward with confidence based on her best judgment as to the right path.

* * *

Leadership Lesson Seven:
LOOK IN THE MIRROR AND BE HONEST ABOUT WHAT YOU SEE

I had the opportunity and high honor to serve America as a Marine Corps infantry officer for three years after college. It was by far the most important developmental experience of my lifetime, but as with many growth journeys, it was painful in some ways. One of the most important lessons I took away was that as a leader, I needed to work to understand my own strengths and weaknesses. And in the end, given that understanding, the best course of action was to simply be myself.

When I entered the military I was a novice as a leader. I had been a varsity athletic captain and member of the student council in both high school and college, but I was still woefully green from a leadership perspective. All of a sudden, at age twenty-two, I was handed life and death responsibility for a Marine rifle platoon. More than forty young men looked to me as an example—or not—of what a good leader should be.

I remember struggling mightily to determine what kind of leader I would become. Should I be a nice guy? Should I be a strict disciplinarian? Should I land somewhere in between—in the realm of the "firm but fair" commander? I must admit, I didn't have a clue. I proceeded to imitate other officers whom I admired, but in the end that did not feel comfortable nor did it work very well. Finally, after about a year's worth of stumbling around, I arrived at an epiphany: How about just be myself?

I felt as if an enormous burden had been lifted from my shoulders. To be sure, I still made many mistakes and had a lot to learn, but things became much easier as I simply made my way being regular old me. I even arrived at a point, probably two years into my service, where when I looked into the mirror to shave every morning, I felt like a pretty good Marine officer was looking back at me. Or at least one who was doing his level best to be himself and to lead his men in the most effective way he knew how.

No leader is perfect. We all have our strengths and shortcomings. What separates good leaders from poor ones, among many other things, is the willingness to examine one's own life and leadership in a realistic way, and to make positive changes accordingly.

We all know leaders like Dan Sickles, who learned everything they think they will ever need to know long ago. There is nothing new under the sun for them. They have little self-knowledge and refuse to assess their own strengths and weaknesses. They proceed with absolute certainty that whatever they do represents the best, truest, and most righteous path. They will work hard after the fact to distort the record in their favor. Those leaders are really a pain in the rear end. Their leadership and life, over time, become nothing but a lie.

Conversely, we have all hopefully been blessed to know a leader or two like Oprah Winfrey. Those leaders are the first to acknowledge their own faults and foibles, and they work to overcome adversity—both personal and professional—and focus on the positive. They are honest with themselves and their followers in a way that allows them to move ahead with a clean conscience and a clear-eyed vision of where they want to go.

Socrates, the ancient Athenian philosopher, said, "The unexamined life is not worth living." Truer words have never been spoken.

Chapter Eight

LITTLE BIGHORN

RENO-BENTEEN DEFENSE SITE: BE FLEXIBLE UNDER CHANGING CIRCUMSTANCES

"Say old man, what is going to be the outcome of this unless we have a commanding officer here pretty damn soon? You are the senior captain, and we would like to see you take the lead in affairs."

—Captain Thomas McDougall to Captain Frederick Benteen—

The dazed survivors of Major Marcus Reno's dash from the woods, across the Little Bighorn, and to the high bluffs beyond, numbered seven officers and eighty-four enlisted men. As they gathered themselves, tired, frightened, and with seven of them wounded, two critical questions stood out. What had happened to their commander, Custer, and where were Captain Benteen's battalion and the pack train? Thankfully, Benteen and his reinforcements quickly appeared on the scene, with the mule-drawn supply train not far behind. Benteen's arrival and decision to stay with Reno and his men was fortuitous. For the remainder of the day on June 25 and throughout the following day

June 26, Benteen—though Reno was his superior in rank—in effect took command of the beleaguered unit and behaved with extreme competence and utmost bravery. Though his overall performance at Little Bighorn has been criticized on other grounds, by virtually every account (including Reno's) Benteen demonstrated great skill in leading the hilltop defense. Above all, despite the chaos and trauma that swirled around him, Frederick Benteen showed that most critical leadership trait—the ability to be flexible under changing circumstances.

When Benteen arrived at the hilltop, he showed his written orders from Custer (telling him to "Come on.... Be quick") to Reno. Reno demanded that Benteen stay with him rather than advance to Custer's aid. There must be no move forward, argued Reno, until the troops were resupplied with ammunition. At that point, even though rifle fire could now be heard to the north, Benteen may have felt that Reno's directive superseded Custer's. Or he may have believed that Custer could handle whatever would come his way. Or he may have been piqued that Custer had earlier sent him on a futile scouting mission. Whatever his logic, Benteen made the choice to stay on, keep his troops in place, and help with the setting up of a defensive perimeter. Altogether, Reno and Benteen commanded probably 367 men including officers, enlisted, scouts, and civilians. For now, most of the attacking Indians had ridden off to the north, and the soldiers enjoyed a brief respite from the storm.

The location now known as the Reno-Benteen Defense Site was hardly ideal in affording protection for the men (see Little Bighorn Map Number Four, June 25–26, Reno-Benteen Defense Site). While the high bluffs that faced west toward the Little Bighorn would be easy enough to defend, the ground to the east and south consisted merely of gentle rolling slopes that left the soldiers exposed. Moreover, a high point about 500 yards to the north, which would later be called Sharpshooter Ridge, gave the Indians unimpeded lines of site into the soldier positions from which they would level deadly sniper fire. In the center of the site, in a shallow swale, acting assistant regimental surgeon

Doctor Henry Porter set up a field hospital to treat the wounded. He was somewhat protected by picketed soldier horses and animals from the pack train, but all points within the perimeter were still vulnerable.

All through the afternoon, Reno's behavior as the senior officer on the scene became increasingly bizarre and even inexcusable. Whether as a result of fatigue, drunkenness, inexperience, the fog of war, or some combination of these, Reno did a poor job of leading the effort. When he had reached the top of the bluff at a few minutes past 4 p.m., Dr. Porter saw Reno anxiously moving about with a red bandana tied around his head. Porter said, "Major, the men were pretty well demoralized, weren't they?" Reno's incredibly odd non sequitur of a retort was, "That was a charge, sir!"

Soon after Benteen's arrival, rather than attending to any number of more important duties—consolidating the perimeter, seeing to the welfare of his men, sending a reconnaissance patrol to determine Custer's situation, or even riding en masse per Custer's orders to the sound of the increasingly loud gunfire to the north—Reno instead personally led a party that included twelve troopers and Dr. Porter down the bluffs to find Reno's adjutant and good friend Lieutenant Benny Hodgson. Hodgson had been reported killed and Reno wanted to verify his fate. They discovered the body, and Reno recovered some of Hodgson's personal effects, but they soon came under fire and abandoned the effort to secure Hodgson's remains. Reno's ill-advised boondoggle resulted in an absence from his command of, by some estimates, forty-five precious minutes.

In addition, another controversial incident took place involving Captain Thomas Weir, commander of Company D. Weir was among the group of officers in the regiment—despite persistent rumors that he had enjoyed a flirtatious and perhaps even romantic relationship with Libbie Custer—who were loyal to Custer, and considered part of his "family." Although most of the Indians had raced away from the scene, there were still pockets of warriors that continued to fire on the soldiers, including a small group positioned to the north, probably at

Sharpshooter Ridge. The men of Weir's Company D formed a skirmish line and drove the Indians away. They then stood to horse, ready to mount up and ride to the gunfire they continued to hear to the north. They assumed Custer was engaged and needed their assistance. Lieutenant Winfield Edgerly, one of Weir's subordinate officers, reported later, "We ... waited for the order to advance, which we felt sure would be given ... every man apparently anxious to move down to the firing."

Captain Weir had been pacing back and forth, wondering how he should proceed. Suddenly, the men heard the crash of two or three simultaneous volleys in the distance—a known sign of distress. Edgerly approached Weir and said, "We ought to get down there." When Weir asked what he proposed that they do, Edgerly said, "Go get Custer, of course." Weir inquired whether Edgerly would be willing to go if only Company D proceeded on its own, with no additional support. Edgerly replied in the affirmative.

Accounts of the battle differ as to whether Weir sought permission directly from Reno to make the move northward. Some witnesses say that Weir did approach the commanding officer, and that a shouting match with much gesticulating followed (not surprisingly, Weir and Reno hated each other). Other versions state that Weir simply saddled up and moved ahead on his own initiative. Weir himself said later that he "hadn't spoken to Reno or Benteen, but rode out on the bluff hoping to see something of Custer's command." Whatever the truth, Weir gave no order to his men but merely began to ride north. Edgerly assumed that Weir had received permission and, with the rest of Company D, followed his leader.

The command rode for just over a mile, moving toward the geographic feature that is today known as Weir Point. It consisted of a series of rugged bluffs interspersed with low-lying areas, all in the shape of a horseshoe. While the hills offered a commanding view out ahead, they also provided precious little cover from a defensive standpoint. Company D took up positions throughout the heights, and could immediately perceive swirling dust clouds, men on horseback, and continued gunfire in the distance, approximately three miles to the north. Edgerly stated that they could see hundreds of horsemen "riding around and firing at objects in the ground and several guidons flying." They believed this was a rearguard action and that Custer was probably covering his own retreat to the north, perhaps to link up with Terry and Gibbon.

At approximately the same time that Weir and his men moved out, Captain McDougall arrived at the Reno-Benteen site with his Company B and the lead elements of the pack train, led by Lieutenant Edward Mathey, a French-born Civil War veteran known as "Bible Thumper" because of his habit of extreme profanity. McDougall reported to his commanding officer and Reno said, "Bennie is lying right over there," indicating Reno's continued lack of focus and preoccupation with the death of his friend Lieutenant Hodgson. Mathey testified later that an inebriated Reno greeted him by revealing his flask of whisky, saying, "Look here, I got half a bottle yet." He did not offer Mathey a drink.

Captain Benteen had observed Weir's move north and assumed the entire command was leaving to join the advance, though Benteen had received no direct order from Reno to that effect. At this point, apparently, either Reno was not delivering orders or, if he was, no one was listening. Benteen directed Companies H, K, and M to join Weir, and they reached his position in about half an hour. Reno did forward a message to Weir, telling him to work to communicate with Custer, and that Reno would follow when the remainder of the pack train arrived. Then, inexplicably, Reno had a trumpeter repeatedly sound the command to halt. Weir, Benteen, and every other officer and man who moved in the direction of Weir Point ignored Reno's trumpeter and continued to forge ahead. Finally, Reno himself moved out with the remainder of the unit, including the pack train and the wounded soldiers, who were carried in blankets.

When Benteen arrived at Weir Point he deployed his three companies in a skirmish line on the bluffs. He scaled the heights, and he too could see vast clouds of dust on the high piece of ground to the north, but now the men heard only an intermittent shot or two. What they saw clearly, however, was an angry horde of Indian warriors moving rapidly in their direction. Lieutenant Luther Hare said later that he believed as many as 1,500 Sioux and Cheyenne were coming at them.

In the first important example of his demonstrating flexibility under changing circumstances—or perhaps just showing simple common sense—Benteen muttered, "This is a hell of place to fight Indians. I am going to see Reno and propose that we go back to where we lay before starting out here."

Benteen tracked back with his men to Reno, who was in front of the pack train about half a mile south and moving toward Weir Point. Weir also came along, leaving Edgerly and one other officer in charge of the remaining troopers at Weir Point. Benteen told Reno of the futility of attempting to defend the advanced position, and Reno agreed. Perhaps because Reno had been previously ignored, he did not direct his trumpeter to sound the signal for a withdrawal. Reno also again failed—just as he had earlier during the frenzied retreat across the river—to take the common tactical precaution of ordering a rear-guard action. Benteen later said of Reno at this critical point in the battle, "If he gave any orders, I did not hear them." The practical result was the second poorly organized retreat of the day under Reno's leadership.

By now, many of the officers were fed up with Reno and feared the dire consequences if he remained in charge. Captain McDougall had conferred with another officer and determined that Reno was incompetent and that unless they took dramatic steps, they were all in danger of being wiped out. McDougall approached Benteen and said, "Say old man, what is going to be the outcome of this unless we have a commanding officer here pretty damn soon? You are the senior captain, and we would like to see you take the lead in affairs." Benteen apparently smiled, but he offered no response. However, when the effort to consolidate and defend the Reno-Benteen position got under way, Benteen took the reins and did not let go until the battle ended.

Confused as to whether they were expected to retreat or not, the soldiers left on Weir Point finally began to hastily withdraw as Indian warriors came ever closer to reaching them. Lieutenant Edgerly and the men of Company D moved rapidly south, but the enemy got near enough that the young officer and his orderly narrowly missed being hit by rifle fire.

In one of the truly heroic individual actions of the battle, Lieutenant Edward Godfrey of K Company took it upon himself to form a rear guard to protect his retreating comrades, who now came sprinting on by. He had twenty-two men in position, dismounted, about 500 yards north of the Reno-Benteen site. The men of Company K were inclined to want to join the sprint to the rear, but through equal parts intimidation and inspiration Godfrey harangued them into standing their ground. He "threatened to kill any man who ran away," as they skillfully executed a fighting withdrawal, pouring alternating fire into the oncoming Indians as each squad leapfrogged the other back to safety. When all of their comrades were securely within home base, K Company joined them. Lieutenant Godfrey had not lost a single man.

Benteen took charge from here. The soldiers quickly deployed in an oval shape. Benteen ensured that not only his men but also the soldiers under Reno's direct command were all properly positioned. Benteen's Company H defended a high ridge on the southern perimeter. To the east, Captain Myles Moylan's Company A defended the hospital, horses, and mules housed in the depression behind them. Company G, under Lieutenant George Wallace, linked in with Company A's left flank. Companies D and K came next, extending the lines facing east and then bending left to defend the northern end of the perimeter. Finally, M Company under Captain Thomas French and Captain McDougall's Company B covered the west-facing bluffs.

Because of the nature of the terrain they occupied, many men were limited by restricted fields of fire, in some cases no more than thirty feet. They were ordered to take their positions quickly and to protect themselves by lying down. They were lacking natural cover such as trees or boulders, so they improvised by using boxes and sacks of food and forage, saddles, and the like. Ammunition was evenly distributed. The officers urged the men to limit their fire to conserve bullets, but when the Indians made their initial charge it took several furious volleys to force them back. The Indians then began to take advantage of the surrounding ground by occupying high points nearby. Several attacks on the eastern flank were stubbornly repulsed, but the Indians maintained an incessant sniping fire into the position. Soldier casualties began to mount.

The Indians also used the tactic of pouring a heavy, smoke-producing fire into the position, and then launching an assault. This dynamic continued throughout the afternoon until the sun went down and even into the night. Soldiers would poke their heads up, unleash a volley or two of deadly rifle fire, and the Indians would scatter and withdraw. The commanding officer, Reno, spent most of his time curled up in his bedding in the safest place he could find, a rifle pit near the hospital, sipping on his whisky. Benteen commented to an enlisted man after a visit to the major, "I found him lying in the same place I saw him before."

Benteen, on the other hand, was the model of the courageous leader, calmly walking the perimeter and exposing himself to constant enemy fire. He encouraged the men, helping them to manage their ammunition and judge aiming distances. They knew he was in command and would do his best to get them through the trial. One man commented later, "He took absolute charge of one side of the hill, and you may rest assured that he did not bother Reno for permission of any kind."

Reno did make the occasional circuit of the defenses, but he always returned to the area of the supplies, where he could hunker down again after refilling his flask from a keg of whisky he had brought with him for the campaign. At one point, an argument erupted between Reno and two civilian mule packers. Reno slapped one of them across the face, spilling whisky onto the men from his flask as he did so. The angry packer made a move toward Reno, but the major grabbed a carbine, pointed it at the man, and threatened, "I will shoot you." The bizarre behavior of Major Marcus Reno continued.

The fighting for the remainder of that afternoon produced twelve additional soldier fatalities and twenty-one wounded. Dr. Porter worked frantically in the center of the storm to treat the injured. As the long, hot, terrible day moved into night, the soldiers faced fearful odds. They were in a mediocre defensive position surrounded by many hundreds of warriors, they lacked water and ammunition, and there were no signs that help was on the way. As the day progressed, in the valley below, the men witnessed a great celebration with huge roaring fires that threw up ominous shadows from the village when darkness finally came. The ceremonies included much singing (both victory chants and mournful death songs for fallen Indian warriors), drums, and dancing. The entire affair had an understandably eerie and unsettling effect on the soldiers, who slept fitfully, if at all, that night.

They still did not know what had happened to Custer. The prevailing opinion was that he had either retreated north to find Terry and Gibbon, or was pinned down in a defensive position somewhere, just as they were. Some men thought Custer had simply abandoned them, much as he had "abandoned" Major Elliott at the Washita some years before. There was no thought that the indestructible Son of the Morning Star and all of his followers could have been massacred. Lieutenant Varnum summarized the consensus among the men when he said later, "The idea of the command being cut up and wiped out as it was, I didn't think of such a thing.... The idea of Custer being killed never struck me, it never entered my mind." Reno himself stated in his subsequent battle report, "the awful fate that did befall [Custer] never occurred to any of us as within the limits of possibility."

Though some historians challenge this assertion, apparently, Reno came to Benteen during the night and suggested that they undertake a forced march under cover of darkness to escape their hellish predicament. Reno advocated that they destroy any supplies they could not take with them, and that every man who could ride join them in a trek to the Yellowstone River and their supply base. The journey would be 120 miles. Benteen inquired as to the wounded, many of whom were unable to mount a horse. Reno stated that those men would have to be left behind. Benteen's immediate response was, "No, Reno, you can't do that." Reno dropped the subject, but when word spread that he had even proposed it, morale—especially among the injured men when they heard of Reno's plan the next morning—plummeted to a new low. After getting wind that Reno proposed to abandon the wounded, Captain Weir sought out Lieutenant Godfrey. Weir asked, "If there should be a conflict of judgment between Reno and Benteen as to what we should do, whose orders would you obey?" Godfrey immediately responded, "Benteen." Weir, apparently heartened to hear the answer he had been looking for, turned away.

Benteen did make a mistake when he allowed his men to rest overnight into June 26, rather than ordering them to dig in and fortify their positions, which Reno had instructed his soldiers to do. Apparently Benteen felt that the worst of the Indian attacks were over. Just before dawn, however, Indian rifle fire from every direction began to pepper the area again. As the sun rose in the sky, the fighting became furious once more. Benteen's men, relatively unprotected as they were and occupying the exposed southern terrain, suffered more casualties. Benteen, with a bullet hole through the heel of his boot, rallied a number of skulkers who had sought safety in the central swale. He repositioned them and then went to Reno to ask for reinforcements. Reno, in his rifle pit, seemed oblivious to the peril they faced. Benteen argued forcefully that the position was about to be overrun, and finally Reno consented to move some of his men to the southern end of the position. In another demonstration of taking charge and showing flexibility, Benteen led soldiers from Captain French's M Company to shore up the defensive line to the south.

When Indians approached close to Benteen's line in apparent preparation to charge, he decided to surprise them. He personally

led a number of his troopers in an assault down the ravines in front
of their position. The Indians, shocked at the audacity of the attack,
scattered. Benteen later said some of them were, "somersaulting like
acrobats." Benteen led a similar attack later from the north side of the
position, which also caused the Indians to disperse. Reno—perhaps in
an attempt to redeem himself—left his fighting hole long enough to
participate in that charge as well.

Benteen's courage was, as on the first day of combat, continually
on display. He walked the perimeter casually, with his shirt untucked,
perpetually under fire, shouting encouragement to the beleaguered
men. He said, "It is live or die with us. We must fight it out with them."
At one point Benteen told a fellow officer, "When the bullet is cast to
kill me, it'll kill me, that's all." Benteen's bravado had an extremely
inspirational effect on all who observed him.

In the increasingly oppressive heat of late morning, as unbear-
able thirst began to torture the men, Benteen called for volunteers to
make a daring 500-yard dash down a steep draw from the south end
of the position west to the river below. About twenty men stepped up.
Benteen assigned a group of them to move to the river to fill canteens
and other receptacles, while four of his best shots covered them from
the bluffs above. They worked for approximately twenty minutes, and
though they came under intense enemy fire, every man made it safely
back to the high ground. They distributed the much-needed water,
which was especially welcome to Dr. Porter's patients, some of whom
were literally dying of thirst. For courage above and beyond the call
of duty, nineteen soldiers who participated in this heroic action were
later awarded the Medal of Honor.

As the day progressed, Indian fire gradually slackened. Many of
the warriors had moved back down to the village. By 3 p.m., the sniping ceased. Indian scouts to the north had seen the Terry-Gibbon column approaching in the distance. The soldiers observed smoke rising
from the valley, as the villagers set fire to the grass to shield their movement away from the area. At around 7 p.m. the men observed a huge

mass of humanity travel south up the valley, in the direction of the Bighorn Mountains. Men, women, and children rode away as a single, mighty host, again chanting their mix of songs, some celebratory, some mournful. Twenty thousand ponies moved with them. Some soldiers estimated that 10,000 people created a column three miles long. It was a sight the men would never forget. Though no one could be positive, it seemed their prolonged, excruciating ordeal was over.

Reno directed that the command move closer to the river. Lookouts were posted. New defensive works were erected. The men watered themselves and their animals. They buried the dead. The cooks put together a meal. The men slept. In two days of intense fighting on the lonely hilltop, fifteen men were killed and fifty-six (five of whom would later die) were wounded.

Through it all, Captain Frederick Benteen had been magnificent. While many have criticized his slow forward progress early in the battle and, in particular, have faulted him for not riding immediately to Custer's aid when he was expressly ordered to do so, no one questions his bravery and adaptability in leading the hilltop defense. Even Reno, in his written after-action report on the battle, commended Benteen's "conspicuous services" and advocated that his courage be recognized by the government.

Benteen demonstrated flexibility in numerous ways. When Weir Point looked impossible to defend, he convinced Reno to back track to their initial position. When it appeared that the consensus was that Reno was unfit for command (though no overt, mutinous action took place), Benteen in effect took charge of the unit. Godfrey and others testified later that Benteen "was exercising the functions principally of commanding officer." Benteen deployed the soldiers, both his and Reno's, in the most effective way within the defensive perimeter. He continuously walked the lines, at considerable personal peril, to encourage and inspire his soldiers. He adapted to new tactical realities by both redistributing men along the lines and, when crisis came, personally leading at least two critical charges that caused the enemy to scatter. He rebuffed Reno's attempt to abandon the wounded to their fate. He organized the heroic expedition to secure much-needed water. Benteen was, in short, the very model of the leader who demonstrates flexibility under changing circumstances.

* * * *

★ ★ Case Study ★ ★

Rascal's Restaurant in Apple Valley, Minnesota: Know Your Business, Know Your Employees, Know Your Customers

While our case studies up to this point have focused on large, multi-million, or even multibillion-dollar enterprises, in fact, small business is the engine that drives our economy. According to the Small Business Administration Office of Advocacy, there were 27.2 million small businesses (defined as an independent business with fewer than 500 employees) in America in 2007. These businesses represent 99.7 percent of all employer firms. They employ close to half of all private sector workers and pay almost 45 percent of U.S. private payroll. Since the middle 1990s, these small firms have generated between 60 and 80 percent of net new jobs. Small businesses create better than half of nonfarm private gross domestic product, hire 40 percent of high tech workers such as scientists and engineers, and produce thirteen times more patents per employee than larger patenting businesses. Entrepreneurs who create and build small businesses are critical to our future economic survival.

There is much that we can learn from studying this powerful force in our national economy. Often, small businesses demonstrate incredible ability to innovate and be flexible as business conditions change. They are nimble in a way that is the envy of larger, more cumbersome organizations. One small business that I know of personally has done a superb job of adapting—both over the long haul and during the current recession—to new economic realities.

In 1994 the husband-and-wife team of Dewey Johnson and Wanda Oland purchased a rough and tumble saloon in Apple Valley, Minnesota, that had metal doors so that glass wouldn't break if anyone got forcefully tossed out into the parking lot. Through hard work, determination, and a passion for the business, Wanda and Dewey have transformed that former rowdy watering hole into Rascal's, one of Apple Valley's most popular family restaurants.

Wanda and Dewey have demonstrated flexibility in building their business over the last decade-and-a-half and have shown particular savvy in navigating through the current recession. They have adapted to changing circumstances, interestingly, by using a tried-and-true formula. The trick has been taking what they have known all along and refining it to a new level. Wanda and Dewey's strategy for success, in good times and in bad, can be summed up as follows: know your business, know your employees, and know your customers.

Wanda and Dewey know their business. Wanda has spent her entire professional career in restaurants. Dewey's background is as a general contractor, but much of what he learned in that discipline translates to the restaurant industry. When revenues started to slide with the economy, Wanda and Dewey applied the principle, "If you want to find out what's happening with your business, work the back room." Dewey spent months in the kitchen working hard, talking with employees, and discovering potential efficiencies.

For example, Dewey built a laundry room and Rascal's now washes its own linens at significant savings. The couple decided to shop different vendors for such things as paper, chemicals, groceries, and credit card processing, and realized additional savings. Wanda says, "We took a good hard look at everything."

Wanda and Dewey have gone through three significant remodels, and Dewey has in effect acted as the general contractor for each. Dewey built every table by hand in Rascal's, and he custom built the bar with thick maple planks formerly used as bowling lanes. He has raised and lowered flooring and installed windows. He put in auto-paper towel dispensers because they are more efficient. He has done it all with the physical facility.

The couple went to a part-time bookkeeper and because margins are small, Wanda pays extremely close attention to every penny that comes in and goes out. She says, "Everything we touch matters." This is all a part of knowing your business.

Wanda and Dewey know their employees, too. Many of their people, including kitchen help, servers, and at least one bartender, have been with them from the beginning. How do they achieve such loyalty? They talk with and listen to their folks, and they treat them right.

With the recession, like countless other businesses, Rascal's watches labor hours closely. But instead of releasing people or reducing hourly pay, Wanda and Dewey developed a flexible schedule that allows employees to swap hours and take time off when they need it. They have not backfilled some positions. Wanda does her best to manage labor efficiently based on the flow of customer traffic and to spread out available hours fairly among the staff.

From a morale standpoint, Rascal's employees see the owners there virtually every day, dressed in blue jeans and ready to work. Wanda says, "Don't ever ask an employee to do something that you're not willing to do yourself."

Finally and perhaps most important, Wanda and Dewey know their customers (Wanda calls them their "guests"). They understand their guests expect high-quality food and excellent service, and in these two areas nothing has changed. Many menu items are homemade. They make their own dressings and sauces. They fillet their own walleye, always fresh, never frozen. They whip up their own batter. They boil and mash their own potatoes. Portion sizes have not changed.

During the down economy, Wanda and Dewey figured their guests would appreciate an opportunity to still go out to eat, but save money. They devised a daily calendar featuring enticements like inexpensive burgers, free video games and musical entertainment, or a kids-eat-free from 10 a.m. to 2 p.m. deal on Sundays. This approach encourages people to come out and enjoy themselves any day of the week without spending too much.

They have also tinkered with the menu, focusing on foods that remind people of good old-fashioned home cooking. Guests can now eat meatloaf (my personal favorite), turkey, or pot roast at Rascal's.

Rascal's offers catering, serving corporate groups, weddings, local schools, and others. Rascal's hosts fundraisers in support of a number of local charities. In short, Rascal's does whatever is necessary to market their product and reward—and hopefully build upon—a loyal guest base.

Survival in the current economy is a struggle even for the healthiest of businesses, large or small. But those organizations that understand their businesses well, treat their employees with respect, and focus continually on the needs of their customers will do best. Wanda Oland says it well, "We touch a lot of lives. We'll make it through, and we'll be stronger for it."

Wanda Oland and Dewey Johnson represent the epitome of smart business leaders who know that in order to survive they must be lean and flexible in adapting to a changing game. They have taken a fundamental, well-tested strategy and refined it in a way that allows them to see new possibilities and set a different, better course of action. They know that things may never be the same as they were, but by continually scrutinizing and closely managing their operations, and changing as necessary, they will endure the tough times and thrive into the future.

Leadership Lesson Eight:

BE FLEXIBLE UNDER CHANGING CIRCUMSTANCES

In the late fall of 2008, the Best Buy Company—in light of reduced performance in a difficult retail environment—offered an extremely generous severance package to any corporate employee who chose to leave the company voluntarily. The departures were to be effective in February 2009. Approximately 500 people out of a total of 4,500 employees at headquarters made the choice to accept the buyout. Many individuals agonized over the decision. Best Buy was, and is, a great American company. People had in some cases worked for many years to build a career there. In the end, most chose to stay, and this was for a variety of reasons. They hoped for Best Buy's successful future and wanted to continue on with a winner. Or they liked their jobs and their co-workers. Or they weren't in a financial position to leave. Or they did not have a more attractive career alternative. Or maybe it was some combination of these reasons. For others, something told them it was time to chart a new path. At the very least, Best Buy forced every single eligible employee to think long and hard about his or her career and life.

This exercise was fascinating on many levels, but particularly so in light of our lesson concerning the need to be flexible under changing circumstances. At a macro level, Best Buy demonstrated flexibility by developing a creative solution for a common business problem: too many employees. Instead of firing people en masse—a course of action that many similarly situated organizations would have taken—Best Buy opted for a more humane and generous approach in allowing employees to opt out voluntarily, with the benefit of a comfortable financial cushion. Best Buy showed humanity, magnanimity, and adaptability all in one stroke.

On the micro level, individual employees also demonstrated flexibility. The opportunity to take a period of time and reconsider life's alternatives certainly represented a changing circumstance. How many of us have fantasized over the question, if I had to do something different, what would it be? Best Buy made this tantalizing dream a reality for its employees.

People like me chose to leave to start their own businesses, or to write. A few people decided to go back to school. Some chose to stay home with kids. Some went right back to work for another company somewhere. Some decided to travel. Some just took time to relax and consider next steps. Everyone who opted for the package was forced to be flexible and, frankly, lucky to have the opportunity.

Those who stayed behind also needed to be flexible in dealing with a whole new scenario at Best Buy. They were now forging ahead without 500 of their former professional colleagues. In many cases they switched jobs or took on different responsibilities. Organizational structures changed. Once the dust settled, the world did not look the same for any of us.

This flexibility skill is imperative in a good leader. Flexible leaders recognize when a situation has changed, and they adapt, rapidly and effectively. Frederick Benteen continually altered his approach during the chaos and danger of the desperate hilltop fight near the Little Big-horn, and the position was saved as a result. Wanda Oland and Dewey Johnson have adapted over many years, but have been especially sharp and focused during the down economy. They will survive and do well in the years to come.

How flexible are you as a leader? Do you recognize change when it happens and move nimbly in response? Or do you continue down the same old path, wondering why nothing is different and your business suffers? In business, as in life, the harsh reality is that we must "adapt or die."

PART FIVE

SHOW ENERGY
& PASSION

Chapter Nine

GETTYSBURG

LITTLE ROUND TOP: WHEN ALL ELSE FAILS, INNOVATE AND LEAD THE CHARGE

"I will take the responsibility of taking my brigade there...."

—Colonel Strong Vincent—

The Confederate advance that began at around 4 p.m. on July 2 at Gettysburg resulted in some of the most ferocious and costly fighting in the entire American Civil War—or any other war. The story of the defense of Little Round Top at the southern end of the field has come to epitomize the intensity and agony of the combat experienced that day. For a variety of understandable reasons, Union Colonel Joshua Lawrence Chamberlain stands out as an American icon and is widely remembered for his heroic conduct as he led the Twentieth Maine Regiment in preserving the Army of the Potomac's endangered left flank. Yet there were a number of other heroes, less well-known, but whose contributions on that critical terrain feature figured just as prominently—or more so—than the vaunted Chamberlain. Without men such as Union General Gouverneur Warren, Colonel Strong Vincent, and Colonel Patrick O'Rorke, in addition to Chamberlain, the day may well have been lost. On the Confederate side, Colonel William B. Oates also demonstrated astounding bravery and determination, along with his Alabama brigade, in nearly capturing Little Round Top. All of these leaders showed great energy and passion when it mattered most. In several important instances, they also modeled the principle that when all else fails, sometimes the best course is to innovate and lead the charge.

For all of the criticism General James Longstreet endured post-Gettysburg, not even his harshest detractor can deny that once he committed his gray-clad legions to combat on Day Two, they fought with incredible fury. Longstreet delivered the order to attack against the fragile salient created by Dan Sickles's reckless move forward. The very capable and extremely pugnacious General John Bell Hood, with his division, personally led the way. Hood had three times requested permission to attempt a flanking maneuver around the Union left, but Longstreet denied his entreaties and ordered him forward. No sooner had Hood stepped off when a shell exploded above him, causing shrapnel to severely wound his left arm. He was carried away to a field hospital and, unfortunately for the Confederate cause, the assault became disorganized without his fiery leadership.

Four of the nine regiments of Hood's two lead brigades attacked thinly defended Union positions in the area known as the Devil's Den, a small, slightly elevated terrain feature that contained gigantic granite boulders that seemed "as though nature in some wild freak had forgotten herself and piled great rocks in mad confusion together," wrote one Union soldier. The remaining five regiments headed straight for the two Round Tops, something they had been expressly ordered not to do. These units were now in effect operating independently and without any overall direction from Hood's replacement, Brigadier General Evander Law. Lee's idea had been to roll up the enemy in echelon, that is, in successive waves, using the Emmitsburg Road as the north-south axis of attack. Instead, the force that moved toward the Round Tops continued in an easterly direction, eventually dividing into two distinct columns, one moving toward large, heavily wooded Round Top, and the other toward the smaller but more open Little Round Top just to the north.

General Meade, immediately prior to riding to meet with Dan Sickles to personally witness the potentially disastrous scenario unfolding in the Third Corps sector, made two important and prescient decisions. First, he directed the men of General George Sykes's Fifth Corps, who rested in reserve two miles to the rear, to move rapidly to their left to reinforce what Meade anticipated would be a threatened Third Corps position. Second, he sent General Gouverneur Warren, his chief engineer, to Little Round Top. Meade had ordered Sickles to anchor on that tactically critical hill, and wanted to make sure that it was properly defended. Instead, to Warren's shock and horror, he found Little Round Top completely undefended, save for a small contingent of Union signalmen. To his further distress, Warren looked into the distance and saw Confederate infantry approaching in mass, less than a mile away. Warren later described the experience as "intensely thrilling to my feelings and almost appalling."

Brigadier General Gouverneur Warren was trained as an engineer (he had also spent time as a math instructor at West Point), and like Meade, he had a reputation for being cautious and deliberate in his approach. But on this day, Warren earned eternal fame for the speed and decisiveness with which he innovated and took action. Warren immediately recognized that if Rebel forces secured Little Round Top, their artillery and rifles would be in position to dominate Sickles's exposed position as well as the tenuous Union line on Cemetery Ridge. Warren dispatched a messenger to Meade requesting reinforcements, then sent his staffer Lieutenant Ranald Mackenzie (who would go on to earn great renown as an Indian fighter after the war) to request that Sickles send a brigade to Little Round Top. Sickles—perhaps wondering what he had gotten himself into and by now fully engaged with a hot combat situation of his own—declined the invitation to send a force to the crest of Little Round Top on the basis that he desperately needed every man to quell the Confederate tide.

Mackenzie rode away in search of any available unit. He happened upon Fifth Corps commander George Sykes, who was in the process of moving his men forward per Meade's orders. Sykes quickly understood the gravity of the situation and sent a courier to find the commanding general of his lead division, James Barnes. No one could find Barnes, but Sykes's messenger was incredibly fortunate to encounter Colonel Strong Vincent, commanding officer of the lead brigade of Barnes' division. Vincent, a 26-year-old Harvard-trained lawyer, was one of those amazing citizen volunteers—of which there were many on both sides in the Civil War—who instinctively took to soldiering with great gusto and skill. He came from Erie, Pennsylvania, and was married the day before he deployed for war. Immediately prior to Gettysburg, he learned that his wife was pregnant with their first child. In lieu of a weapon, Vincent carried a riding crop into battle, which his wife had given him as a gift.

Vincent shouted to the messenger, "Captain, what are your orders?" The captain asked where he could find General Barnes. "Give me your orders," repeated Vincent forcefully. The messenger gestured toward Little Round Top. "General Sykes told me to direct General Barnes to send one of his brigades to occupy that hill yonder." Vincent—in obvious, but wise, circumvention of the chain of command—responded immediately, "I will take the responsibility of taking my brigade there." He ordered his four regiments to scale the rocky heights.

While three Confederate regiments from Hood's division skirted the shoulder of Round Top and headed straight for Little Round Top, two Alabama regiments (the Fifteenth and Forty-Seventh, led by Colonel William C. Oates) took the more laborious direct route up thickly wooded and treacherously steep Round Top. They crested the heights, and then realized that Round Top was militarily useless, with restricted visibility and fields of fire because of the canopy of trees. They distinctly heard the furious fighting to their left in the Devil's

Den. They moved north into the saddle between the two hills and continued on toward Little Round Top.

These Confederate soldiers had already experienced a trying day. They had marched 25 miles to get to the battlefield. They had participated in the ill-fated march and countermarch that delayed the Rebel assault until late afternoon. The weather was beastly hot. The terrain they presently traversed featured heavy vegetation and huge rocks. They were drenched with sweat, tired, and thirsty, and now they were expected to charge into battle against a quickly consolidating and determined enemy. Their commander, Colonel Oates, was a hardy 29-year-old Alabamian, a former teacher and a lawyer. He was known as a tough and demanding leader, but his troops appreciated his willingness to share in their many hardships. The adversity on this day would only get worse.

Colonel Oates and his men of Alabama did not know it, but their comrades in Hood's division had captured the Devil's Den and part of the area just to the north known as Houck's Ridge, in fighting that one Confederate soldier described as "one of the wildest, fiercest struggles of the war." The clash on the boulder-strewn hillock had fragmented into small unit and, in many cases, hand-to-hand combat that was unique and horrible in the experience of these soldiers. Now, like a rapidly spreading wildfire, the conflict surged northward, and would soon engulf the forty-acre woodlot and twenty-acre wheat field owned by farmer John Rose, as well as Joseph Sherfy's peach orchard next to Emmitsburg Road.

All of this evolving action occurred simultaneously with the epic fight for Little Round Top (see Gettysburg Map Number Four, July 2, 1863, Battle for Little Round Top, Late Afternoon). After ordering his brigade up the hill, Colonel Strong Vincent rode rapidly ahead to reconnoiter the position and decide where best to place his troops. Vincent determined that the Confederate threat could potentially come both from the area of the Devil's Den to the west or, more likely, from Round Top to the south. Vincent noticed an advantageous terrain feature in the form of a north-south spur with a rocky ledge running to the west that might serve as a formidable defensive position. As Vincent's four regiments came to the crest, he placed them (1,350 men in all) in order starting with Joshua L. Chamberlain's Twentieth Maine (386 men) on the far left or southern flank, defending the east-west shelf. He positioned the remaining units to the right of the Twentieth Maine in a gradual arc that covered the west-facing front as well. In Chamberlain's words, Colonel Vincent's instructions to him could not have been clearer. Vincent explained, said Chamberlain, "this was the extreme left of our general line, and that a desperate attack was expected in order to turn that position, [and he] concluded by telling me I was to 'hold that ground at all hazards.'"

Joshua L. Chamberlain is a fascinating character in American history. He was thirty-four-years-old at the time of Gettysburg and had been a professor of rhetoric at Bowdoin College in Maine when the war broke out. He abhorred slavery deeply and left his academic career to become lieutenant colonel of the Twentieth Maine Volunteer Infantry Regiment. He was strikingly handsome, brave, and a genuinely kind, humble, and decent man. He was intellectually gifted, trained in theology, and could read seven foreign languages. He possessed a beautiful singing voice and was a compelling public speaker. He was truly a renaissance man, and the nineteenth century beau ideal of the citizen-soldier who unselfishly heeded his country's call to duty.

Chamberlain had fought at Antietam and Fredericksburg, but his moment of highest glory came during the "crowded hour" on Day Two of Gettysburg at Little Round Top. He was awarded the Medal of Honor—just as Dan Sickles was, many years after the war but, unlike Sickles, deservingly—for his courage and leadership in the defense of that critical terrain feature. He was later elevated to brigade command, and General U. S. Grant gave him a battlefield promotion to brigadier general for bravery in action during the siege of Petersburg, Virginia, in June 1864. Chamberlain was also grievously wounded at Petersburg (shot through both hips), and he was not expected to survive.

But survive he did. Grant later honored Chamberlain by directing him to receive the formal surrender of Lee's decimated legions at Appomattox, Virginia, to end the war in April 1865. There, Chamberlain made an unforgettably gracious and endearing gesture by saluting the defeated Army of Northern Virginia.

Chamberlain enjoyed a productive and high-profile career after the war. He was four times elected governor of Maine and served as president of his beloved Bowdoin College. He was a prolific and eloquent writer, and his book *The Passing of the Armies* is still in print and regarded as a classic account of the Army of the Potomac's final campaign. Some critics have contended that Chamberlain overplayed and exaggerated his battlefield contributions in his post-war writings. Nevertheless, over time, Chamberlain has been favorably portrayed in books and movies such as Michael Shaara's historical novel *Killer Angels* and the film *Gettysburg*, in which the actor Jeff Daniels played Chamberlain. Chamberlain died an old man in 1914, in part due to complications from the Civil War wounds that had always troubled him. Chamberlain is an iconic figure in the lore of the Civil War as well as the present day. It is in large part because of the ongoing fascination surrounding his personality and gallantry that Little Round Top is the most-visited portion of the Gettysburg National Military Park.

During the battle, at that soon-to-be famous place, Strong Vincent placed his men and they immediately saw the enemy. Vincent had acted none too soon. The three Confederate regiments that moved over the shoulder of Round Top directly at Little Round Top appeared first. Due to the difficulty of terrain and lack of command and control, these three Rebel units fought loosely and not in any coordinated fashion. As the tough Maine lumberjacks and fishermen of Colonel Chamberlain's regiment positioned themselves, the enemy also came into sight for them in the form of Colonel Oates's Alabamians, approaching from the saddle between the two hills. Oates and his two regiments also fought independently of any other command. The exchange of musketry gradually began to escalate. Chamberlain later said, "It did not seem to me that it was *very* severe at first. The fire was hot, but we gave them as good as we sent, and the Rebels did not so much attempt at that period of the fight to force our line, as to cut us up by their fire."

Oates finally directed an attack against the Twentieth Maine, but was repelled by what he described as "the most destructive fire I ever saw." Chamberlain remembered, "They pushed to within a dozen yards of us before the terrible effectiveness of our fire compelled them to break and take shelter." Oates responded by taking his Fifteenth Alabama on an end run to the east, beyond the Union left flank. Chamberlain countered by thinning out his ranks to only one man deep and "refusing," that is, bending back his left flank to meet the Confederate threat. The action was becoming decidedly more violent and uncertain at the extreme left end of the Army of the Potomac.

As the drama in Vincent's sector of Little Round Top continued to unfold, Gouverneur Warren maintained his frantic pace in ensuring the defense of the entire hilltop. He breathed a sigh of relief as Battery D of the Fifth U.S. Artillery, commanded by Lieutenant Charles Hazlett, appeared on the scene. The rugged ground and limited space made placement of Hazlett's guns difficult, but Warren himself assisted with wrestling the weapons into position, facing west. Once the Yankee artillery commenced firing, the effect on Union troops below the hill and Vincent's brigade to the left was inspiring. Warren suffered a minor wound at this point when an enemy bullet grazed his throat. He continued to push, however, and though he could not see that far—he had not communicated directly with Vincent at all—he now heard the combat raging at the southern end of the line. Reinforcements were again needed, and quickly.

Warren clambered down the hill in search of help. Fortuitously, a Fifth Corps brigade commanded by Brigadier General Stephen Weed was on its way via the Wheatfield Road, and Weed had spurred ahead to Little Round Top to scout the scene. The lead regiment in that column (the 140th New York) was commanded by an outstanding young officer, Colonel Patrick Henry O'Rorke. O'Rorke was born in County Cavan, Ireland, and came to America with his parents as a young child to live in Rochester, New York. His many friends and admirers held him in high esteem and knew him as "Paddy." He was twenty-six years old at Gettysburg, and he was brilliant, having graduated first in his class out of West Point in June 1861 (the same class in which George Armstrong Custer finished at the bottom). O'Rorke had distinguished himself in several previous battles. Warren had been O'Rorke's commanding officer earlier in the war, and now shouted, "Paddy, give me a regiment." O'Rorke hesitated momentarily, stating that General Weed had ridden on ahead and expected his brigade to follow him. Warren shouted, "Never mind that, Paddy! Bring them up on the double-quick—don't stop for aligning! I'll take the responsibility!" With that, O'Rorke ordered his men forward in a mad scramble up the east slope to the crest of Little Round Top.

Strong Vincent saw that his Sixteenth Michigan Regiment, which occupied the far right flank of the line, was wavering under the Rebel attack. The Sixteenth pulled its colors back to a safer position, and put the entire defensive effort in jeopardy. In an attempt to rally the remaining men, Vincent jumped up and, waving his riding crop, shouted, "Don't give an inch!" He was immediately struck with a rifle shot to his groin. Vincent cried out, "This is the fourth or fifth time they have shot at me, and they have hit me at last." He would linger painfully until his death on July 7. One soldier lamented of Vincent's sacrifice, "Throwing himself in the breach he rallied his men, but gave up his own life."

With Strong Vincent mortally wounded, the Union right continued to crumble. Paddy O'Rorke and his 140th New York arrived just in time. As the New Yorkers hastily formed their line for battle, O'Rorke surveyed the situation. He saw Confederates nearby and approaching rapidly, and realized that he must immediately shore up the disintegrating wing. O'Rorke jumped off his horse and, brandishing his sword, cried, "Down this way boys!" An enlisted man wrote later, "It was about this time that Colonel O'Rorke, cheering on his men and acting as he always does, like a brave and good man, fell, pierced through the neck by a Rebel bullet." His spine was severed and he was killed instantly. His men, who were furious at the loss of their valiant leader, rushed into the breach and poured a volume of fire into the enemy. With much intense exchange of musketry, the New Yorkers attacked and the Rebels withdrew. A Union soldier wrote later, "They soon fell back, our boys being too much for them; but they did cut us down dreadfully while we were advancing." Casualties on both sides ran to a quarter of the number of men engaged in the brief but sharp firefight. For now, the Yankee right at Little Round Top was secure.

At the other end of the line, Joshua Chamberlain and the Twentieth Maine continued in their monumental struggle with Colonel Oates and his determined Confederates. As casualties multiplied and ammunition ran out, the situation became desperate for Chamberlain. Oates decided to try one last all-out attack. He too had suffered heavy casualties, but rallied his men by leading the charge himself. He explained later, "I passed through the column waving my sword, rushed forward to the ledge, and was promptly followed by my entire command in splendid style."

The Rebels attained the rocky ledge and fierce, point-blank, hand-to-hand combat ensued. Chamberlain recalled later, "The edge of conflict swayed to and fro, with wild whirlpools and eddies. At times I saw around me more of the enemy than of my own men: gaps opening, swallowing, closing again with sharp convulsive energy...." Chamberlain's line had bent back severely enough to the left—it was now shaped like a hairpin—that some of his men faced east, and fought almost literally back-to-back with their comrades. The Union officers held their swords with both hands and using all of their might, pressed the weapons flat against the backs of their own enlisted men to stem the furious Confederate onslaught. Finally, after much savage fighting, the Twentieth Maine held the line and the exhausted Rebels were forced to withdraw. It had been a close call.

Colonel Oates now believed that he had no alternative but to retreat from the field entirely. Chamberlain, however, did not know what his counterpart was thinking. Chamberlain said later, "our ammunition utterly failed," and his perception was that the Rebels were gathering at the base of the hill not for a withdrawal but for one more charge, which he would have no hope of repelling. In an innovative stroke of genius, Chamberlain shouted the command, "Fix bayonets!" In the smoke and din, the order had run down the right side of the line only, and Lieutenant Holman Melcher led his company forward down the hill. On the left, the directive had not been heard, but when Captain Ellis Spear saw his comrades moving forward he too led his troops in a bold attack into the enemy. The result was devastating. One man explained, "The Rebel front line, amazed at the sudden movement, thinking we had been reinforced... [threw] down their arms and [cried] out 'don't fire! We surrender,' the rest fled in wild confusion." Colonel Oates issued his retreat order even though the route was already well underway. Oates said, "When the signal was given, we ran like a herd of wild cattle." Many Confederates were captured, and the fight for the rocky heights was over. Both sides at Little Round Top had sustained one-third casualties.

Elsewhere on the field, the brigades of Dan Sickles's Third Corps that were tasked with holding the left side of his salient at the Devil's Den, the Wheatfield, and the Peach Orchard—positioned such that they were unable to support each other—were overwhelmed and destroyed piecemeal. After much hard fighting, the Confederates retained possession of those areas. Only as a result of the heroic efforts of Second Corps commander General Winfield Scott Hancock, who spent the afternoon personally directing the shoring up of the Union line, was complete disaster averted. As the day wore on and the fight moved north, Rebel forces nearly penetrated the Union defenses in the center of the line at Cemetery Ridge, near a copse of oak trees that would become famous the next day. But again and again, Yankee reinforcements were thrust into the fray in the nick of time (see Gettysburg Map Number Five, July 2, 1863, Confederate Assault, Late Afternoon).

On the far northern end of the line, at dusk, General Ewell (who had been ordered by Lee to coordinate his assault with Longstreet's and had failed to do so) and his Second Corps finally commenced furious attacks over many hours continuing into the darkness in an effort to wrest control of Cemetery Hill and Culp's Hill from their determined Federal defenders. Except for the capture of some empty trenches on the lower slope of Culp's Hill, those efforts were in vain. Second Corps contributed nothing but additional casualties to the Confederate cause. By midnight, the firing died down and the Union line from the two Round Tops north to Cemetery and Culp's Hills was unbroken. There was sporadic gunfire during the night, but the predominant sounds were the cries of the wounded. Combined casualties on the second day of Gettysburg were almost 20,000, making it perhaps the second bloodiest day in American history (there were 23,000 casualties in one day at Antietam on September 17, 1862).

Amidst this incomprehensible carnage, leaders and common soldiers on both sides displayed incredible energy and passion. At Little Round Top, General Gouverneur Warren deserves enormous credit for recognizing the threat and moving immediately, without orders, into action. He fetched Strong Vincent's brigade none too soon. He helped to place critical artillery into position. He personally ordered Paddy O'Rorke into the breach. Warren served out the remainder of the war and never approached the glory he earned at Gettysburg, but without his efforts there, the incredible and timely heroics of Vincent and O'Rorke would not have been possible. Both Vincent and O'Rorke led the charge that day, but in the end gave the last full measure of devotion. Colonel William Oates led the charge as well, and survived the war to be elected governor of his native Alabama. But he suffered the misfortune of fighting on the losing side.

It is interesting to speculate about Vincent and O'Rorke and their place in history. Had either, or both of them, survived the conflict and, perhaps, gone on to become state governors or college presidents or had the opportunity to write and speak extensively about their wartime experiences, undoubtedly they would be remembered differently. Their very lucky colleague Joshua L. Chamberlain lived to do all of those things. He had the chance to be portrayed in books and movies. While Chamberlain's outstanding personal qualities, as well as his accomplishments and bravery at Gettysburg and throughout the war speak for themselves, he has probably benefited from a disproportionate share of credit for the victory at Little Round Top. In any event, all of these leaders were indispensable in their own way. Each of them ably demonstrated the principle that when all else fails, innovate and lead the charge.

★ ★ CASE STUDY ★ ★

HARLEY-DAVIDSON:
BACK FROM THE BRINK

William Harley and Arthur Davidson built a prototype motorcycle in 1901, but they were not satisfied with their machine. When Arthur's brother, Walter—with his unique combination of skills as a machinist, bicyclist, and organizer—joined them in 1903, they were officially in business as the Harley-Davidson Motor Company. A third Davidson brother, William, came on board five years later. In 1908, the fledgling Milwaukee-based company produced 450 motorcycles. By 1913, Harley-Davidson turned out 13,000 machines annually. Harley-Davidson has enjoyed an incredibly colorful corporate history, and out of more than 300 American motorcycle manufacturers in business before World War I, Harley is the only one that has survived continuously to this day. Yet the company almost did not survive.

Harley went through a near-death experience in the late 1970s and early 1980s as poor quality, manufacturing and marketing problems, and intense competition from the Japanese threatened to put Harley out of business. The story of this great American company's rebirth constitutes an important reminder that sometimes, in business as in war, the smartest move is to innovate and take a completely different course of action.

By the middle 1970s, motorcycling had become an incredibly popular pastime in the United States. The widely recognized Harley brand was seen as a unique icon. The familiar, raw power and low, staccato wump-wump-wump sound that reverberated from a Harley engine gave true aficionados a genuine thrill. Yet Harley was struggling. The company had been purchased by American Machine and Foundry (AMF) in 1969 and in just four short years was pushed to increase production almost threefold, to 75,000 units annually. In the rush to build more bikes, serious quality issues arose. Fifty percent of the machines came off the assembly line literally missing parts, and dealers were frequently forced to make a significant investment just to get their product ready for sale. The world-renowned Harley engine dripped oil, rattled, and generally failed to compete with the sleek, masterfully made Japanese models. Veteran Harley owners were willing to tinker with their bikes to get them up and running but newer, less dedicated customers generally had no such desire. Japanese motorcycles—Hondas in particular—gobbled up market share.

Better quality control and an improved engine design became an immediate imperative. In 1975, AMF appointed Vaughn Beals to take over Harley-Davidson. Beals quickly set about developing quality control and inspection processes—expensive though they were—to address critical manufacturing problems. For the first time in company history, Beals worked with top managers to develop a product strategy that looked ten years into the future. The plan involved improving existing engine designs and working to create newer, more competitive motors that could compete with the Japanese over time.

But the new family of engines would take many years to introduce. Near term, the company turned for help to William G. Davidson, grandson of one of the founding Davidson brothers and Harley's design director. Willie G., as he was widely known, was an avid motorcyclist whose signature beard, blue jeans, and black leather biker jacket gave him tremendous credibility with many of Harley's core customers. But Willie G. was also a talented artist with a superb sense of design. He had been deeply concerned about the partnership with AMF but, fortunately, the corporate power players left him alone to pursue his creative passions.

Beals asked Willie G. to improve the cosmetics of various models. Willie G. had a deep connection with and understanding of Harley customers, saying, "They really know what they want on their bikes: the kind of instrumentation, the style of bars, the cosmetics of the engine, the look of the exhaust pipes, and so on. Every little piece of a Harley is exposed, and it has to look just right.... It's almost like being in the fashion business." Willie G. had already put together a terrifically successful factory-built custom motorcycle, known as the Super Glide, which brought together styling components from other Harley models. Now, the company needed him to continue to innovate and help hold on to customers while longer-term issues were fixed. Willie G. created a number of custom cruiser motorcycles, such as the Wide Glide and the Low Rider. Many members of the Harley-Davidson team gave Willie G. personal credit for saving the company during this difficult run. Chief engineer Jeff Bleustein said, "The guy is an artistic genius. In the five years before we could bring new engines on-stream, he performed miracles with decals and paint. A line here and a line there and we'd have a new model. It's what enabled us to survive."

Despite this innovative survival plan, by 1980, AMF's interest in Harley-Davidson began to wane. In February 1981, Beal and twelve other Harley executives, including Willie G. Davidson, signed a letter of intent to purchase Harley-Davidson for $81.5 million. With the help of lender Citicorp, by mid-June 1981, the buyback became official.

Harley-Davidson was an independent company again and promoted the rallying cry, "The Eagle Soars Alone."

But serious challenges, particularly in manufacturing, remained. In 1982, after an eye-opening visit to a Honda assembly plant, Harley leadership realized that the key to improvement lay in building professionalism among its managers and in enlisting the help of its workers to solve problems. Beals said, "We were being wiped out by the Japanese because they were better managers. It wasn't robotics, or culture, or morning calisthenics and company songs—it was professional managers who understood their business and paid attention to detail." Harley leadership made a decision to go to a just-in-time inventory program. In addition to dedicated, knowledgeable managers, Harley would also need the help of its workers in order for the effort to succeed. The Materials As Needed application was piloted at the Milwaukee engine plant. Harley decreased production costs and improved quality by purchasing raw materials and parts only as they were required. This process eliminated costly inventory and the consequent need for sophisticated handling systems. Management consulted employees closely. Beals said workers generally told him, "Well, we have some problems, but it's a lot better than it was before, and we'll get those problems fixed." The process did not produce results overnight, but the foundation for dramatically improved quality and efficiency had been established.

Next, Harley made a decision to dedicate itself to improving market share exclusively in the big-bike niche, rather than attempting to compete against the Japanese at every level. Harley petitioned the International Trade Commission (ITC) to win tariff protection against Japanese big bikes, specifically those that were 700cc or larger. Harley asserted that the Japanese were stockpiling huge inventories of unsold bikes in the United States, and the ITC agreed. In April 1983, an additional tariff of 45 percent was attached to the existing 4.4 percent, with the tariff scheduled to end in five years.

Even with help against the Japanese competition, Harley continued to lose market share. A central challenge involved convincing the motorcycle-buying public that Harley was back on track from a quality standpoint. With that incredibly challenging marketing goal in mind, in 1983, Harley established the Harley Owners Group, or H.O.G. (Harley owners refer to their motorcycles as HOG's). The employee-run Harley Owners Group hosted events all over the country and quickly became the largest factory-sponsored motorcycle club on Earth. By 1989 H.O.G. membership stood at 90,000 and grew to exceed half-a-million members by 2000. In 1984, Harley came up with another unique idea in the form of a demonstration program called SuperRide, which allowed 40,000 bikers, over three weekends, to go to any Harley dealer in the country and take a ride on a new Harley. Harley also worked hard to establish good relations with its customers by doing a better job of supporting its dealers.

Despite these initiatives, Citicorp officials remained concerned about the long-term future and made a decision to back out of their relationship with Harley. After much haggling, Harley was able to cobble together a deal with a new group of lenders, led by Heller Financial Corporation, in 1985. But Citicorp had miscalculated. As a result of the concerted effort to improve quality in manufacturing, and the new outlook in marketing that focused on keeping loyal customers as well as securing new ones, Harley came back from the brink. In 1986 profits came in at a much-improved $4.3 million on gross sales of $295 million. Harley's market share for big bikes continued to climb. The company went public and succeeded in raising an additional $20 million, which it used to service debt. Harley even requested, confident in its future, that the tariff against Japanese big bikes be phased out a year early.

Today, Harley-Davidson remains a going, vital concern, and one of the most recognized and respected brands in America. As with many companies everywhere, large and small, it is also true for Harley that a difficult recession—featuring weak consumer spending and tough credit markets in particular—has caused production and profitability to fall. There have been layoffs as well.

Nevertheless, many analysts predict that Harley will rebound again. If the past is any indicator, it is unwise ever to count Harley-Davidson out. In the late 1970s and early 1980s, through a short-term survival plan hinging on the creative-design genius of Willie G. Davidson, coupled with a long-term program to improve quality in manufacturing and management techniques, Harley hung on despite dire odds. Harley made a point of listening to and enlisting the expertise of its workers. Through smart marketing and a renewed focus on its dealers and customers, Harley showed how imaginative it could be. In the end, Harley-Davidson represents the epitome of the leadership principle that when all else fails, innovate and lead the charge.

Leadership Lesson Nine:

WHEN ALL ELSE FAILS, INNOVATE AND LEAD THE CHARGE

Most of us have been fortunate enough in our lives to benefit from the opportunity to know at least one really special teacher, coach, or mentor. I played high school football in Edina, Minnesota, for just such a person. My coach was Stavros Canakes, a.k.a., "The Greek." He died in late October of 2008, and with his passing he was widely eulogized by those whose lives he had touched. Patrick Reusse, a well-known Twin Cities sportswriter and commentator, called Stav Canakes "perhaps the most famous high school football coach in Minnesota history." Stav coached at Edina from 1961 through 1989 and during that time won 203 games, 16 conference titles, and 5 state championships. He was a big, burly guy who had been a football star himself, playing at the University of Minnesota and later, professionally, in Canada. He was a Korean War Army veteran. He was old-school and tough. Occasionally, he treated us harshly and we feared his wrath. He loved to win, and he had incredible energy and passion for the game of football.

But there was much more. He was a profoundly skilled teacher, a brilliant motivator, and a master psychologist. One time, when my hair had grown out a little long (it was the 1970s after all) he sidled up to me at practice and gently stroked the locks cascading from the back of my helmet. He did not say a word. My girlfriend at the time had told me she loved the flowing blond mane; The Greek clearly did not. I was uncertain as to whether he was smiling, but I was pretty sure the answer was no. It was a faint, Mona Lisa smile at best. The next day, I came to practice properly shorn and looking like a football player again.

Stav Canakes knew when to communicate a message without words, and when to scream out loud. He knew when he needed to support and encourage us. He knew when he needed to kick our butts. He knew when to use intimidation, when to use inspiration, and when to use love. He was hugely adaptable in his approach, and able to navigate any changing circumstance during the heat of battle with great deftness and then lead us forward, almost always to victory. He taught us not just about football, but about our obligations as young men. He taught us about life. In the end, perhaps most important, though he never said it out loud, we all knew that he cared for each of us not just as football players, but as individual human beings. We would have stormed the gates of hell for him.

The Harley-Davidson story provides a powerful example of a similarly passionate and courageous group of leaders who, against great odds and despite all the collective wisdom that predicted they would fail, also showed tremendous adaptability. They cobbled together a creative short-term plan, and then forged ahead with the major changes they knew had to be undertaken over the long haul to survive. And survive they did.

Finally, no level of courage ever displayed on the football gridiron or in the corporate arena can compare to the fortitude displayed by all of the men, officers and enlisted, Union and Confederate, who struggled desperately for control of Little Round Top on July 2, 1863. Several leaders that day—Warren, Vincent, O'Rorke, Chamberlain, and Oates—proved especially critical to the final outcome. Each of them modeled, in his own way, the ability under chaotic circumstances to innovate and lead the charge.

Chapter Ten

LITTLE BIGHORN

CRAZY HORSE-KEOGH FIGHT: CARE FOR YOUR PEOPLE

"He was a very quiet man except when there was fighting."

—He Dog—

In the late afternoon of June 25, 1876, a young Hunkpapa Sioux woman named Moving Robe was digging wild prairie turnips with several companions about a half-mile southwest of their encampment along the Greasy Grass River. Suddenly, in the distance to the east, she saw a huge cloud of dust rising in the air, which indicated many horsemen coming her way. A frantic Indian rider appeared, shouting that soldiers were nearby and that the women, children, and elderly must run to the hills opposite their camp. There was no time to lose. The alarm sounded, spreading like wildfire throughout the six great village circles. The approach of the wasichu was truly a surprise. The Hunkpapa woman Pretty White Buffalo said later, "I have seen my people prepare for battle many times and this I know: that the Sioux that morning had no thought of fighting."

As the women and children rushed about in the chaotic effort to flee, the many young warriors in camp hurriedly readied themselves to confront the hated white soldiers. Among the number of experienced war leaders who would be counted upon to help win the battle this day, none stood more prominent than the one they knew as Tasunke Witko, or Crazy Horse. Along with Sitting Bull, Crazy Horse had won many battle honors, counting coup more than 200 times in his storied career. Also like Sitting Bull, he was regarded as a mystic, who excelled in the four virtues held sacred in Sioux culture: bravery, fortitude, generosity, and wisdom. Fierce warrior though he was, he was particularly noted for his unselfish kindness toward his tribesmen, his willingness to teach and mentor the young, and his ability to keep his men alive in combat. Crazy Horse was a chief who embodied the critically important leadership principle: care for your people.

Crazy Horse was born in the late autumn of 1840 near Bear Butte, South Dakota (just north of the hallowed Black Hills), to a beautiful young mother named Rattle Blanket Woman and a father who, like his father before him, was called Crazy Horse. The newborn child's skin was comparatively pale, and he had his mother's wavy hair, with a brown luster. He became known by any number of combinations of the name Pehin Yuhaha, or Curly Hair. He was born of the very powerful Oglala tribe of the Teton Lakota Sioux. His father was a noted hunter who became an Oglala holy man. His mother was a Minneconjou, famed for her gorgeous appearance and for being an exceptionally fleet runner. Curly Hair had one sibling, an older sister named Looks at Her. He was a quiet child who in his boyhood knew the unconditional love of close family relationships. In addition to his immediate family, he was a part of a "tiyospaye," or extended family group, that consisted of people related by blood and through marriage. These lodge groups provided structure and stability to Sioux society, and might contain between fifty and one hundred kinfolk each. But young Curly Hair also knew great personal tragedy, which shaped his worldview in ways we can only imagine.

His parents had an unstable marriage. Both of their names were linked with sexual scandals within the tribe. After a particularly nasty fight with her husband, Rattle Blanket Woman committed suicide by hanging herself. Curly Hair was around four years old and there is evidence, sketchy though it may be, that he was understandably devastated by the loss of his mother. A Sioux boy was usually taught to ride at age five. Curly Hair acquired the skill quickly, and soon took to riding into the hills for long periods by himself. His extended family worked to mitigate his grief, and he continued to be deeply loved by those around him, but forever afterward there was a certain melancholy in his demeanor.

Curly Hair became interested in the Lakota belief system and matters of the spiritual world. His father and grandfather taught him about Wakan Tanka, the mysterious totality of all powers. Curly Hair became attentive to his dreams and continued to brood introspectively, as he would throughout his life. He also loved the active life of the budding Sioux warrior, and horsemanship, marksmanship (with bow and arrow and later, with the gun), and hunting buffalo became second nature by the time he was ten or eleven. When he was fifteen, Curly Hair had an intense visionary experience, in which he came to believe he had acquired the power and protection of Thunder, one of the most significant gifts Wakan could provide.

Curly Hair was a natural warrior. He helped his tribe fight their age-old Indian enemies, such as the Crows, Pawnees, and Shoshones. At the age of sixteen, he began to demonstrate the extreme physical courage, to the point of recklessness, that would characterize his conduct in battle for the rest of his life. Like his future dread adversary George Armstrong Custer, he had many horses killed from underneath him. Also like Custer, he was extraordinarily lucky. Except for a leg wound early in his career, he was never seriously injured in combat. When he showed exceptional bravery in a battle with an enemy tribe, his father finally bestowed the name Crazy Horse upon him. In dozens of raids and fights, Crazy Horse became so proficient and his reputation so secure, that he would sometimes sit back and let another warrior count coup ahead of him. Despite his fearlessness in always leading his men from the front, he was also a diligent planner and used sound judgment in battle. His followers knew he would fight aggressively, but be careful with their lives at the same time. He was a brilliant tactician and became an inspiring war chief. Even his hated rivals the Crows commented on his high-profile leadership. A Crow warrior asserted (whether intending to create a poetic rhyme or not), "We know Crazy Horse better than we do you other Sioux. Whenever we have a fight, he is closer to us than to you."

By the middle 1860s, the encroachment of the white man upon Indian territories became a more pressing military concern than inter-tribal warfare. In 1866, a U.S. Army captain named William Fetter-man, who was stationed at Fort Phil Kearney along the Bozeman Trail in Wyoming, boasted, "Give me eighty men and I would ride through the whole Sioux nation." In a demonstration of tactical skill that won him enormous accolades, Crazy Horse led a classic decoy and ambush maneuver. He drew Captain Fetterman away from the fort, and into a trap from which he could not be saved. In an ironic twist of fate, Fetterman and his entire command, numbered exactly eighty, were surrounded by Crazy Horse and his fellow fighters and wiped out to a man. His role as the chief tactical leader in the Fetterman massacre meant that Crazy Horse was now viewed not just as a talented and courageous warrior, but as a possible future leader of his people.

The fully mature Crazy Horse stood about 5 feet 8 inches or 5 feet 9 inches tall, and was extremely slender. His hair grew waist length, and it retained the brown sheen and wave of his youth. His skin was light, and his features sharp. Those who met him took note of his eyes, which were mesmerizing. One white observer wrote that his eyes were "exceedingly restless and [they] impress the beholder fully as much as does his general demeanor." He was his stunning mother's son, and his fine, fair, almost feminine appearance caused one white person who met him—even though Crazy Horse was thirty-six years old at

General Robert E. Lee, commander of the Confederate Army of Northern Virginia, was a great soldier who won many victories. But he did not perform well at Gettysburg where he relied on faulty information and rejected an alternate scenario.

Brigadier General John Buford was the highest ranking Union officer on the scene at the beginning of the Battle of Gettysburg. His swift and accurate assessment of the situation and bold decision to defend the town until help arrived were critical to the final outcome of the battle.

Lieutenant General James Longstreet was Lee's "Old War Horse," who never failed to provide his commanding officer with sometimes blunt feedback. Longstreet disagreed vehemently with Lee's battle plan at Gettysburg and told him so, but to no avail.

Lieutenant General Thomas J. "Stonewall" Jackson was Lee's most trusted subordinate and one of the truly gifted field commanders of American military history. He was tragically shot by his own troops at Chancellorsville, so that Lee faced his greatest test at Gettysburg without his ablest soldier.

Lieutenant General Richard Ewell took over command of the Second Corps of the Army of Northern Virginia after Jackson's death. Unfortunately, Ewell could never measure up to his former commander and his failure to capture the critical high ground at Gettysburg has generated controversy ever since.

Major General James Ewell Brown "Jeb" Stuart commanded the cavalry of the Army of Northern Virginia. He was a capable soldier with a dashing presence, but his reckless ride around the Union army prior to Gettysburg cost Lee his "eyes and ears" for eight critical days.

Major General George Gordon Meade commanded the Union Army of the Potomac. He had been in position only a few days when Gettysburg commenced and managed the battle well, but his failure to aggressively pursue the defeated Southern army deeply disappointed President Lincoln.

Major General Daniel Sickles was a rogue and a maverick who commanded the Union Third Corps at Gettysburg. His decision, without orders, to move his corps forward of the position he had been directed to occupy almost cost the Union the battle.

Colonel Joshua L. Chamberlain, commander of the Union Twentieth Maine Regiment, was a true renaissance man and the beau ideal of the citizen-soldier. He won the Medal of Honor for his actions in defending Little Round Top, but has perhaps been given too much credit historically for what was truly a team effort in winning the fight for that critical piece of terrain.

Major General George Pickett commanded a division of Virginians in Longstreet's First Corps. He was a colorful figure who led the famous but failed charge on the third day of Gettysburg, which left him forever embittered against Robert E. Lee.

SITTING BULL.

Sitting Bull was a powerful and charismatic
Hunkpapa Sioux chief who combined great skill and
bravery as a warrior with the wisdom and mysticism
of a holy man. He was the unquestioned leader of
the thousands of Indians who gathered in the valley
of the Little Bighorn in June 1876.

George Armstrong Custer, in his favorite photograph of himself, wearing a flamboyant version of the uniform of a major general of volunteers near the end of the Civil War. Custer attacked boldly and took a tremendous gamble by splitting his forces at the Little Bighorn, but he failed to consider a simple question: What if the Lakota Sioux and Northern Cheyenne turn to fight?

George Custer with his beautiful and intelligent wife, **Elizabeth Bacon Custer**, who was known as Libbie. They had an extremely close if occasionally turbulent marriage, and she spent the remainder of her days after his death writing, lecturing, and doing everything in her power to defend and preserve his memory.

Major Marcus Reno was Custer's second-in-command at the Little Bighorn. He was a deeply troubled man, and was later accused of incompetent, irrational, and even cowardly behavior during the battle.

Captain Frederick Benteen was criticized for being slow to arrive at the scene of action and for his failure to obey Custer's orders to "come quick" during a critical phase of the Little Bighorn battle. But Benteen also provided exemplary leadership by in effect taking command from a flustered Reno and organizing the desperate hilltop defense at the Reno-Benteen site.

the time—to say he was "a bashful girlish looking boy." We do not have an authenticated photograph of Crazy Horse; like many Indians, he probably believed that to have his photograph taken would steal his soul and shorten his life.

He dressed simply, and in battle never donned a war bonnet. Instead, he wore one eagle feather upside down behind his head. He typically fought naked, wearing only a breechcloth and moccasins. His body paint consisted of hailstones and a lightning streak. He wore his long hair in two braids. He carried a good luck charm in the form of a tiny white stone in a small bag under his arm. Away from the battlefield, at home with his people, he wore a plain shirt, leggings, and a simple necklace of shells.

Around the village, he was enigmatic and reticent in a way that some of his tribesmen regarded as off-putting and even peculiar. He had no desire to be a chief and did not participate in tribal councils. Black Elk described Crazy Horse succinctly: "Never was excited." He Dog, a long-time friend, said, "He was a very quiet man except when there was fighting." But Crazy Horse was also noted for legendary kindness and generosity. After a successful buffalo hunt, he made sure that the meat was distributed first to the poor, the sick, and the elderly. He kept no loot from raiding for himself except weapons, ensuring that horses and other spoils of war were donated to others. By every account, he gave material things away and helped others with no political agenda or expectation of anything in return. In another demonstration of his generous spirit, he took a great interest in the young warriors of the village. He was an extremely popular mentor and role model to these developing fighters.

There is no dispute that Crazy Horse was a terrifically charismatic leader, in significant part because he cared for the people around him. A woman named Lucille Runs After (who was descended from a relative of Crazy Horse called Lone Horn) said, "My mother and aunts all said that Crazy Horse ... was an outstanding person; there was something magic about him; he made people happy in his presence."

Crazy Horse experienced a tumultuous personal life, which was punctuated again and again by tragedy. He carried on an open affair with a married woman, whose jealous husband shot him with a pistol at point blank range just below the left nostril, shattering his jaw. The resulting scar disfigured him for life and gave his already striking face an even more unique look. Following on the heels of this incident—which caused Crazy Horse no end of embarrassment within the tribe—a younger half-brother, Little Hawk, was killed in an attack on white miners. In the autumn, an older warrior named Hump, with whom Crazy Horse was extremely close (Hump had served as a mentor and friend for many years) was killed in an ill-advised raid against the Shoshones.

In his late twenties, Crazy Horse finally married. His bride was a woman named Black Shawl, and they enjoyed a stable union that was initially passionless but grew in closeness as the years went by. The marriage lasted until Crazy Horse's death in 1877. The couple had a daughter named They Are Afraid of Her, whom Crazy Horse adored. It is said that she looked like her father. When she was two-and-a-half years old, she died suddenly of illness, sending Crazy Horse into grief and depression. Historian Kingsley Bray wrote of Crazy Horse after the little child's passing, "... it is safe to say, after They Are Afraid of Her, no death, least of all his own, would ever mean so much again."

In the early 1870s, Crazy Horse and the great chief Sitting Bull finally met. In 1872, the two men took part together in an attack on army troops in which both leaders performed admirably. They each hated the white man with a passion and committed themselves to preventing him from conquering their territory. When they finally brought their people together in the summer of 1876, it was Crazy Horse who again showed keen tactical abilities to go with his obvious physical bravery in taking on George Crook and his Wyoming column at the Rosebud River, eight days prior to the Little Bighorn fight. Crook retreated south and was never a factor in the upcoming drama. Another important result of the Rosebud battle was that Crazy Horse, as well as those whom he led, felt renewed and abundant confidence in his capacity as a combat leader.

On June 25, as the white cavalry approached from the south and began to fire into the village, confusion reigned. Mothers frantically rushed about to gather their children. There was panicked screaming amidst the rattle of gunfire. Some of the elderly sang death songs to inspire the younger men to great deeds in the upcoming fight. Women called the tremolo on eagle bone whistles. The warriors moved quickly to organize themselves. Sitting Bull, along with a handful of others, exchanged rifle fire with the enemy. Sitting Bull then provided tactical instructions to the younger men (the honored, battle-hardened old chief would not have been expected to participate directly in the fighting when there were abundant numbers of youthful warriors on hand; Sitting Bull spent the remainder of the day ensuring the protection of the women and children) and sent them on their way.

The eager Lakota and Cheyenne fighters began to mount their horses and ride toward the enemy in defense of their homes and loved ones, first in small groups and then in larger bands. A group of Arikara scouts from Reno's command got close enough to kill a number of women and children in the Hunkpapa camp before they were angrily repulsed. There were warrior casualties as well. Eventually, the soldiers were overwhelmed on their open left flank and retreated, taking a position in the woods near the river. It was at this time that the cry went up: "Crazy Horse is coming! Crazy Horse is coming!"

Crazy Horse had heard the first distant shots as he bathed, and while he knew there was a battle to come and time was short, he insisted on meticulously preparing himself. As other warriors eager to follow him anxiously awaited, he applied his war paint and assembled his gear. Some, like his brother-in-law Red Feather, lost patience and rode away without him. Finally, the war chief emerged from his tipi and mounted his white-faced pinto. He led a contingent of Oglala warriors—one soldier eyewitness estimated the number of Crazy Horse's followers at 200—who were even joined by some Cheyennes who knew of the power of Crazy Horse's medicine. They galloped south toward the wasichu soldiers trapped in the woods. Many hundreds of Indians now surrounded the desperate, beleaguered men of Major Reno's command.

Crazy Horse entered the action at a critical moment, and thrust himself violently into the fray. A number of warriors had assembled near the river, on the opposite side of his approach. When they saw Crazy Horse and his frenzied band smash into the white soldiers in the woods, they too were inspired to attack, causing pressure from both directions. The white soldiers broke just as the onslaught commenced and rode in a chaotic retreat to the river and across, toward the hilltop beyond. Crazy Horse led the way in the chase across the river, killing white soldiers with his war club and pulling some off their mounts as they hesitated at the steep riverbank. Once the terrified soldiers reached the high ground, they were harassed by Indian fighters until it became apparent to Crazy Horse and the others that a sizeable body of white troopers was moving rapidly north, threatening the village from a different direction.

The Oglala warrior Short Bull, who had been so intent on fighting Reno's men, did not notice that Crazy Horse had been a part of the action or that blue-clad cavalrymen could be seen to the north. When Crazy Horse rode up Short Bull shouted, "Too late! You've missed the fight!" Crazy Horse laughed and said, "Sorry to miss this fight! But there's a good fight coming over the hill." Just then, to Short Bull's surprise, Crazy Horse pointed at the soldier column in the distance. In his typical understated manner, almost as a joke, Crazy Horse said, "That's where the big fight is going to be. We'll not miss that one." With that, Crazy Horse wheeled and began to gallop downstream, with many warriors—including the newly inspired Short Bull—following close behind (see Little Bighorn Map Number Five, Approach to Crazy Horse-Keogh Fight, Late Afternoon).

Crazy Horse took a brief diversion to assist some warriors who had been wounded in the combat safely back to the village. He stopped at his own lodge for prayers to Wakan Tanka. Finally, his medicine strong again, Crazy Horse lit out to cross the river a mile north of the village's Cheyenne circle. As they splashed across the river, he and his friend Flying Hawk could see Custer's soldiers on a high hill in the distance. Crazy Horse galloped east for half a mile, up Deep Ravine, then turned south for a quarter mile. The ravine became narrow, and Crazy Horse dismounted to climb to higher ground. As he reached the rim of the gully and peeked to the south, he saw a line of bluecoats, and immediately began to pour accurate rifle fire into their ranks. His cohorts joined him, and they began a process of moving stealthily in the direction of the soldiers, using terrain to their advantage, and keeping up a steady barrage of bullets, along with a hail of arrows from those who were not armed with guns.

These white men were from Company C under the immediate command of Captain Myles Keogh, not Custer. When Custer divided his forces, he retained overall leadership of one five-company battalion, but designated that Keogh would command not only his own Company I, but also Companies C and L. Captain George Yates would lead Companies E and F. Custer, along with Yates and his two companies, had continued to move north—with a brief diversionary maneuver toward the river at Medicine Tail Ford—in an apparent effort to draw attention away from Reno to the south.

Indian warriors from other bands now began closing in from every direction on the men of C Company, some of whom had been ordered to form a skirmish line along a ridge toward the river, and the soldiers began to drop under the withering assault. Finally, in a multi-pronged mounted attack led by the Hunkpapa Crow King, the Oglala Low Dog (who shouted to his men, "This is a good day to die—follow me!"), and the Cheyenne war chief Lame White Man, many of the remaining soldiers at this position were shot and clubbed to death, while others scrambled to reach their brethren further north.

The next group of soldiers to the north were the men of Company L, commanded by Lieutenant James Calhoun, Custer's brother-in-law.

They held a position at an elevated piece of ground that would become known to history as Calhoun Hill. At this point—in the interests of staying ahead of and between the advancing soldiers and the women and children in the village—Crazy Horse rode with his men to a spot about 400 yards northeast of Calhoun Hill. With this flanking maneuver, Crazy Horse could direct fire into both Calhoun's Company L and Keogh's I Company, which was dismounted and located on the east slope of the ridge further north.

Crazy Horse received reinforcements as more Indians moved east to join him. One Minneconjou warrior called White Bull expressed frustration with Crazy Horse and his long-range sniping, asserting that now was the time for a charge. Crazy Horse, with his astute tactical sense, knew that White Bull was wrong. Crazy Horse understood that there was a contingent of warriors further north who could engage Custer and, hopefully, pin him down. If Crazy Horse waited for the right moment to destroy the Keogh wing of the command, then Custer's lines of communication to Reno and Benteen to the south would be broken, and every warrior could turn his full attention to Custer's destruction. To attack too soon would invite failure and also waste lives. Crazy Horse waited patiently for the most opportune moment to present itself.

Calhoun's Company L proved a tough bunch to kill. They fought with good order, repulsed one direct Indian assault from the south, and made an extended stand. Warriors in increasing numbers crept forward through the coulees toward the position. The two platoons gradually became surrounded and defended themselves back-to-back. The Indians noted later that the two officers who led them (Calhoun and platoon commander Lieutenant John Crittenden) stood bravely in their proper positions, orchestrating the action from directly behind their men. Meanwhile, the survivors of Company C rushed panic-stricken to join their L Company comrades on Calhoun Hill. This event created temporary disorder, and invited another more concentrated Indian attack from the south. Many of the bluecoats were now cut down by the swarming Lakota and Cheyenne warriors, and those soldiers who were still able to do so moved quickly north in the direction of Keogh and I Company. The breaking of the defensive perimeter at Calhoun Hill was the beginning of the end for Keogh's wing, and the critical tactical opportunity that Crazy Horse envisioned.

The Minneconjou White Bull, from his position near Crazy Horse to the east, finally lost his patience. He was determined to count coup and could not do it from a distance with his Winchester repeater. As the Calhoun Hill defense disintegrated, White Bull took off on his pony, riding bareback and leaning low. He galloped toward a gap in the soldier line and came under withering fire from the army carbines. He dashed through the line, and then cut back through another opening to return to his original spot. He said later, "The soldiers shot at me but missed me. I circled back to my friends." White Bull approached Crazy Horse and shouted, "This life will not last forever! This time I will not turn back!"

The display of incredible bravery by White Bull was infectious. White Bull shouted, "Only heaven and earth last long!" Crazy Horse knew the moment was right. He mounted his pinto, blew on his eagle bone horn, and his intrepid band of warriors followed him and White Bull directly at the enemy. As the terrified soldiers continued their northward trek, the Indian warriors smashed into their flank. Some soldiers were on foot, others on horseback. Those who were riding were shot or pulled from their mounts, and a stampede of horses ensued. There was much violent hand-to-hand combat as wasichu and warriors mixed in a wild melee.

Crazy Horse realized that some of the retreating soldiers from Company I would have the potential to link up with Custer's unit on the high ground further up the ridge. The war chief would need to act with great speed if he wanted to realize his goal of isolating this wing. In an inspired moment of original thinking, he spurred his mount and rode the length of the I Company line. The startled cavalrymen let loose an intense volley of fire in the direction of Crazy Horse and his followers as they swiftly galloped by. Crazy Horse was unhurt, and as he neared the end of his run he turned his pinto ninety degrees and penetrated straight through the soldier line. The bluecoats were now effectively divided into two groups, and their destruction became only a matter of time. One Arapaho eyewitness said later, "Crazy Horse, the Sioux Chief, was the bravest man I ever saw. He rode close to the soldiers, yelling to his warriors. All the soldiers were shooting at him, but he was never hit."

Crazy Horse had conceived an incredible tactical gem. As a result of his intelligent sense of timing and amazing heroics, the battle now turned decidedly in his favor. Captain Keogh and the remainder of his battalion (his own I Company and what was left of Companies C and L) continued their struggle to break away from the increasingly large and emboldened masses of Indian warriors and to link up with Custer to the north. But Keogh's luck finally ran out, as he received a shot that went clean through his knee to hit his mount as well (the famous warhorse Comanche who, though wounded multiple times, survived the battle), and both man and animal tumbled to the ground. Though the bulk of his I Troop came to Keogh's defense, surrounding him in an effort to fend off the Indian onslaught, they perished with their captain in a cluster together. The Indians estimated that only twenty survivors of this desperate action ever succeeded in linking up with Custer. Those soldiers would all meet their demise in short order at Last Stand Hill.

It is easy to attribute superhuman characteristics to Crazy Horse. Indeed, many chroniclers of the battle—both Indian and white, and eyewitnesses and historians who came later—have ascribed mythical feats to him. The most persistent falsehood concerning Crazy Horse is that he led as many as a thousand warriors in a triumphant northern flanking movement, which was perfectly timed and proved to be the crushing blow to Custer at Last Stand Hill. It never happened. Crazy Horse apparently did arrive on Last Stand Hill just as the fight was ending, but this was not his critical contribution.

Crazy Horse was a human being, who was very much a product of his time and the environment in which he grew up. He was a fierce and uncompromising warrior, who killed men and women, and who occasionally scalped and mutilated his enemies. In his culture a war chief did not command others, but led by example. Warriors were tactically independent and trained to take individual initiative, but they would definitely follow the lead of a trusted chief such as Crazy Horse. Historian Gregory Michno said it well, "Crazy Horse was an extraordinary warrior, courageous, daring, and a stellar example for his followers. But he was no figure from Homeric legend, touched and guided by the gods." Biographer Kingsley Bray echoed the thought: "The most famous Lakota victory of all time was not Crazy Horse's triumph alone. He was no Caesar or Napoleon, moving warrior brigades like chess pieces across the field."

Yet Crazy Horse was undoubtedly instrumental in the defeat of Custer. No one did more to bring about that result. Crazy Horse's effort in leading the charge against Reno in the woods, and the subsequent "buffalo hunt" as the white troopers raced across the river was important. But even more critical was the outstanding and perfectly timed "bravery run" along and through the I Company line, which cut Keogh's force in two and led to the destruction of that wing of Custer's battalion.

Crazy Horse was certainly recognized by his own people for his contributions to victory. Standing Bear said, "After the battle, I heard a lot about Crazy Horse." Many individuals witnessed his acts of courage, and they praised him in song and oral tradition. As much as anything, his tribesmen appreciated Crazy Horse's genuine concern for them as reflected in his lifelong habit of kindness and generosity. They knew that he sincerely cared for their welfare. He also trained and mentored many young men. His warrior followers deeply appreciated, among his many other attributes, the concern that Crazy Horse showed for their lives in battle. They would have followed him anywhere.

Interestingly, Crazy Horse and his mortal enemy George Armstrong Custer had much in common. They were born within a year of each other. They were both raised in extremely loving family environments. They loved horses and the thrill of the hunt and were expert marksmen. They were physically attractive, energetic, athletic, and charismatic leaders of men. They both possessed the heart of a true warrior and loved nothing more than the turbulent, noisy, savage swirl of combat. They died violent deaths each at the age of thirty-six, just over a year apart.

But in one significant respect, Crazy Horse and Custer were different. Custer acted with a callous disregard for the men who served under him. In contrast, Crazy Horse showed steadfast faithfulness to the members of his tribe, and he demonstrated time and again the power of that crucial leadership principle: care for your people.

★ ★ Case Study ★ ★

Google: Don't Be Evil

"Google was started when Sergey and I were Ph.D. students at Stanford University in computer science, and we didn't know exactly what we wanted to do." So began Larry Page—co-founder along with Sergey Brin of Internet search giant Google—in a speech to a group of Israeli math students in the fall of 2003. Page continued, "I got this crazy idea that I was going to download the entire Web onto my computer. I told my advisor that it would only take a week. After about a year or so, I had some portion of it." The students were greatly amused by Page's story, and he held their rapt attention as he went on to conclude, "So optimism is important. You have to be a little silly about the goals you are going to set. There is a phrase I learned in college called, 'Having a healthy disregard for the impossible.' That is a really good phrase. You should try to do things that most people would not."

212

Brin and Page began an extensive research project in the spring of 1995 as graduate students at Stanford that yielded a new internet search system. The University offered to sell the system at a price of $1 million to a number of venture capital firms, and such search engine and high-tech enterprises as Yahoo! and AltaVista. Everyone turned them down. Thus, with reluctant hearts, Brin and Page felt compelled to quit school in 1998 and run Google themselves. They initially worked out of a garage that they leased in Menlo Park, California. From these humble beginnings, Google became one of the outstanding growth companies in corporate history. In August 2004, Google went public in the largest technology IPO ever, offering stock at $85 per share and raising almost $2 billion. The stock catapulted to $300 a share in less than a year and over its first decade in business, Google soared to a market capitalization of over $160 billion. Today, Brin and Page are worth approximately $14 billion each.

Google prides itself on doing business differently, and has earned its reputation as a technology "innovation machine." Google tries to do business ethically, with a mantra that says, "Don't Be Evil." But perhaps the key to Google's staggering achievements lies in its attitude toward and treatment of its employees, known as "Googlers." Google—identified by *Fortune* magazine in both 2007 and 2008 as the "Number One Best Company to Work For" in all of corporate America—embodies the critical concept: care for your people.

Brin and Page hired Eric Schmidt—an experienced industry executive who worked for Sun Microsystems and Novell and holds a Ph.D. in computer science—as CEO in 2001. That triumvirate envisions and articulates a future in which Google organizes all of the world's information and makes it available to people for free. Despite intense competition, they are well on their way. Today, Americans conduct approximately 7 billion searches per month through Google. This figure represents two-thirds of all searches, compared to around 20 percent for Yahoo! and less than 10 percent for Microsoft.

One critical component of Google's success as a search engine is that people can seek information anonymously. There is no requirement to provide any personal data. Google's highly sophisticated PageRank algorithm uses the search phrase to draw on information that sits on web pages, and to determine the relative merits of one page over another to produce effective, speedy search results. Google earns 97 percent of its enormous revenue through online ads. Despite a natural aversion to advertising, Brin and Page have said, "Our search results are the best we know how to produce. We do not accept payment for them or for inclusion or more frequent updating. We also display advertising, which we work hard to make relevant, and we label it clearly."

The obvious key to this well-financed, technologically innovative business model is quality people. From the very beginning, Google has been determined and very express in its desire to "hire only the best." While other enterprises in the software industry may focus primarily on hiring undergraduate students in computer science with "high upside potential," Google pursues Ph.D.'s, or at the very least candidates with a master's degree from a highly rated school. Forty of the company's first 100 engineers held doctorates. Google's elitist approach is based on several premises. First, because the methods of empirical science (develop and revise hypotheses repeatedly based on experimentation) guide Google's work processes, those who are trained in that methodology are in high demand. Second, people who have stayed in school tend to be passionate, disciplined, and motivated by a desire for intrinsic rewards rather than money alone. Finally, employees with the highest levels of education tend to be extremely competent, intelligent "A Players," who help in the recruitment of other A Players. Recruitment at Google is considered an extremely important function, and a flex staff of human resource recruiters works hard to meet the demand for employees at any given time.

Google has also, from its earliest days, mounted a significant effort to take care of these A Players. Amenities abound at Google's headquarters, known as the "Googleplex," in Mountain View, California. Brin and Page insisted from the start that Google be a fun place to work, that their employees be treated like family, and that any benefit they could reasonably provide to increase productivity would be worth the investment. Google hired a chef and kitchen staff to provide gourmet meals (breakfast, lunch, and dinner) for free. A free shuttle service of charter buses that provide wireless internet access covers the entire San Francisco Bay area, so Googlers can focus on work, instead of the stress of traffic, during their commute. Two full-time physicians provide free on-site medical care. There is a company child care facility, a fitness center with personal trainers, and a professional masseuse. For a fee, Googlers can do their laundry, pick up their dry cleaning, get a haircut, repair their bikes, and wash their cars and change the oil. Googlers play beach volleyball, foosball, and roller hockey. They race scooters. They relax in beanbag chairs and bring their dogs to work. There is really no reason for Googlers, many of whom are young and single, to do anything other than hang out at work.

In another concept borrowed from the world of academe, where professors are encouraged to spend time pursuing their own projects, Googlers enjoy the benefits of the "20 percent rule." For Google's engineers and developers, 80 percent of their time involves project work that earns them a paycheck. The remaining 20 percent of their workweek is dedicated to research of their own choosing. While many companies would fear that such freedom might be abused by employees, Google puts protections in place. The overriding assumption is that an individual's personal project will align with Google's goals and objectives. In return for Google's generous gift of time, employees provide innovation, information, and loyalty. To that end, personal projects are subject to stringent peer review. The most promising projects will receive funding. Googlers understand that their professional reputation is at stake with respect to their research. And they have come up with any number of bright ideas. Such Google products as Google Suggest, Google News, Google Toolbar, AdSense for Content, and Orkut were directly developed out of the 20 percent process.

Google also takes care of its people and promotes innovation by creating small, autonomous work teams. Google assigns teams (usually from three to six people) to pursue projects with limited, clearly stated objectives and short timelines (rarely longer than six weeks). Both research and practical experience demonstrate that small teams are generally more efficient and productive. With short deadlines, projects are easy to track and problems surface and can be dealt with rapidly. Small teams tend to focus less on political turf wars around resource allocation and more on solving technical problems. With less need for control and greater employee autonomy, management can pay attention to higher-level objectives. Small work teams allow Google to maintain its famously non-hierarchical structure. Googlers clearly get enormous energy out of the opportunity to work independently with a few colleagues on challenging, ever-changing projects. These processes are the key to Google's incredible capacity to innovate.

Like any other company that has expanded rapidly, Google faces many challenges today. In June 2009, competitors Microsoft and Yahoo! entered into an agreement (government approval is pending) to develop a search engine to challenge Google's dominance. Microsoft is a formidable, well-financed rival that intends to spend $100 million to market Bing, its new search program. Google has ventured into other areas of business, such as scanning and selling books, and is under government antitrust investigation around a legal settlement the company reached with the publishing industry. Conflicts have arisen over Google's e-mail, office, phone, and desktop operating systems. Many people are concerned that Google has simply become too big, and they worry that Google will not adequately protect the reams of personal information in its possession. Google purchased YouTube for $1.6 billion in 2006, and while YouTube continues to grow dramatically, Google has experienced less than stellar advertising revenues out of the acquisition. Google has lost a number of talented employees, who have chosen either to strike out on their own or to join glamorous new start-ups such as Facebook.

Problems aside, Google remains a huge company with an incredibly bright future. Marketing research demonstrates that the Google brand is the most valuable in the world—worth more than $100 billion—and has been for the last three years running. Google has achieved this feat while only rarely advertising itself. Brin, Page, and Schmidt appear determined to continue to do business differently, and to count on Google's unique and powerful culture to deliver continued outstanding business results. The key component of that culture remains an approach that involves hiring only the most qualified people, taking care of their every need, and freeing them up to innovate both individually and as a part of small project teams. Google demonstrates the power and potential every day of an organization that truly cares for its people.

Leadership Lesson Ten:
CARE FOR YOUR PEOPLE

In the middle 1990s, I worked for the Target Corporation in the Community Relations area. My boss at the time, one of the best I have ever had, was a woman named Gail Dorn. At that time, and for many years, Gail was Target's vice president for Community Relations and Communications. Gail was (and is) incredibly bright, professionally competent, vivacious, and funny. She has energy and passion for her work. But as I look back over all these years, perhaps the quality that most stands out was that she genuinely cared for her people.

We had a great team, all women except for me and one other guy, and we achieved excellent business results. Gail set high standards, made clear to each of us individually and as a team what she expected, and then she got out of our way and let us go. If we needed her help, she jumped in to help. We had amazing team meetings that generally began with about ten minutes of silliness and laughter. We teased each other relentlessly. We occasionally got scolded for "having too much fun." We always got down to business eventually, and we were the very definition of a high-performing team. People from other parts of the organization wanted to be a part of our team. We liked and respected each other, and frequently socialized together. We are all good friends to this day and, though we have gone our separate ways, we still stay in touch more than fifteen years later.

I remember when I sat down with Gail for my individual status meetings that she always began by inquiring about me personally. How are you doing? How are Faith (my wife), Anna, and Luci (my daughters) doing? Are you enjoying what you are working on? Is it challenging? How can I be helpful to you? I know Gail did this with all of her other direct reports as well. But here is the key. She was not just going through the motions. She carefully listened to and was genuinely interested in the answers to those questions. She cared for her people.

Are you a leader who cares for your people? Does your boss care about you? Does your organization or team promote a culture that cares for people? Or is everyone just going through the motions?

George Custer never even went through the motions. His men were pretty confident that their welfare was low on his priority list. Crazy Horse, on the other hand, reaped the benefit of a lifetime of countless overt, sincere acts of kindness and generosity. His people, and particularly the warriors who chose to follow him into battle, loved him for it.

And the Googlers of Mountain View, California, must also know that they are led by people who truly care for them. That care is manifested in multiple ways, through amenities and employee-friendly work processes, which go to the very heart of Google's outstanding success and bright future as an enterprise. Care for your people, and you will reap the rewards.

PART SIX

MAKE GOOD DECISIONS

Chapter Eleven

GETTYSBURG

PICKETT'S CHARGE: USE THE RIGHT DATA

"Never, never, never, did General Lee himself bollox a fight
as he did this."

—Confederate Colonel Edward Porter Alexander—

In 1870, frail and in ill-health as he neared the end of his life, Robert E. Lee received a visit from John S. Mosby (famed guerilla leader during the Civil War who was known as the "Gray Ghost of the Confederacy") and George E. Pickett, who led the desperate but futile assault that forever bore his name against the Union center on the final day at Gettysburg. Pickett, by then an embittered and broken man, only reluctantly agreed to call on Lee, at Mosby's urging. The substance of the meeting is unknown, but it was surely a strained affair. As they left, Pickett muttered to Mosby, "That old man had my division massacred at Gettysburg." Mosby replied, "But he made you immortal."

Robert E. Lee is undoubtedly one of the great captains of American military history, and perhaps all of military history. On his best days, he was a superb strategist, shrewd, confident, and audacious. He led his beloved Army of Northern Virginia to victory time and again. He successfully battled an enemy that was almost always superior in men and material. But the three critical days of the Battle of Gettysburg were not his best days. After the war, he said of Gettysburg, "Its loss was occasioned by a combination of circumstances. It was commenced in the absence of correct intelligence. It was continued in the effort to overcome the difficulties with which we were surrounded, and [a success] would have been gained could one determined and united blow have been delivered by our whole line. As it was, victory trembled in the balance for three days...."

Not only did Lee commence the battle with faulty information, but he also relied on inaccurate assumptions on the second and third days. Lee provides a vivid example of a leader who tragically led his team in the wrong course of action because of his failure to use the right data.

The initial "absence of correct intelligence" that Lee identified after the war, of course, referred to the loss of his "eyes and ears" in the form of Jeb Stuart and his cavalry. Lee had been operating under the erroneous impression that as he began his northern invasion, the Union army was demoralized, poorly led by Fighting Joe Hooker, and spread thin in a long arc designed to protect the approaches to the capital city of Washington. Stuart had argued that instead of staying close to protect General Ewell's flank, the cavalry could advance farther and faster by heading east and then north in a path around the presumably disorganized and widely dispersed Yankee units. Lee assumed Stuart would be gone no more than three days, but some of Lee's senior commanders were wary of the plan. James Longstreet felt that the young and rash Stuart needed "an older head to instruct and regulate him." Lee disagreed and gave Stuart broad discretion to carry out his plan. This was an unfortunate decision for, in fact, the Army of the Potomac would consolidate quickly in pursuit of Lee.

Stuart took his three best brigades and began his infamous ride on June 25, 1863. General Meade would soon take over command from

Hooker, and the Confederates would be incredibly surprised by how rapidly the Yankee army organized itself, moved north, and brought its full weight to bear at Gettysburg. While Stuart succeeded in causing some commotion in the Union rear by cutting communication lines, capturing a supply train, and generally frightening the population of Washington, D.C., he was badly hindered in his effort to re-establish contact with Lee and his infantry. Transport of the supply train slowed Stuart down considerably, and he was further delayed by several sharp skirmishes with Union cavalry and Pennsylvania militiamen.

In all, Stuart was gone eight days, and his exhausted horsemen did not appear on the scene at Gettysburg until late on Day Two. Stuart severely let Lee down by forcing the commanding general to stumble blindly into a battle he did not yet want, at a location he had not chosen. Lee certainly bears significant responsibility for not managing his impetuous subordinate more closely. The net effect of the entire fiasco was that Lee had very little accurate data about his enemy until Longstreet's scout appeared on the scene on June 28 to inform him that the Yankees were nearby, and in force.

Lee pulled his units together, and in a bloody day of confused fighting on July 1 succeeded in pushing the Federal forces through Gettysburg to Cemetery and Culp's Hills south of town. Lee was still under the distinct impression that most of the Union army was not close enough to help and that if he moved rapidly, he could defeat the enemy before it achieved full strength.

Until mid-morning of the second day of battle, Lee worked to collate the reports that came to him from a party of engineers he had sent to scout the Union left flank and other officers who had information to offer. Lee felt pressed by time, and though he asked a few questions when he received his reports, he did not seek to further verify or update any of the information he possessed. This too was unfortunate, because the information he possessed was dead wrong, or at least not timely. His engineers informed him the Yankee left was uncovered— when in fact there was enemy activity all throughout the area they were supposed to have scouted—and that an ideal attack should focus on rolling up the Union line from south to north, starting at the place that came to be known as the Peach Orchard. Thus, Lee formulated his plan to "deliver a determined and united blow."

General Ewell would take his cue from General Longstreet. When Longstreet commenced his attack on the Yankee left, Ewell would bombard and then assault the Yankee right—especially if Meade sought to reinforce his left by moving units from his right. Longstreet was delayed, however, and did not begin his attack until 4:00 p.m. When Ewell finally heard the cannon fire to the south, he opened up on Cemetery Hill, but after a two-hour duel with the more powerful Yankee artillery, Ewell's guns were silenced. Meade actually did redeploy units away from Culp's Hill when the exchange of artillery fire ceased. But Ewell once again failed to capitalize on a potential opportunity. He did not attack with his infantry until about 9:30 p.m., and he fought futilely into the darkness, at great expense in casualties. Ewell captured some unoccupied trenches at the base of Culp's Hill and held them overnight, but it was a meaningless achievement.

Earlier in the day, many critical hours had lapsed from mid-morning until late afternoon while Longstreet got his men ready, marched and countermarched. During this timeframe, Dan Sickles moved his Third Corps forward to occupy positions in and near the Peach Orchard. Hypothetically, if Sickles had aligned his two divisions per Meade's orders—tying in with General Hancock on his right and anchoring at Little Round Top on the left—Lee with his existing plan would have missed the extreme left flank of the Union army entirely and, even if he had redirected his effort, would have had extreme difficulty rolling up the Union line. Little Round Top, however, was still unoccupied. Lee must have known that the enemy would use whatever time was available to reposition his forces, but the Confederate commander did nothing to verify or update the faulty intelligence that the Union left was open to a flanking movement perpendicular to Emmitsburg Road at the Peach Orchard. Accurate and current information would have told him the Peach Orchard was heavily occupied, but the far left flank at (and even behind) the two Round Tops was vulnerable.

When Longstreet's divisional commander John Bell Hood realized that Sickles's Third Corps sat dead in his path, he quickly and wisely scouted farther south. Hood forcefully appealed to Longstreet that he go completely around the Union left, which may with rapidity of movement still have been possible. By this time Longstreet, who had himself repeatedly advocated just such a maneuver with Lee, was resigned to the fact that Lee wanted the assault to take place now, and on the path he had designated.

Longstreet ordered Hood forward, and incredibly bloody fighting ensued. While delay and confusion unfolded at the level of the Confederate high command, Gouverneur Warren also had sufficient time (barely) to cover up Sickles's gross oversight and fortify Little Round Top. More bloody fighting took place, and at the end of Day Two, the Confederates occupied the Peach Orchard, the Devil's Den and the Wheatfield, but the Union line held fast. Sickles's recklessness in exposing his corps—though his men fought valiantly—had been remediated by quick thinking and hard fighting on the part of others. The Yankee defenses had not been rolled up accordion-like, pursuant to Lee's vision and as they had been at Chancellorsville. Most important, the Federals retained the high ground at both ends of the battlefield. For want of accurate intelligence, Lee had failed to strike the battle-winning blow. That goal would be left for Day Three.

At the end of Day Two, Lee once again failed to appropriately gather good data. He did not receive first-hand, in-person status reports—which he should have demanded—from two of his three corps commanders, Ewell and Longstreet. Those two generals instead sent staff officers to brief Lee, and the information thus conveyed gave Lee a false picture of his army's situation. Lee said later that based on these updates he believed that, "Longstreet succeeded in getting possession of and holding the desired ground ... [and] Ewell also carried some of the strong positions which he assailed." While it is true that Longstreet held the Peach Orchard, which is the "desired ground" that Lee referenced, possession of that terrain feature gave Lee no particular advantage. Lee assumed that his artillery, placed in an elevated position in the Peach Orchard, could dominate the Yankee line on Cemetery Ridge. In fact, Cemetery Ridge itself rose to an elevation of about forty feet at the critical point of resistance. Therefore, Lee was completely mistaken in his assessment of the value of the ground, hard-won though it was, that Longstreet had secured.

Lee also had an erroneous sense of the outcome of Ewell's late evening attacks against the Union right. Lee believed that Ewell had breached the Yankee defenses such that, according to Lee, Second Corps "would ultimately be able to dislodge the enemy." In truth, Ewell spent the night in possession only of some abandoned Yankee trenches at the base of an incredibly well-fortified Culp's Hill. Lee was the victim of poor communication and bad data, but he brought those troubles upon himself. Had he insisted on being properly and directly briefed by his principal subordinates, he would have had a truer picture of his army's status. As it was, Lee the offensive-minded optimist continued to engage in wishful thinking and, as a result, formulated a plan of battle for Day Three that would ultimately fail.

Lee's plan for July 3 entailed much of the same. Lee himself explained his thinking when he wrote later, "The result of this day's [July 2] operations induced the belief that with proper concert of action, and with the increased support that the positions gained on the right [by Longstreet] would enable the artillery to render the assaulting columns, we should ultimately succeed, and it was accordingly determined to continue the attack. The general plan was unchanged. Longstreet, re enforced [sic] by Pickett's three brigades ... was ordered to attack the next morning, and General Ewell was directed to assail the enemy's right at the same time." Lee also ordered Jeb Stuart and his cavalry to protect the left of Ewell's Second Corps, to create a diversion if possible, and to attack the enemy in his rear if the planned infantry assault was successful.

General Meade, unlike Lee, had physically assembled all of his corps commanders in his tiny farmhouse headquarters for a council of war on the night of July 2. While it is clear that Meade knew in his own mind he would stand his ground on July 3 (he had previously wired his superiors in Washington telling them as much) he wanted consensus among his subordinates. After much discussion amidst a hazy cloud of cigar smoke, Meade finally asked for a vote of his generals as to whether they should stay and fight or retreat. They voted unanimously to fight. They each left the conference that evening resolute in their common purpose, and clear as to their respective duties for July 3. This stroke of genius on Meade's part—asking for input and achieving uniform agreement among his leadership team as to their plan for July 3—may as much as anything he did as commanding general over three days have won the battle for the Army of the Potomac. The great Robert E. Lee could have taken a page from the upstart and novice General Meade's notebook.

While Lee clearly desired a coordinated attack on July 3, literally from dawn's first light his plans went awry. At 4:30 a.m., on the northern end of the field, Union artillery commenced a bombardment of the trenches occupied by Ewell's soldiers, and the fight was underway. Apparently, there was no mention in the orders that the forever out-of-step Ewell conveyed to his subordinates that indicated a need to attack in tandem with Longstreet to the south. Ewell had intended to initiate combat at dawn, too; the Yankees simply beat him to the punch. The Confederate Second Corps fought furiously to gain the heights before them. By 11:00 a.m. they were defeated, having suffered twice as many casualties as their enemy. Longstreet would have to proceed on his own, with no help from Ewell.

When Lee met with Longstreet just after dawn, he was distressed to hear his lieutenant again arguing for a flanking move. Longstreet had sent out scouts in the night, and he believed a move around the two Round Tops could succeed. Lee shut him down. Lee was also surprised to find out, apparently for the first time, that the two of

Longstreet's divisions that had fought on Day Two were in extremely tough shape, and in no way ready to resume the offensive. The ever resilient—and at this point arguably obsessed—General Lee hatched a new plan.

Lee determined that he would attack the Federal center, using Major General George E. Pickett's fresh division (the all-Virginia unit had arrived on the field late on July 2) of Longstreet's corps. Pickett was an incredibly colorful character. Like George Custer, he had graduated last in his class at West Point (in 1846). He had a drooping mustache and wore his long hair in perfumed ringlets. He had a teenage fiancée whom he adored. He was chomping at the bit for his moment of glory, as he had seen little action since being wounded at the Seven Days Battles a year earlier. Pickett's three brigades would comprise nearly half of the primary attacking force, but would be supplemented by six brigades from A. P. Hill's Third Corps. Hill's units had been roughly handled and sustained many casualties on Day One, but the survivors had enjoyed a day of rest on July 2. There would also be two brigades of Hill's corps available in reserve. About twelve thousand men would comprise the attack force. The offensive would be preceded by a massive artillery bombardment.

Though A. P. Hill would send a greater number of his Third Corps brigades into the fray, Lee designated Longstreet as principal assault commander. Hill had been strangely non-participatory in the battle throughout the three days, apparently because he was not feeling well. Lee once again demonstrated his trust in Longstreet, or perhaps he felt compelled to teach Longstreet a lesson by reminding him of who was in command. Whatever Lee's motives, Longstreet reacted to the assignment with shock and dismay. He disagreed vehemently with the plan and told Lee, "General, I have been a soldier all my life. I have been with soldiers engaged in fights by couples, by squads, companies, regiments, divisions, and armies, and should know, as well as anyone, what soldiers can do. It is my opinion that no fifteen thousand men ever arrayed for battle can take that position." Lee was not swayed.

Longstreet remembered sorrowfully many years later, "My heart was heavy. I could see the desperate and hopeless nature of the charge and the cruel slaughter it would cause. That day at Gettysburg was the saddest of my life."

Two cannon shots barked out from Seminary Ridge toward a copse of oak trees to the east that Lee had identified as the central target for the assault. The time was 1:07 p.m. With that, a deafening roar of artillery fire, representing the combined thunder of 150 Rebel guns lined up wheel-to-wheel for three-quarters of a mile, rained shot and shell in the direction of the Union lines. The volume of noise was such that it could be heard in Pittsburgh, 150 miles to the west. Some experts assert that the barrage that preceded Pickett's Charge generated the loudest man-made noise ever heard on the North American continent, until the testing of the atomic bomb at Alamogordo, New Mexico, in 1945.

But for all its sound and fury, the bombardment was ineffectual. Within minutes, the Confederate shells began to fall long. Because of the heavy smoke created by the intense firing, which hung in the air on this still and humid day, Rebel gunners could not see the impact point of their rounds. The explosions wreaked havoc behind the Union lines, but artillery and infantry at the front went unscathed. Some soldiers argued later that the safest place to be during the cannonade was at the Union front lines, and a number of men—in their extreme exhaustion—even fell asleep as the errant shells soared over their heads. Some historians have blamed faulty fuses for the inaccurate fire. Others say that as the guns recoiled, the carriage trails became embedded in the earth, thereby raising the barrels slightly. Some say the barrels overheated, causing a more powerful explosion of powder. Whatever the reason, the result was unsatisfactory. Once again, General Lee forged ahead based on a false assumption, that is, that his artillery had done its job.

The Confederate infantry staged itself in the trees along Seminary Ridge, behind its own cannons, in preparation for the advance.

Union artillery responded to the Rebel barrage, and soon some 250 combined guns were engaged in a monumental, cacophonous duel back and forth. Some of the Union rounds fell long too, but although they missed the enemy batteries at the front line, they landed squarely amidst the now vulnerable Rebel foot soldiers who lay in waiting. The men took cover as best they could, but still sustained many casualties. At one point, a frightened rabbit scurried from the woods to the rear. A grizzled Rebel soldier was heard to mutter, "That's right old hare, you run. If I was a old hare, I'd run too." The Union guns eventually ceased firing both to preserve ammunition and, in a calculated ruse, to give the Confederates the impression that their counter-battery fire had been effective in taking out at least some of the Yankee artillery. The Confederate rate of fire also began to fade as ammunition ran low. Now, just before 3:00 p.m. on July 3, 1863, it was finally time to commence Robert E. Lee's greatest gamble (see Gettysburg Map Number Six, July 3, 1863, Pickett's Charge, Late Afternoon).

Two of Pickett's brigade commanders, Brigadier Generals Richard B. Garnett and Lewis A. Armistead, gazed solemnly across the three-quarters of a mile of open, rolling fields, crisscrossed with post-and-rail fencing, that they would be expected to traverse before meeting their well-entrenched, determined enemy. Garnett said to Armistead, "This is a desperate thing to attempt." Armistead responded contemplatively, "It is. But the issue is with the Almighty, and we must leave it in his hands."

Young Colonel Edward Porter Alexander, who commanded Longstreet's artillery, passed the word to Longstreet that now was the time to go. Pickett looked at Longstreet, waiting impatiently for the order. "General," he said, "shall I advance?" Longstreet later described his emotions at that moment, saying, "My feelings had so overcome me that I could not speak, for the fear of betraying my want of confidence." The best that Longstreet could do was to slowly, reluctantly nod his head and, with that, Pickett was away. He galloped to the head of his division and, in a fiery speech that only those immediately in front of him could hear, reminded his soldiers of their duty. He exhorted them, "Up men, and to your posts! Don't forget today that you are from old Virginia."

Renowned Civil War historian Bruce Catton eloquently described what happened next, "The smoke lifted like a rising curtain, and all of the great amphitheater lay open at last, and the Yankee soldiers could look west all the way to the belt of trees on Seminary Ridge. They were old soldiers and they had been in many battles, but what they saw then took their breath away, and whether they had ten minutes or seventy-five years yet to live, they remembered it until they died. There it was, for the last time in this war, perhaps for the last time anywhere, the grand pageantry and color of war in the old style, beautiful and majestic and terrible: fighting men lined up for a mile and a half from flank to flank, slashed red flags overhead, soldiers marching forward elbow to elbow, officers with drawn swords, sunlight gleaming from thousands of musket barrels, lines dressed as if for parade. Up and down the Federal firing line ran a low murmur: 'There they are.... There comes the infantry!'"

When the Confederate brigades moved out, they came almost immediately under intense artillery bombardment, giving the lie to the idea that the enemy's guns had been knocked out. The long lines of gray-clad men were raked by devastating, enfilading cannon fire from the abundant and accurate Yankee batteries. As Union shells tore bloody, yawning holes through their ranks, the Rebels bravely closed the gaps, aligned themselves, and continued the attack. We can speculate and wonder in awe as to what causes human beings to carry on in such a desperate situation but, for many a warrior on both sides, the most powerful motivation was a simple desire not to disappoint his comrades, the men immediately to his right and to his left. One soldier confessed in a letter to his sister, "You ask me if the thought of death does not alarm me. I will say that I do not wish to die.... I myself am as big a coward as eny [sic] could be, but give me the bullet before the coward when all my friends and companions are going forward." And so forward they went.

As they came nearer the Union position, Pickett's men turned north in an oblique move intended to close the gap with units on the left, but that made the Virginians even more susceptible to fire on their right flank. When they reached the vicinity of the Emmitsburg Road, all the Confederates now came under withering rifle fire. An audible moan, which could be heard above the din and echo of gunfire, emanated from the Confederate ranks when the first massive volley of musketry struck home. The Rebel infantry leaned forward as if moving into a violent hailstorm. The Yankee artillerists leveled their pieces and used them like gigantic shotguns, blasting canister (small, encased metal balls that sprayed directly from the mouth of the gun) into the ranks of the oncoming Rebel warriors. The remaining Southerners presented a 600-yard front as they approached. They veered in the direction of a low stone wall that ran north and south for 300 yards, with a ninety-degree turn east that ran sixty yards, before turning north and south again. This spot would forever afterward be known as "The Angle."

Some 200 courageous Confederates, led by the seemingly invincible General Lewis Armistead, hat perched atop his sword so the men could see him, succeeded in breeching the Union lines at the angle in the stone wall. They fought furiously. Union soldiers from General Hancock's Second Corps (primarily New Yorkers and Pennsylvanians) stood toe-to-toe and fought hand-to-hand with the Rebels in a pitiless struggle for control of that piece of earth. Bruce Catton described the scene, "This was the climax and the bloody indisputable pay-off; the next few minutes would tell the story, and what that story would be would all depend on whether these blue-coated soldiers really meant it.... [E]very man was firing in a wild, feverish haste, with the smoke settling down thicker and thicker.... A fresh Union regiment was moving up.... and as the men came out into the open they heard the uproar of battle different from any they had ever heard before—'strange and terrible, a sound that came from thousands of human throats, yet was not a commingling of shouts and yells but rather like a vast, mournful roar.'" Armistead was struck down, mortally wounded. Hancock (who had been Armistead's close personal friend in the pre-war army) was also shot, a bullet piercing his saddle and driving a nail and bits of wood into his groin. He was badly injured but would survive.

Suddenly, like an ocean wave that crashes furiously ashore and then gently recedes, the Confederate assault lost its energy and momentum. It was not yet 4:00 p.m. Longstreet determined that to send additional reserve units into the fight now would be suicidal, so he did not order them forward. More than half of the men who had made the charge became casualties. A significant percentage of these were North Carolinians, in addition to Pickett's Virginians (many historians today refer to the charge as the Pickett-Pettigrew Charge to acknowledge the significant contributions of the North Carolinians). All three of Pickett's brigade commanders and all fifteen of his regimental commanders were either killed or wounded. The valiant fighters who survived reluctantly fell back in dazed agony to the safety of their own lines. General Lee was waiting for them upon their return. "It's all my fault," he told the men, "It is I who have lost this fight, and you must help me out of it the best way you can. All good men must rally." When told that the Confederate assault had been repulsed, General Meade's succinct but heartfelt response was, "Thank God."

Simultaneously with the Southern bombardment of Cemetery Ridge, three miles east of the main fighting in the Yankee rear, Jeb Stuart and his cavalry had battled enemy horsemen furiously and at close quarters, to a draw. Stuart soon withdrew—his total contribution to the Confederate effort amounting to virtually nothing—to rejoin Lee and the rest of the army.

Lee's first thought was to prepare for a Union counterattack. He told the despondent General Pickett, "place your division in the rear of this hill, and be ready to repel the advance of the enemy should they follow up their advantage." "General Lee," replied Pickett, "I have no division now." But there would be no counterattack, for General Meade and the Army of the Potomac were exhausted as well.

The two armies faced each other warily, like two wounded animals, overnight. The next day, July 4, the skies opened up with rain. Lee began his retreat in the afternoon, first evacuating the wounded in a train of wagons that stretched for seventeen miles. The bulk of the Army of Northern Virginia moved south from Gettysburg on July 5 and continued the march to cross the Potomac River back home into Virginia. Despite being trapped for a time at the river's edge by rain-swollen waters, Lee made his escape to safety on July 14. Meade pursued cautiously the whole way, but did not endeavor to deliver the killing blow. Meade has been subjected to withering criticism over the years for his failure to follow up upon his success. President Lincoln knew no end of disappointment over Meade's inability to finish the job, for he felt that had his general moved aggressively, the war could have been ended quickly, in one final stroke. As it turned out, the conflict would last almost two more years, and there would be more casualties after Gettysburg than before. But Gettysburg, along with the nearly simultaneous Union capture of the strategic city of Vicksburg, Mississippi, would prove to be a pivotal turning point.

After the battle, in a private letter, Longstreet's artillery chief Colonel Edward Porter Alexander (who was widely admired for the straightforward and truthful nature of his post-war memoirs) summed up the feelings of many when he wrote, "Never, never, never, never did General Lee himself bollox a fight as he did this one." Lee accepted immediate responsibility for the debacle as the battle ended. He told his soldiers, "It's all my fault." Lee did not directly criticize A. P. Hill, who was sick and essentially passive for the entire three days of battle. Lee also never openly blamed Longstreet, who argued with Lee the whole way from a strategic standpoint but, once the fighting commenced, did his duty.

But later, in his writings and commentary, Lee seemed to be casting about for other explanations as to what happened. He did identify causes other than his own missteps. In an official battle report, he bluntly blamed Stuart, saying, "The movements of the army preceding the battle of Gettysburg had been much embarrassed by the absence of cavalry." Lee faulted Ewell for his hesitancy in taking Cemetery and Culp's Hills. After the war, Lee told a trusted cousin, "[Stonewall] Jackson would have held the heights." Lee also, in an indirect way, seemed to point to his soldiers as well. He wrote to President Jefferson Davis saying, "No blame can be attached to the army for its failure to accomplish what was projected by me.... I am alone to blame, in perhaps expecting too much of its prowess & valour."

There was enough dissatisfaction with Lee's performance in the popular Southern press that he submitted his resignation to Jefferson Davis on August 8. Davis rejected the idea. In that letter, Lee implied that his health may have been a factor. Lee had suffered what some modern medical doctors think may have been a myocardial infarction in March 1863. Lee said, "I am so dull that in making use of the eyes of others [probably a veiled reference to the intelligence problems of Day Two] I am frequently misled." Heart disease would kill Lee in 1870. Some historians have suggested Lee may have been suffering from a bout of diarrhea during the battle as well. The fact that Lee may have been feeling poorly certainly could have affected his performance.

In the end, the officer commanding bears the responsibility, whether it is fair or not, for the outcome of a battle. At Gettysburg, General Lee continually operated on the basis of incomplete or incorrect information. He took a poorly judged risk in allowing Jeb Stuart his joyride and suffered from the result. He wrongly believed the Union army would not come together and move to strike him as quickly as it did. He received bad information on Day Two, in the morning from his inept scouts, and late at night from emissaries sent in the place of his two key lieutenants, who should have briefed their commanding general personally. On Day Three, he tragically assumed his artillery had softened the Union defenses, and that his brave soldiers could overcome all obstacles. This series of errors and misjudgments by Robert E. Lee cost the Confederacy a pivotal battle and, perhaps, the war. Lee reminds us that success in decision making can only come when a leader uses the right data.

POSTSCRIPT TO CHAPTER ELEVEN

The town of Gettysburg was devastated by what happened there, and was decades in recovery. Almost every public building and many private homes had been turned into field hospitals to treat the all-but-unbearable suffering of the wounded. The battle produced approximately 50,000 casualties (killed, wounded, missing, and captured) including 7,000 fatalities during the three days. Four thousand mortally wounded men died later. Five thousand horses were killed and were placed in piles and doused with oil for mass incineration. The men were buried for the most part in shallow graves. The stench of death hung in the air, as did the danger of disease. Gettysburg residents kept their windows shut during the remainder of the long, hot summer of 1863.

Some prominent Gettysburg citizens proposed that land be acquired to create a national cemetery in order to establish a proper burial place for the thousands of Union dead. They received political support from Northern governors, and in the months after the battle some 3,577 soldiers were reinterred state-by-state (eighteen in all), in a semi-circle of graves adjacent to the private Evergreen Cemetery where so much of the fierce combat had taken place. Almost half of the graves are marked "unknown," which makes it a virtual certainty that Confederate soldiers lay resting there as well. Many of the Confederate dead from other locations around the field were disinterred and reburied in the South after the war. In 1895 the War Department officially established Gettysburg as a national military park, and in 1933 control passed to the National Park Service, where it remains to this day.

On November 19, 1863, a formal dedication ceremony took place. President Abraham Lincoln was invited to attend, not to be the main speaker that day, but to simply offer "a few appropriate remarks." The Gettysburg Address was 272 words long and took Lincoln about three minutes to deliver in his high-pitched Kentucky twang. In it, he explained the meaning of the loss of so many lives on the battlefield just four months prior. Lincoln, the lawyer, for the first time anywhere asserted the Declaration of Independence as a matter of founding law. The Declaration's central principle—equality—became a principle of the Constitution (which does not mention equality). To Lincoln, the Civil War was the great struggle around and testing of this powerful idea that "all men are created equal." Historian Garry Wills wrote, "The Gettysburg Address has become the authoritative expression of the American spirit—as authoritative as the Declaration itself, and perhaps even more influential, since it determines how we read the Declaration.... By accepting the Gettysburg Address, its concept of a single people dedicated to a proposition, we have been changed. Because of it, we live in a different America."

★ ★ CASE STUDY ★ ★

BILLY BEANE AND
THE OAKLAND A'S: MONEYBALL

In 1990, a middling professional baseball player named Billy Beane was struggling to make the roster of the Oakland A's big league franchise. In a surprise move, Beane decided to abandon his career as a player. He approached A's General Manager Sandy Alderson and asked him for a position as an advance scout. In that job, Beane would be responsible for going on the road to scout future opponents. Alderson said, "Nobody does that. Nobody says, 'I quit as a player. I want to be an advance scout.'" But not for the last time, Billy Beane would defy conventional thinking. Beane rose through the ranks to an assistant general manager role by 1993 and, in 1998, he was named to replace Alderson as team general manager. Beane continues in that role to the present day. During his tenure, Beane has become famous for his willingness to eschew accepted wisdom in favor of scientific principles and statistics to assemble a winning team, despite severe cost constraints. Billy Beane has turned the world of Major League Baseball on its head, defied his many critics, and become a well-known consultant and guru in the wider business arena, simply by doing a better job than anyone else of identifying and using the right data.

Beane's story came dramatically to light with the publication in 2003 of Michael Lewis's best-selling book, *Moneyball: The Art of Winning an Unfair Game*. Beane had been a phenomenal high school athlete who excelled in football, basketball, and baseball. He was judged by baseball scouts as having unlimited potential as a big league player. He was what they called a "five-tool player"; he could run, field, throw, hit for average, and hit for power. The scouts liked Beane's body; he was tall and angular and looked good in a baseball uniform. Some of the scouts even thought they could predict future aptitude by looking at a ballplayer's face. If an athlete had "the Good Face," which Billy Beane surely did, then he would go on to greatness. But despite all of the abundant prognostications of success for him, Beane was basically a flop as a pro baseball player. Beane hated to fail, and when he struggled in pro ball, his intense personality got in the way of his growth and development. From 1984 through 1989, Beane played in 148 major league games for four different teams. He batted .219 and hit three career home runs.

When Beane finally landed as general manager of the A's, he knew that there had to be a better way to identify and develop baseball talent. He was living proof that the old system, which consisted of scouts making judgments about an athlete's future potential based on what they saw, was fundamentally flawed.

Beane's theories of talent evaluation evolved from many different sources (he was an especially devoted student of iconoclastic baseball writer Bill James), but revolved around several fundamental beliefs. First, Beane believed that hitting was more important than fielding. He would take a lousy fielder who could create offense any day. Second, the single most important baseball statistic—aside from the obvious one of runs scored—was not batting average but on-base percentage. Beane sought to find players who did not make outs and got on base, whether through a hit or a base on balls. Players with good on-base percentages created runs. Runs created victories. Next, Beane believed in drafting college players over high school players, because they were easier to evaluate and, on average, tended to succeed much more often in big league careers. Finally, and perhaps most important, Beane believed that the system of scouts relying on what they saw to judge future performance was wrong. Instead, he favored using detailed statistical analysis to evaluate players based on what they had already done. As Michael Lewis said in *Moneyball*, "The human mind played tricks on itself when it relied exclusively on what it saw, and every trick it played was a financial opportunity for someone who saw through the illusion to the reality. There was a lot you couldn't see when you watched a baseball game."

In that spirit, Beane hired Paul DePodesta as an assistant GM. DePodesta was definitely not a baseball guy. He had never played the game. He graduated from Harvard with distinction in economics, and he was fascinated by the concept of irrationality. More specifically, he was interested in how to take advantage of irrational behavior. And the world of major league talent evaluation was brimming with irrational behavior. DePodesta ran reams of information through statistical analysis on his laptop, and he spit out conclusions that defied conventional baseball wisdom. Long-time scouts and other members of what Michael Lewis called "The Club," looked down their noses at DePodesta and his laptop. But Beane listened closely to what DePodesta's numbers told them. Lewis said, "Billy had his own idea about where to find future major league baseball players: inside Paul's computer. He'd flirted with the idea of firing all the scouts and just drafting kids straight from Paul's laptop."

The primary challenge Beane faced was a lack of financial resources with which to compensate ballplayers. During his tenure, Oakland has consistently had one of the lowest payrolls in baseball. In 2002, the sport's richest team, the New York Yankees, would pay their players $126 million. In contrast, the A's had the second-lowest payroll in baseball at around $40 million. But Beane knew that by taking players from DePodesta's laptop, players that the rest of baseball's scouting system had overlooked, he could afford to be competitive.

And competitive the A's have been. With Beane at the helm, the A's have made the playoffs five times. In 2000, the A's spent $26 million to win 91 games and a division title. In 2001, the spent $34 million and won 102 games. They went one better and won an astounding 103 games in 2002. By the beginning of the 2008 season, the A's had the fourth-best record in baseball since Beane took over in 1998. Critics delight in pointing out that since 2006, Oakland has not made the playoffs or fielded a .500 team. They argue that the "*Moneyball* experiment" is surely a failure.

But others argue that no person in the last several decades has had a more powerful impact on the business of baseball than Billy Beane. Thanks to Beane, there exists a much more widespread viewpoint that using technology to render careful qualitative and quantitative analysis of hard data is a better way to judge baseball talent and to develop players than solely relying on the opinions of scouts. Even Joe Girardi, manager of the 2009 world-champion New York Yankees, carries with him at all times a 200-page binder chock full not just of scouting reports, but of statistics and other data that help him make critical managerial decisions.

The information revolution is here to stay in baseball. The game has changed significantly in that now it is standard practice to bring highly educated, analytical people—who don't necessarily need a baseball pedigree—into front offices. Paul DePodesta is now the GM of the Los Angeles Dodgers. Beane's friend J. P. Ricciardi became the general manager of the Toronto Blue Jays in 2001. Yale graduate Theo Epstein, who is a Beane disciple, runs the Boston Red Sox (who have enjoyed enormous success and won two World Series titles over the past several years—albeit with an extremely high payroll). The field manager's role has been diminished, and the general manager's role enhanced, as a result of Beane's influence. Beane said, "We're going to run the organization from the top down. We're controlling player personnel.... There's this belief that a baseball team starts with the manager first. It doesn't."

Billy Beane's methodologies have had an impact far beyond the business of baseball. Thanks mostly to the fame and notoriety gained from the publication of *Moneyball*, Beane has become something of a phenom in the corporate world. He has consulted with world-class investor Warren Buffett. He is a sought-after speaker—with a typical honorarium of $40,000—on the subject of his philosophy of assessing risk and gaining a competitive advantage through efficient use of undervalued resources. He sits on corporate boards, including Net-Suite, a software company, and sporting goods company Easton-Bell Sports. He has become enormously wealthy, and in 2005, Beane was awarded a roughly four percent ownership interest in the A's, along with a contract extension through 2012.

Billy Beane is an individual who loves to compete and win, and has never shied away from challenging conventional thinking in pursuit of those goals. He believes in fact over fancy, and hard information over gut feel. Billy Beane provides a terrific example of a leader who has succeeded by using the right data.

Leadership Lesson Eleven:

USE THE RIGHT DATA

Sometimes, measuring results in business is an extremely easy proposition. In retail, where I spent so many years of my career, we can measure things like gross revenue, profitability, and year-over-year store sales with absolute precision. At other times, however, deciding which data to use in order to evaluate performance and make critical decisions is maddeningly difficult.

In my new business—which involves delivering individual leadership and team development training—I am facing a really interesting challenge in determining how to measure results and make decisions, so that I can more effectively market the program. I conduct a survey after each of my seminars. Fortunately, so far, participants have indicated a high level of satisfaction with the training itself. I also have lots of anecdotal evidence in the form of testimony from leaders that they found the training useful. The fact that companies are willing to spend scarce dollars to send people through the seminars, and that I have had repeat business, are strong indicators of perceived value.

Nevertheless, my goal is to create a program that delivers lasting value over the long haul, not just an outstanding one-time experience. I want to be able to point to improved business outcomes and a measureable, healthy return on investment for my customers. Because of the nature of the training, this is a hard thing to accomplish. Right now, we are working on developing a set of measures that focuses on four things: participant satisfaction, knowledge and skills acquired, behavioral changes in the form of new habits and practices, and organizational impact resulting from improved knowledge, better skills, and changed behaviors. We will need to collect data over a period of time and figure out how to be consistent and factual in our reporting of results. My effort to identify and use good data is admittedly a work in progress.

The point in explaining all of this is that deciding which information to use in evaluating your business and making decisions about the future is a very real challenge that requires time and effort and, in some cases, new ways of thinking.

Robert E. Lee was hindered at Gettysburg by his refusal to consider a different way of thinking about the problems that faced him. He took in information, much of which was wrong, failed to ask probing questions, and then compounded his predicament by making assumptions and selectively filtering the data in a way that supported his flawed plan of action. Billy Beane, on the other hand, does nothing but think differently and question established wisdom. He has forced the rest of the baseball world to use new and different kinds of data in assessing their business. He has forced the rest of the baseball world to come with him into the age of technology.

What information do you use when you make decisions in your business? Is the information right, that is, correct? Do you question the data you receive? And even if it is factually correct, is it the right information? Or should you be using other data? Using flawed information is fatal. And correctly measuring all the wrong things also does you no good at all. The next time you make an important decision, simply ask yourself if you are using the right data. The answer can be the difference between victory and defeat in the competitive world in which we live.

Chapter Twelve

LITTLE BIGHORN

LAST STAND HILL: IF THE SITUATION LOOKS FAMILIAR—BEWARE

"Let us bury our dead and flee from this rotting atmosphere."

—Captain Walter Clifford—

Western historian Don Russell once said, "No single event in United States history, or perhaps even in world history, has been the subject of more bad art and erroneous story than Custer's Last Stand." The authors of the wonderful book *Where Custer Fell: Photographs of the Little Bighorn Battlefield Then and Now* agreed, saying, "The fight that occurred on Custer Hill has so often been portrayed in art and film—from grandiose canvases to humorous caricatures, heroic epics to satirical burlesques—that even the most pragmatic researchers and historians find their quest for the truth obscured by the pervasive imagery of the Last Stand. The buckskin-clad figure of the Seventh's commander, standing amid the dwindling shambles of his two battalions and blazing away at hordes of assailants can be hero or fool, inspire veneration or contempt, but the image endures."

Indeed, the path to the truth is difficult. There are countless details about the battle that we will never know for sure, either because there were no survivors to tell the tale, or because eyewitnesses have offered such grossly contradictory stories that the absolute facts are impossible to discern. Therefore, the following narrative—as is true with any description of Custer's final hours—represents at best only an educated approximation of what probably transpired.

We do know that Custer's chain of decision making, however it unfolded in his head, resulted in the death of every man under his immediate command. But, contrary to popular opinion, that series of decisions was not stupidly careless or profoundly illogical. The decisions Custer made in the heat of combat ended up being tragically wrong, but they were neither careless nor illogical. Given everything Custer had experienced in his long career as a war fighter up to June 25, 1876, and based upon everything he observed on that particular day of destiny, his decision making was not at all surprising. In fact, he did what many another aggressive cavalry commander and Indian fighter might have done in the same circumstance. The fatal flaw in his thought process involved his inability to envision a more complex scenario than the one that he thought he saw. Custer failed to contemplate a simple question: What if the Lakota and Cheyenne decide to hold their ground and fight? Custer's Last Stand represents possibly the most dramatic example in American history of a failure to consider the cautionary warning that every good leader should heed: if the situation looks familiar—beware.

Just before 4:00 p.m. on June 25, 1876, as Major Marcus Reno's battered command frantically situated itself on the high bluffs east of the Little Bighorn, Custer and his contingent halted in the low-lying area to the north known as Medicine Tail Coulee. Custer had organized his command into two battalions—Companies C, I, and L led by Captain Myles Keogh and Companies E and F commanded by Captain George Yates. Custer allowed his men a break to dismount, adjust their saddles, and ready their gear in preparation for a continuation of the advance.

Custer ordered his adjutant W. W. Cooke to dispatch orderly John Martin with a written message for Benteen, directing the captain to move forward quickly and to bring ammunition. Martin rode away, and as he turned to look back he observed Custer and his five companies galloping with enthusiasm down Medicine Tail Coulee in the direction of the river. Continuing on his way, Martin soon noticed Custer's younger brother Boston (who had accompanied the expedition as a civilian) riding toward him. Boston asked Martin for Custer's location, and then spurred his mount toward the ravine in order to join his brothers. He could not bear the thought of missing the upcoming action.

Meanwhile, scout Mitch Boyer, from the elevated position at Weir Point, had observed Reno's panicked retreat. Boyer was accompanied by four of Custer's Crow Indian scouts, and he had authorized them to leave. Three of the four did so, but the scout Curley remained at Boyer's side. Curley survived the battle, and though some historians consider him to be an unreliable witness (he issued contradictory statements over the years), his testimony helped to make some sense of this segment of the unfolding drama. Together—according to the story told after the battle by Curley—Boyer and Curley rode in a northeasterly direction from Weir Point to intercept Custer's command, which was on the move, and to deliver their discouraging report. At about 4:00 p.m., the scouts reached Custer. We do not know the specifics of the conversation between Boyer and Custer, but Custer must have been deeply disappointed by the defeat of Reno. This bit of bad news would necessitate a change in plans.

Custer's idea all along had been to prevent the scattering of the Indians. At the Battle of the Washita in 1868, Custer had split his forces, surprised the Cheyenne Chief Black Kettle in his village, destroyed the encampment, slaughtered an Indian pony herd, and

taken several dozen women and children prisoners. In addition, however, because he had not properly reconnoitered the area, Custer also
faced a surprise counterattack from a force of perhaps 1,000 warriors
from other camps nearby. In a bold offensive move, Custer feinted
aggressively in the direction of the assembling Indians, causing them
to hesitate long enough that the Seventh Cavalry was able to make
good its escape. Custer also faced subsequent withering criticism for
his perceived abandonment of Major Joel Elliott, who had ridden off
in pursuit of Indians and was found slain with his entire contingent
of soldiers two weeks later. We can only speculate as to which scenes
from this incredibly vivid experience eight years earlier at the Washita
may have played out in Custer's mind at the Little Bighorn.

There is no doubt that Reno's predicament must have caused a
change in thinking for Custer. If Reno could have held the Lakota and
Cheyenne at bay at the southern end of the encampment, Custer may
have succeeded in swiftly flanking the village from the north, taking
captives, and thereby causing the enemy to surrender. Now, though
Custer was loath to give up the initiative, Reno needed help. Custer
did not want to bring about accusations that he had again abandoned
a subordinate in need.

At this point, young Boston Custer approached the column bearing positive news. He had ridden all the way from the pack train, and
had passed Benteen's unit along the way. He undoubtedly informed
his older brother that Benteen was nearby and the pack train not far
behind. Custer now made an attempt to visually assess the situation.
He moved his command out of the ravine to a ridge to the north, from
which he could get a better view of the village (it was more immense
than he had imagined) and also see the dust rising from Benteen's
column, approximately four miles to the south. If Benteen obeyed
Custer's orders and hurried forward, he would arrive in no more than
thirty minutes.

Custer, the inveterate gambler, now chose to take a further risk.
He decided to split his force once more. He ordered Captain Yates

and Companies E and F (with seventy-six men total) to attack toward the river, about a mile away, at the mouth of Medicine Tail Coulee. This movement would place Yates opposite the Cheyenne circle, at the northern end of the encampment. Company E was known as the Gray Horse Troop, and its uniformly gray mounts gave the unit a distinctive and even intimidating appearance. A Cheyenne warrior named White Shield said these animals were "pretty white," and "could be seen a long way off." Many Indians commented later on the attempt of the men on gray horses to ford the Greasy Grass.

Custer would remain in place with Keogh and his three troops, waiting for Benteen's arrival. It is possible that Custer believed if Benteen joined him quickly enough that he could follow Yates to the ford, cross the river, and attack the village from that position. Some historians argue that this is an unlikely scenario, given that the women, children, and elderly villagers had already left their tipis and were assembling outside of the encampment on the west bank of the river. Custer probably surmised that he would have fallen upon a mostly empty village for purposes of securing captives.

More likely, Custer intended the Yates maneuver strictly as a feint, designed primarily to draw Indian attention away from Reno, or even from Custer himself. If Indian warriors could be occupied near the river, Custer might either buy precious minutes to wait for Benteen and reinforcements, or simply continue with an attack on his own in a northerly direction. Custer may have also believed that this feint would give the impression that there were more soldiers than there actually were, and that the soldiers were so confident and abundant that they were able to mount multiple attacks at different locations on the field. At this point it seems clear that Custer was determined to continue in an offensive mode. It is highly probable that he still believed that "Custer's Luck" would prevail again, and that he could snatch victory from the jaws of defeat.

Custer arranged with Yates before his departure that if Benteen did not arrive in a timely way, Custer would continue north along the ridgeline and have his troops fire a volley or volleys in unison to signal Yates to leave the area of the ford and rejoin the main column. Yates would then rendezvous with Custer and Keogh on a long, high ridge one-and-a-half miles to the northeast.

By virtually every Indian account, the movement toward the river was stopped several hundred yards short of the ford. Subsequent recovery of artifacts indicates that some sort of action took place, but the skirmish was brief and the attempted feint aborted. Some of Yates's troopers dismounted to fire at the warriors who gathered on the west side of the river to oppose them. Indians were now also moving north away from the fight against Reno. They were heartened by their victory on that part of the field and anxious to continue the battle—and to protect their village—against the hated wasichu.

Eventually, Indian numbers became sufficiently menacing that Yates chose to withdraw. This decision may have also occurred simultaneously with Custer's decision to give up on Benteen (Custer had waited perhaps fifteen minutes), continue the move north, and signal Yates to join him with coordinated volleys of rifle fire (these were the same volleys heard by the troopers at the Reno-Benteen Defense Site to the south). As Custer moved forward along the high ground that is today known as the Blummer or Nye-Cartwright Ridge, the battalion spotted an Indian war party of perhaps fifty men ahead to the north. There were also warriors gathering to the south and the east, slowly but surely making their way in Custer's direction. Custer's troops received scattered incoming fire in the form of steel-tipped arrows, but also delivered long-range rifle fire in return, which caused the warriors to disperse. A few dead soldiers were found in this vicinity after the battle, and many empty carbine cartridges indicated that an engagement had been fought from a distance, rather than at close quarters, at this location.

Yates led his men through the coulee and up to the high ground to rejoin Custer and Keogh. The time was now probably shortly before 5:00 p.m., and with many angry Indians pressing in from every direction, Custer briefly called his officers together. His new plan required Keogh and his three companies to continue to hold their position around the elevated terrain, which is today known as Calhoun Hill. They would protect Custer's rear and, hopefully, be able to rendezvous with Benteen should he appear. Custer and Yates, with their smaller contingent of two companies, would proceed rapidly in a flanking maneuver around the northern end of the camp with the goal of securing prisoners. Custer very likely harkened back to his experience at the Washita, where he was able to grab captives and cause the enemy to hesitate with a bold offensive move. Cheyenne oral tradition vividly describes an attempt by white soldiers late in the Little Bighorn battle to cross the river at a location to the northwest. We do not know for sure whether Custer accompanied Yates in this attack toward the river, but given his propensity for leading from the front, and his undoubted desire to see this maneuver succeed, it is highly likely that Custer did personally lead the effort. This last-ditch stratagem represented a desperate attempt to save the rapidly deteriorating situation. It was the only hope.

Custer proceeded for a half mile along the ridge in a northwesterly direction, and then turned west directly toward the Little Bighorn. From this elevation, he surely saw the thousands of Indian elderly, women, and children huddling across the river to the west and south. He must have recognized with a sunken heart that he simply did not possess the manpower—he currently had only about eighty men under his command—to corral so many prisoners. But Custer continued in his mission, moving down into the low ground toward the river. Indians who had followed him poured fire into the harried troopers from the heights they had just vacated. When he finally reached the river with the intention of crossing, Custer came up against the stiffest resistance yet. Warriors in hiding on the western bank unleashed volley after volley of rifle fire and swarms of arrows.

Custer now knew that he must rejoin Keogh, and quickly. He ordered his men to withdraw to a high knoll in the distance. About halfway to his destination, Custer paused. He looked through field glasses to the southeast, and there was no sign of Keogh. Custer saw only rising clouds of dust and smoke approximately a mile away. He heard a roar of gunfire that could only mean that Keogh was intensely engaged with the enemy. It was at this moment, very likely, that George Armstrong Custer realized that this would be his final battle.

Keogh did indeed have his hands full. He had deployed L Company, commanded by Custer's brother-in-law, the handsome Lieutenant James "Jimmi" Calhoun, who had married Custer's sister Margaret in 1872 (Maggie Custer would lose her husband, three brothers, and a nephew at the Little Bighorn), into two platoons occupying a spur connected to the ridge. The men concerned themselves mostly with threats of Indian encroachment from the west and from the south. Lieutenant Calhoun and his second-in-command Lieutenant James Crittenden stood behind their skirmish lines in order to direct the fire. Every fourth man was detailed to hold four horses, freeing three of his comrades to wield their carbines. Keogh placed C Company behind Calhoun and Keogh's own I Company in reserve in some low ground to the east, below the crest of the spur.

The Indians, stealthily using terrain to their advantage, continued to pour arrows and rifle fire into the soldier positions and to gradually encircle Keogh's command. Keogh ordered a group of C Company troopers to form a skirmish line along a ridge toward the river, past the area occupied by L Company. The Indians scattered with this move, but soon rebounded in even greater numbers to overwhelm the men of Company C. At this point, the Brule Lakota Two Eagles said, "some of the soldiers were mounted and some were dismounted. Most of those dismounted had lost their horses." The soldier's horses in many cases had either been killed or wounded by incoming enemy fire or had bolted in panic. Some of the horses, crazed with thirst, raced toward the river. The C Company soldiers themselves were now also in a panic, and those who survived rushed to rejoin their comrades of Company L.

This sudden redeployment of frantic men back into the L Company fold caused further confusion and disarray. Keogh's beleaguered force now faced pressure from all sides. Companies I and L came under fire from the east, as groups of warriors (including Crazy Horse) began to apply increasing combat power from that direction as well. The soldiers who were detailed as horse-holders now received bullets and arrows, and found it increasingly difficult to manage the terrified animals. Some simply let the horses go and attempted to join their comrades in the fight. The Cheyenne Wolf Tooth said, "Horses were running over the soldiers and over each other." The Oglala Low Dog recalled, "Their horses were so frightened that they pulled the men all around, and a great many of their shots went up in the air and did us no harm." The Indians tightened the noose.

The men of L Company, in particular, battled valiantly and put up a disciplined defense. They were tactically stable for perhaps thirty minutes. The number of shell casings subsequently found in the area of Calhoun Hill provided proof of the volume of fire that had been produced. There were as many as forty expended carbine shells around some of the dead cavalrymen. The bodies of Lieutenants Calhoun and Crittenden were found in their proper places, directly behind the skirmish lines of their respective platoons and within a few short yards of each other. It appears that they had been fighting almost back-to-back. Empty cartridges from their revolvers testified to the fact that they each fought at close range and to the last moment. Crittenden was the son of an army general, and he had recently lost an eye in a hunting accident. The young lieutenant's body was later identified in part by virtue of his glass eye, which had been shattered by an Indian arrow.

Calhoun Hill was finally overrun, and the survivors of Companies C and L ran panic-stricken to join Keogh and I Company further north. As Crazy Horse realized the possibility that these men might link up with Custer, he executed his famous "bravery run" along and through I Company's line. This was the death knell. The combat was now hand-to-hand, with the Indians exerting overwhelming force.

At a point about halfway between Calhoun Hill and Last Stand Hill, Keogh was killed, surrounded by loyal troopers who had come to his aid when he fell wounded. After the battle, the remains of many white soldiers—the men of Myles Keogh's battalion—were found scattered in a fashion that proved that they had been routed, and were killed one-by-one in a desperate attempt to reach Custer at Last Stand Hill.

As Keogh met his demise, Custer began to feel increasing pressure as well (see Little Bighorn Map Number Six, Custer's Advance to Last Stand Hill, Early Evening). The Indians still respected the firepower of even this relatively small contingent of wasichu, so they were reluctant to get too close just yet. But as their numbers began to swell they became emboldened, and like a python working to slowly strangle its prey, they gradually surrounded Custer and endeavored mightily to hold him in their grip.

While Indians sniped at the soldiers from long range and infiltrated from all sides, it became apparent that there was a large ravine feeding upward from the river toward the high ground (known today as Deep Ravine) that had become a particularly convenient and well-used avenue of approach for the warriors. There is great controversy on this point among students of the battle, but it seems possible that at some point Custer ordered a contingent of men, probably from Lieutenant Algernon Smith's E Company, to form a skirmish line (known by battle analysts who support the theory as the "South Skirmish Line") down into the gulch to prevent Indian approach from that direction. Some historians assert that no such concerted action ever took place, and that to the extent that soldier bodies were discovered in a line running down Deep Ravine they represented not an organized tactical defense but a contingent of men who rushed toward the river and were overtaken in a final attempt to escape near the battle's end. Testimony on this subject is inconsistent, and we will probably never know the full truth.

Custer led what remained of his troop, including the regimental staff, his brothers Tom and Boston, and his nephew Autie Reed, up to the elevated ground that is today known as Custer or Last Stand Hill. In doing so, Custer heeded the age-old military maxim to occupy the high ground, but this particular piece of terrain was a difficult one to defend. Cover was limited and the men were exposed. Custer set up a defense on the western slope of the hill and took up a position himself at the very crest. In a desperate move to buy time, which had to have signaled to the remaining soldiers that the end was near, Custer ordered that most of the horses be shot and their bodies laid out to form a makeshift breastworks. The men huddled behind the slain animals and returned fire against the ever-increasing numbers of Lakota and Cheyenne warriors that moved closer and closer to surround them.

Custer was joined by what the Indians later said was about twenty men, most of them from Company C of Keogh's shattered command, who frantically dashed to the hilltop, shot more horses to create protection for themselves, and then turned to face the Indians who pursued them from the south. Any relief that these soldiers felt at having finally reached the high ground had to have been short-lived.

At some point during the final melee, a group of men that included the scout Mitch Boyer, Boston Custer, and Autie Reed made a sprint down the hill toward Deep Ravine in an attempt to escape. These men were quickly overtaken and killed. There has been deep controversy, again, concerning the events in Deep Ravine. Some witnesses assert that many men, either as a result of a tactical deployment (the South Skirmish Line theory) or in an effort to escape the slaughter, or both, were slain in Deep Ravine. Other eyewitnesses say that a group of soldiers actually made it into the gully at the end of Deep Ravine and were shot there by pursuing Indians. Many soldier bodies (several witnesses counted twenty-eight corpses) were apparently seen in the gully, but were so difficult to reach that they were simply covered up with mounds of dirt by burial parties after the battle. Over the many decades subsequent to the battle, the landscape has shifted and none of those bodies, to the extent they still rest there, have ever been recovered from the bottom ground of Deep Ravine.

Incoming rifle fire and a rain of arrows steadily took their toll against the stalwart, dwindling defenders of Last Stand Hill. The Indians gradually crept closer. The time was now probably around 6 p.m. The final handful of soldiers was dispatched at close quarters. An Arapaho warrior called Waterman said, "We rushed to the top of the hill and finished off all that were still alive." There is a popular image in the lore of the battle of hordes of warriors on horseback riding in a tight circular formation around the Seventh Cavalry, but that is not what happened. The last phase of the Battle of the Little Bighorn was a matter of progressive attrition. It was a terrible, inexorable strangulation.

When Custer fell and who killed him will never be known. It is clear that the Indians did not know they were fighting Custer that day, and they did not know what he looked like. He had cut his hair short prior to the campaign, so any warrior searching for the soldier leader called "Long Hair" would not have found him. White eyewitnesses say there were many empty cartridges from Custer's Remington sporting rifle surrounding his corpse. He ultimately took a shot to the upper torso and then another to the temple. Those who observed his body disagreed as to whether he received those shots to the left or right torso, or the left or right temple. But either one was a fatal injury, so the wound to the breast probably quickly preceded the shot to the head. Witnesses said that there were no powder burns at the temple, indicating a shot from distance rather than a suicide. We do know that a number of Seventh Cavalry troopers chose that day to take their own lives rather than fall into the hands of their dreaded enemy. We do not know whether a decision to kill himself was the final one of Custer's eventful life. Finally, the noise and tumult ceased, and every last man in Custer's command lay dead with him upon the field.

Now the warriors turned south again to move against Reno's soldiers on the bluff. As they did so women, children, and elderly from the village, who had waited patiently out of range for the battle to end, moved onto Last Stand Hill and the surrounding area to finish off any wounded soldiers, strip them of their belongings, and mutilate their bodies. The warrior Iron Hawk said, "The women swarmed up the hill and began stripping the soldiers. They were yelling and laughing and singing now." Historian James Donovan said, "There were skulls to crush, eyes to tear out, muscles and tendons to sever, limbs to hack off, and heads to separate from bodies. These soldiers would not move through the next world in comfort."

During the late afternoon of June 26, the attack against Reno and Benteen slackened, and warriors began to move back down into the village. The survivors of the hilltop defense observed the massive horde of Indians moving away from the valley of the Little Bighorn later that evening. Indian scouts had seen the Terry-Gibbon column approaching from the north, and they knew that they could stay in this place no longer. Late in the morning of June 27, Terry and Gibbon came into view. Their march had been a hard one, and what they saw when they arrived at Last Stand Hill horrified and sickened them. They proceeded through the abandoned village. The overjoyed men of Reno and Benteen's command were soon shocked and saddened to learn what Terry and Gibbon had to tell them. Custer with all of his men was dead.

The men of the Seventh commenced the grim task of burying their comrades on June 28. They found 210 men who had perished with Custer. The bodies, most of them naked, and having lain out in the blistering sun since June 25, were bloated, discolored, and fetid. The interpreter Frederick Girard said, "The horror of sight and feeling over the bodies of all these brave men after lying in the hot sun for three days I will not attempt to describe.... The stench of dead men was nauseating." Lieutenant Edward Godfrey described "a scene of sickening, ghastly horror." Many of the bodies were mutilated. Captain Walter Clifford said later that what he saw was "horrible in the extreme.... Here a hand gone, here a foot or a head, gaudy gashes cut in all parts of the body, eyes gouged out, noses and ears cut off, and skulls crushed in." First Sergeant John Ryan recalled, "I served through the Civil War and saw many hard sights on the battlefield, but never saw such a sight as I saw here."

Custer was found at the very top of Last Stand Hill, near the spot of the present-day Seventh Cavalry Monument and mass grave. He was stripped naked and sitting half-upright against two dead troopers underneath him. One officer commented on his tranquil visage, saying, "He looked as natural as if sleeping." He had wounds to the torso and to the head, but he was not badly mutilated compared to others, further evidence that the Indians did not know his identity. He was not scalped, perhaps because his hair was too short, but his thigh had received a slash and an arrow had been inserted into his penis. Benteen looked at Custer's body and said, "By God, that is him." Tom Custer was located fifteen or twenty feet away, so horribly mutilated that he could only be recognized by a familiar tattoo on his arm. Custer's other loyal officers lay nearby. Boston Custer and Autie Reed were found about a hundred yards away from the crest of the hill in the direction of Deep Ravine. Lieutenant Godfrey said, "A short distance below his [Custer's] position a number of bodies were found, indicating an attempt to escape." Captain Clifford succinctly summed up the prevailing sentiment of the survivors: "Let us bury our dead and flee from this rotting atmosphere."

Over the generations, Americans have developed a hard and enduring perception that the Battle of the Little Bighorn represented the height of folly. Custer's arrogant, careless foolhardiness cost his men their lives. Yet in analyzing the battle, it is interesting to speculate what many another talented cavalry commander—such as Nelson Miles, George Crook, Ranald Mackenzie, Wesley Merritt, or even General Phil Sheridan himself—may have done in the same circumstance. Arguably, any one of them might have used the same tactics as Custer. Based on all of the hard-won knowledge and experience of the day, the principle concern in approaching any group of Indians was that they would scatter, making capture or defeat incredibly difficult. No force of armed soldiers greater than eighty men (Captain

Fetterman and his command in 1866) had ever been wiped out by a contingent of Indians. There were many examples of white soldiers who were inferior in number defeating larger Indian forces. Custer had been a hard-driving, offensive-minded cavalry leader in the Civil War. He also had his experience of success on the Washita to draw upon. There, though his performance was far from perfect, he had split his forces, attacked boldly, and won the battle.

In his book *Lakota Noon*, historian Gregory Michno argued, "Whereas it may be best to avoid dividing up a command in the proximity of an enemy during large-scale maneuvers with army-sized units ... such is not the case during small-scale tactical cavalry maneuvers. Custer Battle student Bruce Trinque has very ably pointed out Custer's adherence to the principles for a successful engagement in fighting a small, guerilla-type, mobile enemy. Citing the successful tactics used by the British army in scores of their 'Small Wars,' Trinque showed that Custer did nearly everything necessary to defeat his foe. For example, proven tactics called for individual initiative, mobility, maintaining the offensive, acting without delay, playing not for safety but to win, and fighting whenever the opportunity arose. It was accepted that regular soldiers would never shirk an encounter even with a superior irregular force of enemies, and that division of force for an enveloping attack combined with a frontal attack was most preferable...."

Why then, if his fundamental tactics were sound, was Custer so badly defeated? What might he have done differently?

Custer was defeated precisely because he failed to look past his own experience and consider that he might be facing a unique scenario. The situation looked—at least on its surface—very familiar to him, and so it called for a familiar set of responses. In fact, the situation probably looked so similar to the event at the Washita eight years earlier that Custer, until it was too late, failed to consider any other possible course of action or potential outcome. He would succeed by doing just what he had done at the Washita, where he split his forces, surprised and destroyed a village, and took prisoners. Even when a large group of warriors from nearby encampments moved toward him at the end of the battle, Custer was able to intimidate his enemy temporarily with an offensive thrust and then to withdraw in good order. This time, on the Little Bighorn, he again split his forces and achieved surprise, but the massive horde of warriors he encountered defied his expectation by standing to fight. To what was undoubtedly Custer's shock and dismay, the Indians failed to be intimidated or to scatter. One profoundly significant reason Custer lost that day was the simple fact that he faced a very competent, energized, and determined opponent.

Would there have been any chance of success for Custer had he taken a different approach? We will never know for sure. He might have waited for Terry and Gibbon, for example, but there is a good chance the Indians would have either discovered Custer or seen the northern column approaching and dispersed by June 26 or 27. Custer might have stuck with his original plan by reconnoitering the area, letting his troops rest, and waiting until June 26 to attack on his own. We now know that the Indians may very well have been surprised by his attack, even had it commenced on June 26, but Custer could not have known that. He had ample evidence that his regiment had been discovered on June 25, and it would be unfair to criticize him too harshly on this point.

What if Custer had kept his attack force united? This possibility would probably have presented him with the greatest opportunity to succeed but, even then, he may still have failed. If he had kept Benteen with him, Custer's manpower would have been enhanced by 130 soldiers. Perhaps he and Benteen could have followed Reno into the southern end of the village. The element of surprise coupled with the additional firepower of almost 350 of Custer's and Benteen's soldiers—on top of Reno's 150—might have tipped the scales. Maybe the addition of Benteen's unit to Custer's wing would have given him sufficient strength to succeed in capturing prisoners with a northern flanking movement. Again, we will never know the answers to these questions.

George Armstrong Custer was ignominiously defeated because he relied solely on skills, abilities, and methodologies that had proven successful for him in the past. In his case, reliance on personal experience was a severely limiting factor and hindered new insights that might have allowed him to see the complex and unique set of circumstances at the Little Bighorn differently, and to try different tactics as a result. In the end, Custer failed to heed the important and cautionary leadership lesson: if the situation looks familiar—beware.

POSTSCRIPT TO CHAPTER TWELVE

For understandable reasons, the initial burial of soldier bodies at the Little Bighorn on June 28 was carried out in a hurry. The officers generally were buried in deeper graves than the enlisted men, but all of the excavations were shallow at best and, for the most part, simply covered over with dirt. The soldiers were presumably buried where they fell, and a wooden stake was placed at the head of each grave. No formal record was kept of who fell where or of how many men were interred on the field. Today, the modern visitor notices the abundant white marble markers that lay scattered across the hardscrabble landscape, which seemingly indicate where the soldiers died. But these markers are in many cases inaccurately placed.

In 1877, the army disinterred the officer's remains—those that could be identified—for return to their families. Custer was reburied at the U.S. Military Academy in West Point, New York, where he rests today with Libbie by his side. In 1881, a huge granite shaft bearing the names of the enlisted dead was erected atop Last Stand Hill, and as many human remains as could still be found were disinterred and reburied in a mass grave beneath the monument. The places of original burial were restaked. In 1890, the marble markers that we still see today were installed. Regrettably, the army detail that carried out this task made mistakes, such as erecting 246 markers on Custer's portion of the field, where only 210 men had fallen. Since that time, the placement of additional markers has brought the total number to 259. On Last Stand Hill, where only forty-two bodies were initially buried, there are fifty-two stones. The result of this confusion over the years is that there may be as many as seventy markers at the battlefield today that are misplaced and stand in a location where no body was found.

There were Indian casualties at the Little Bighorn as well, but the exact number is unknown. The Indians removed their dead from the battlefield immediately. A reasonable estimate seems to be around sixty fatalities. In 1991, the U. S. Congress changed the name of the battlefield from Custer Battlefield to Little Bighorn Battlefield National Monument. In 1996, the Park Service, working with an advisory committee made up of members from Indian nations who fought in the battle, historians, artists, and landscape architects, conducted a national design competition, with a theme around "Peace through Unity." In 1997 the winning design was selected and in 2003 the Indian Memorial was dedicated. So it is only in the last few years that Native Americans finally have a fitting and meaningful tribute to the courage of those on their side who fought, sacrificed, and died at the Little Bighorn. In 1999, the Park Service also began erecting red granite markers at the sites of known Lakota and Cheyenne fatalities. There are currently about twenty such monuments on the field. The markers all indicate the name of the warrior who fell, and that he died "defending his homeland and the Sioux or Cheyenne way of life."

Subsequent to the Little Bighorn battle, Crazy Horse and Sitting Bull parted ways. Crazy Horse continued to lead a group of his people in eluding government forces, but in the spring of 1877, plagued by cold and hunger, Crazy Horse and his band surrendered at Camp Robinson in Nebraska. On September 5 of that year, in a physical struggle to arrest him, Crazy Horse was bayoneted and killed by an army guard.

After the battle, Sitting Bull took a body of his people and escaped to Canada where they lived until 1881. Upon their ultimate surrender, they were placed on reservations. Sitting Bull overcame his animosity toward whites long enough to spend time touring with Buffalo Bill Cody's Wild West Show, which, ironically, included a re-enactment of Custer's Last Stand. The famous chief enjoyed great celebrity across America.

In the late 1880s, a ceremonial religious ritual called the Ghost Dance spread rapidly among many Native American tribes. The Ghost Dance and its proponents promised the coming of an Indian messiah, that the old Native way of life would be restored, and that Indians would be impervious to white men's bullets. White political and military leadership became increasingly concerned about what was seen as the growing militancy of the movement and the possibility of a violent uprising.

Though he was ambivalent about the claims associated with the movement, Sitting Bull nevertheless encouraged the organizing of the Ghost Dance at the Standing Rock Agency in North Dakota. Soon, he became a recognized leader of the groundswell despite his own uncertainty about its legitimacy. For his perceived advocacy of the Ghost Dance and status as a troublemaker, Sitting Bull was ordered arrested by the army at Standing Rock. In the attempt to take him, Sitting Bull was shot and killed by Indian police on December 15, 1890, in a confused melee that left six of his followers dead as well.

Two weeks later, on December 29, in a great and tragic irony of American history, troops of the Seventh U.S. Cavalry surrounded a group of 350 Lakota men, women, and children at Wounded Knee Creek in South Dakota. The men of the Seventh had been detailed to transport the Indians to a railroad for shipment to a military prison in Omaha, Nebraska. The soldiers were armed with high-powered Hotchkiss rifled guns. In an attempt to disarm the Indians, a violent confrontation erupted. When the shooting was done, by some esti-mates, as many as 300 Indians lay dead. Twenty-five cavalrymen also perished, mostly killed by "friendly fire" from their own weapons. With this senseless event, the series of conflicts between Native Ameri-can and white cultures that had endured for almost 400 years and that were known collectively as the "Indian Wars," came to a heartbreak-ing conclusion.

★ ★ CASE STUDY ★ ★

THE WALT DISNEY COMPANY: FIGHTING THE THIRD BATTLE OF MANASSAS

The Walt Disney Company was founded in the autumn of 1923 by brothers Walt and Roy Disney as an animation studio. Over the decades, the company grew into a massive enterprise, becoming one of the largest media and entertainment empires in the world. Today, in addition to movie production, the company owns theme parks and television networks, and has its hands in radio, publishing, merchan-dising, and travel. Disney's 2008 revenues were almost $38 billion. Through the years Disney, with its beloved and iconic mascot Mickey Mouse, has become one of the best-known global brands of all-time. Disney's wholesome, family-friendly culture and focus have served it well time and again.

But in 1993–94, Disney fought and ultimately lost what many commentators called the "Third Battle of Manassas" (two major Civil War engagements were fought at Manassas, Virginia, the first in July 1861 and a second in August 1862). The company had proposed to build a $650 million historical theme park called Disney's America on a 3,000-acre site in Haymarket, Virginia, just four miles from the

Manassas National Battlefield Park. On several previous occasions, Disney had prevailed in negotiating the placement of theme parks by wooing politicians, business leaders, and local citizens with promises of capital investment and tax dollars, thousands of jobs, and a chance to be a part of the Disney magic. The Virginia situation looked familiar to Disney. Yet Disney failed to account for or skillfully counter the intense grassroots opposition that would arise against the project. Disney stepped into a unique scenario unlike anything ever previously experienced, but failed to adapt its methods. The result was an embarrassing defeat that tarnished the Disney brand.

On Veterans Day in 1993, Disney announced with great fanfare the creation of Disney's America, which would depict and allow visitors to experience important eras and events in American history. For two years prior to the announcement, Disney had quietly gone about assembling various parcels of property—on land owned primarily by the Exxon Corporation—sufficient to house the massive new theme park with its complementary hotels, golf courses, restaurants, and retail outlets. Michael Eisner, Disney's CEO, explained his vision for the park to his creative team (known as the "Imagineers") saying, "The most difficult job won't be to tell important stories about our history, or to deliver an enjoyable experience for our guests, but to achieve both these goals without having either one dilute the other.... We need to keep working to create a daylong experience that makes our guests laugh and cry, feel proud of their country's strengths and angry about its shortcomings." Accordingly, the Imagineers put together ideas for seven differently-themed areas that would depict such things as a working family farm, a state fair, Ellis Island, a Civil War fort, and an Indian village.

Disney crafted a meticulous plan to court key stakeholders. The company had used this strategy on previous occasions—most notably in establishing Disneyland in California—which involved selecting a large, inexpensive parcel of land near a good highway system, and then to begin promoting the economic benefits of their project with the objective of receiving public financial concessions in return.

Starting with Virginia's new governor, the Republican George Allen, Disney wooed politicians at the state, regional, and local level. Disney also met with business leaders and prominent local citizens. Regional chambers of commerce formed a Welcome Disney Committee. The Virginia state legislature approved the issuance of $140 million in bonds to support wide-ranging improvements in infrastructure. The state also committed $20 million to assist Disney by promoting tourism in Virginia. Polling data showed that Virginia's citizenry supported the project by a two-to-one margin.

But trouble was brewing. On the very day of Disney's announcement, which was presented as a fait accompli, Bob Dennis, president of the Piedmont Environmental Council (PEC was a rural preservation group), began contacting his membership. Dennis was terrifically concerned about Disney's proposal. The park would sit adjacent to thirteen historic towns, sixteen Civil War battlefields, and seventeen historic districts. Members of PEC—which included a number of highly affluent business leaders and philanthropists—were similarly outraged, and the organization succeeded in raising and spending $2 million to oppose Disney. Within a few short days, the PEC unleashed a campaign that it labeled the "Scream of Pain." The group reached out to the media and used radio and print to depict Disney as an acquisitive and greedy corporate citizen with a terrible reputation for bullying communities into submitting to its demands. One newspaper ad depicted Mickey Mouse's four-fingered hand, palm skyward, saying, "Brother, can you spare $158 million?"

Another grass-roots organization was formed in Prince William County specifically to oppose Disney. Known as Protect Prince William (PPW), the group achieved non-profit status and recruited 2,000 members by the summer of 1994. This organization was less well-funded than PEC, but its energized members traveled in buses to the state capital in Richmond in order to be present for any key legislative activity. Despite Disney's support from the governor and the state legislature, the members of PEC and PPW agreed to work together and vowed to defeat the project.

A number of key environmental organizations, such as the Sierra Club and Citizen Action, also thrust themselves into the fray. These groups opposed Disney's America on the grounds that the park would violate federal air pollution and traffic regulations. All of the various anti-Disney activists realized that they must coordinate their campaigns, so they met on a regular basis to meld their efforts. The word was getting out.

Disney responded to these attempts to quash the theme park, predictably, by putting together a talented team of its own to trumpet their message. Disney retained fifteen well-known Virginia political consultants and lobbyists to carry the torch at the legislature. The *Washington Post* said, "Disney has hired some of the most familiar faces in Richmond to make its case. The lobbyists are well-connected, they are experienced, and they are everywhere." The result of this investment was passage of the massive financial aid package from the state. Disney's public relations team said, "Our intention is to continue our process of education and communication so that by the end.... we're going to be able to allay almost all private fears and concerns."

The opposition, however, had a new trick up its sleeve. The PEC's Bob Dennis contacted Richard Moe, president of the National Trust for Historic Preservation. The highly influential National Trust took out a full-page ad in the *Washington Post*, signed by many important historians and preservation groups, urging Michael Eisner and Disney to choose a new site. The argument had now shifted. In a newspaper commentary, Richard Moe asked, "What will 'Disney's America' mean for the teaching of American history?" Disney failed to respond to this very important question and instead pursued its typical approach, which was to enhance its image by offering land to local units of government for schools, a library, a fire station, and ball fields.

Now many prominent historians entered the fight. A group of National Trust members that included renowned Civil War historian and Pulitzer Prize winner James McPherson formed Protect Historic America (PHA) to challenge Disney. At a news conference organized by PHA, a group of historians that included among others McPherson, Doris Kearns Goodwin, and David McCullough argued that Disney would destroy our history. McCullough said that Disney's America would "create synthetic history by destroying real history," and the alternative would be "plastic, contrived history, mechanical history."

Michael Eisner, who seemed particularly insensitive and tone deaf throughout the debate, responded by saying, "The First Amendment gives you the right to be plastic.... We have a right to do it. It's private land that is not in the middle of a historic area.... It's not the middle of a battlefield." Eisner also angered people when, on the television show *CBS This Morning*, he responded to a question about the concern that the plastic atmosphere of Orlando would be transplanted to Virginia by saying that Virginia residents "should be so lucky as to have Orlando in Virginia."

The controversy now raged at the national level, with editors and columnists decrying Disney's plan to "plasticize" American history. Yet throughout, Disney continued to play its cards as if it were working to solve a local dilemma. Disney had failed to adequately account for the particular historical and environmental sensitivities prevalent in Virginia. Disney failed to court national historians or environmental leaders who might have helped its cause. Disney failed in allowing its opponents to frame the argument. Disney failed to listen to its consultants (for example, by not using television to provide a broader range for its message). And Disney failed to understand and respond to the national implications of the project.

In the end, after a vicious national pummeling, and based on dismal financial predictions and the enormous difficulty of ever completing the project, Michael Eisner recommended to his board that it pull the plug on Disney's America. The board unanimously agreed. Eisner still could not fathom the forces that had dealt Disney this rejection. He said, "I thought we were doing good. I expected to be taken around on people's shoulders ... the issue was no longer who was right or wrong. We had lost the perception game." The Walt Disney Company had failed to adapt to a new set of circumstances and to heed the cautionary principle: if the situation looks familiar—beware.

Leadership Lesson Twelve:
IF THE SITUATION LOOKS FAMILIAR—
BEWARE

When I left the practice of law in the early 1990s, I went into business for myself. After a great deal of soul-searching and research of different options, I decided to scrape together the money to open a restaurant, which was a fast-food franchise connected to a large national chain. I knew nothing about the restaurant industry, but I was confident that with hard work and a little luck I would be successful. I had always thrived on challenge, even required it in some ways, and had been more or less successful throughout my life whenever I applied myself with energy and determination. This formula had worked for me in athletics, in college, in the military, in graduate school, and even in my legal practice. The new opportunity (running a small business) was undoubtedly different in many ways, but it looked familiar enough that I had few reservations about forging ahead. But I had a rude awakening coming.

After a thorough education in Small Business 101—which involved forming a corporation, purchasing the franchise, going through training, selecting a site, constructing a building, hiring and training a team, marketing the product, and all the other necessary preliminary details—I was ready to open for business. I worked horrendously long hours, lost fifteen pounds, and loved every minute of being my own boss. But guess what? The customers did not show up. No matter what I tried, business was terrible. I closed my doors after just six months. I don't know whether it made me feel better or worse that every other franchisee for this particular chain also went belly-up (as did the national franchisor). Despite my best intentions, I had made a really poor decision.

I was a young guy with a wife and an infant daughter who were depending on me. I was bankrupt and unemployed. We had lost all of our savings, such as they were at the time. I was mortified and confused. While my family and friends, God bless them, stuck with me, I was jobless for seven months. I had failed badly, in a way that had never happened before.

I learned never to take any challenge for granted. I learned that sometimes, even if you are smart and work hard, you may still lose the competition. I learned to focus on what I could control and not fret about the rest. I learned that, forever after that experience, I need to acknowledge what I don't know, try to recognize complexity, and be flexible. I learned to be thankful for what I have, especially for good health, family, and friends. I learned humility.

George Custer failed to recognize complexity at the Little Bighorn. He paid for it with his life, and his team was destroyed. The Walt Disney Company failed to acknowledge a new scenario in Virginia and suffered a dismal public relations loss.

Simply put, wisdom is not enough. Most of the time our lifelong learning serves us well (don't put your hand on that hot stovetop or you will feel pain). The challenge for today's leaders is, first, to recognize and acknowledge situations that may on their surface appear familiar, but are in reality new and more complicated than what has come before. Next, the trick is to marshal resources and elevate understanding. This can come through reading and study, discussion with knowledgeable people, feedback from diverse and unbiased sources, or development of rigorous processes. The goal, in the end, is to achieve better awareness and the higher level of decision-making capability necessary to make good choices in uniquely challenging scenarios.

Conclusion

WHY STUDY HISTORY?

"History teaches us that men and nations behave wisely once they have exhausted all other alternatives."

—Abba Eban, Israeli Diplomat—

There are many excellent reasons to study history (prior to exhausting all other alternatives), but among the most important and practical are:

1. History provides the gift of perspective.

2. History helps us to appreciate complexity.

3. History proves the importance of cultural understanding.

At the beginning of this book, there is a quotation attributed to countless business leaders since commerce began that says, "Business is war." I actually don't agree with that statement. We hear it all the time: "business is war," "politics is war," "international diplomacy is war," "litigation is war," even "football is war." But the plain truth is that only war is war. In its absolute pervasiveness over time and geography, and in its stark brutality, there is no other activity undertaken by human beings that is quite like war. George Patton is supposed to have said, "Compared to war, all other forms of human endeavor shrink to insignificance." I am not sure whether I agree completely with Patton's assertion either, but it is clear that if we put as much effort into pursuing peace as we do into making war, the world would be a better place.

When I take leadership teams to the battlefield, it is not surprising therefore that I sometimes get the question, "Aren't we dishonoring the sacrifice of the people who fought and died here by comparing war to our mundane, day-to-day business world?" The answer is no. I always tell my teams that what they do is important. Does it require us to deliver orders that will send people to their deaths? No. Are we asked to potentially lay down our own lives for a cause? No. But our organizations and teams are depending on us. So are our families. The collective efforts of business people all over the world make the global economy hum. I strongly believe we have an obligation to study these historical events and to take something away that we can use to improve our businesses, our own leadership, and our personal lives. We need to use what we learn to become better citizens of Earth.

It is this conscious, deliberate process of examining with an open mind our own circumstances in comparison to what others have experienced in the past that provides one of history's most important lessons: the gift of perspective. Somehow, if we acquire an understanding of the sacrifices made by people who have gone before us, our own situation seems less pressing and critical than it did before. We have a deeper understanding of what the word "crisis" truly means. We are able to pause and reflect on our own existence with a broader view of the world and a more informed wisdom about life. Hopefully, we see the world more clearly and function more effectively as a result. We have gained perspective.

With this broadened perspective, those who study history also tend to do a better job of recognizing complexity. Quite simply, they have a larger base of knowledge, insight, and experience from which to draw upon. While the fundamental challenges that leaders faced long ago are in many ways the same as those that leaders encounter today, the lessons of history are not absolute. In his book *Leading the Charge: Leadership Lessons from the Battlefield to the Boardroom*, retired

Marine General Anthony Zinni (who was commander-in-chief of U. S. Central Command and a special envoy to the Middle East) said, "I've learned to use the lessons of the past but not to trust them blindly."

There are consistent skills and abilities that effective leaders throughout all eras have demonstrated. General leadership principles remain unchanged. But the situations against which those skills and principles must be applied are forever fluid and constantly changing. Great leaders know this and they respond accordingly, showing the strength, insight, and flexibility that allow them to successfully manage new scenarios.

General Zinni said, "Many times I've worked through a problem or a decision process that produced good results. The success felt good: 'Man, I got it right this time. I know how to do it. The next time I'm in this situation, I know what to do.' But then months—or more likely years—later, I realize that what I did the first time only works in that particular situation. It doesn't carry over. The situation may look the same on the surface, but the decision I have to make requires a very different option, approach, or angle." George Custer showed us the danger inherent in applying the same old approach in a seemingly familiar but, in reality, distinctly different situation. History helps us see complex patterns and to better navigate the maze that constitutes the modern world of business.

Finally, history provides a compelling cautionary tale about what can happen when cultures refuse to make the effort to understand one another. In the Civil War, two vastly different cultures, the North and the South—though forged out of the same basic foundational national experience—could not come together and resolve their regional differences through peaceful means. Sometimes even within an apparently homogeneous nation, organization, or team there are dual or multiple cultures that clash with each other.

In the more obvious case, where two cultures that have been formed based on distinctly different historical, experiential, geographical, or racial factors come into conflict, the capability and willpower to reach across cultural boundaries frequently becomes even more difficult to achieve. The violent struggle between European white immigrants and the original Native American inhabitants of the North American continent provides a vivid example. Neither race had any particular interest in learning about the other. While white arrogance and the prevailing view toward Indians as "uncivilized savages" is well documented, it is also true that the Indians were condescending in their outlook as well. The Indians even looked down their noses at each other. Studies of North American Indian tribes show that the vast majority of original tribal names reflected some version of a translation of the words "human being," "people," or "us." This nomenclature originated from a highly ethnocentric worldview. The idea of the central importance of each individual tribe versus all the others played itself out in the furious, ongoing conflicts that existed between and among Indian tribes long before the white man ever arrived on the scene. Once the white man came, other than by threat of force, very few tribes expressed interest in learning white culture. The white man, of course, showed strikingly similar contempt for Indian culture.

In today's increasingly complex, fast-paced, interconnected world, in which the growth plans for many companies (small, medium, and large) include some form of globalization or international expansion, the imperative to achieve sensitivity and awareness with respect to other cultures becomes, literally, a matter of survival. It is not a nice-to-have; it is a must-have. If we work collectively to achieve this appreciation of differences, our economic fates will become increasingly intertwined and, therefore, interdependent. Nations and organizations that do business together in a spirit of cooperation, understanding, and shared desire for economic gain are much less likely to want to undermine or destroy one another. Perhaps, through this process of working together to achieve better cultural insight, though it may be a distant dream for a faraway future, the human race will someday arrive in the promised land, and truly experience a world in which "Peace through Unity" prevails.

Afterword

Sacred Ground Today

"But, in a larger sense, we can not dedicate—we can not consecrate—
we can not hallow—this ground. The brave men, living and dead,
who struggled here, have consecrated it far beyond our
poor power to add or detract."

—Abraham Lincoln—

McPherson's Ridge: Gettysburg Battlefield Tour Stop Number One[*]

Today a traveler at the Gettysburg National Military Park can explore McPherson's Ridge, located just northwest of town, while riding northbound on Reynolds Avenue. The positions occupied by the Federal forces on July 1 are clearly visible to the right along this roadway. The Confederates approached down Chambersburg Pike from the west or left. Varied markers commemorate the different regiments that fought. Smaller stone flank markers, generally side-by-side, designate the positions where one unit's line ended and another's began. Each of these markers contains the name of the regiment and a LF (left flank) or RF

---

[*]   Battlefield tour stop numbers represent the official tour stop number, as designated by the National Park Service, that visitors see at each of the two battlefields today.

(right flank) designation. They can be found all over the battlefield. In front of McPherson's Woods (known as Herbst Woods at the time of the battle and sometimes as Reynolds Woods today), sits a monument that identifies the approximate spot where Union General John Reynolds was tragically shot out of the saddle. At Stone Avenue south of the Chambersburg Pike sits the large white McPherson Barn. It is the only original structure still standing from the McPherson farm and was the scene of intense fighting on July 1.

On the north side of the pike are two large statues, one of Union General John Buford and the other of Reynolds. Ironically, Buford the cavalryman is not depicted on horseback. He stands with binoculars peering off to the west, forever waiting for a ghostly Confederate army to approach. Reynolds sits astride his horse with two of the animal's hooves in the air. There is a sometimes disputed tradition at Gettysburg, and other battlefields around the world, that a man's fate in a given battle can be determined by looking at the horse that he rides in his commemorative sculpture. Two hooves in the air mean he was killed in the battle. One hoof airborne signifies that he was wounded. All four hooves planted firmly on solid ground indicate he came out unscathed. This pattern is true of the seven equestrian statues at Gettysburg with one notable exception, which we will discuss in a moment when we get to the Longstreet Memorial.

THE INDIAN VILLAGE: LITTLE BIGHORN
NATIONAL BATTLEFIELD MONUMENT
TOUR STOP NUMBER ONE

For a visitor today at the Little Bighorn National Battlefield Monument (just a couple of miles south of the tiny town of Crow Agency, Montana, and about an hour southeast of Billings on Interstate 90), the very first official stop is a tablet called "Indian Encampment." It is on an elevated position about a half mile from the Visitor Center and Last Stand Hill, along the winding paved avenue called Battlefield Road that meanders through the park. From this high ground, and thanks to a colorful depiction on the tablet (designed and erected by the National Park Service) a visitor can peer off to the southeast and see in her mind's eye what the village might have looked like in the valley below on that sultry morning in 1876.

The verbiage on the tablet at the Indian Encampment stop says that 7,000 people, 1,500 to 2,000 of whom were warriors, camped in the valley that day in 1876. This too is an interesting story. Despite the large number of eyewitnesses on both sides who reported then and later on the size of the village, the wide disparities in their opinions of the encampment's dimensions and population make it hard to believe they were all looking at the same scene. Blackfeet Lakota Chief Kill Eagle said the village was six miles in length and one mile wide. Iron Hail, a Minneconjou warrior who outlived all of the combatants, described six camp circles that ran for four miles along the river. Sitting Bull's version depicted a camp three miles long. This disparity can be partially explained in that Indians did not use mileage as a measurement. Instead, they thought in terms of the time it took to travel from one point to another. When the Indians described the camp this way the opinions coincided much more closely.

The whites did not fare any better as estimators of size or numbers. Captain Myles Moylan said there were 3,600 warriors in the village. Lieutenant Winfield Edgerly guessed 4,000. Lieutenant George Wallace believed there were 9,000 warriors, with 1,800 lodges in a camp that ran three miles long by one-half mile wide. The soldiers generally described a larger village than the Indians. The best estimate of Indian numbers is probably the one offered by the Park Service of 7,000. Numerous credible historians and students of the battle are in accord with this basic estimate. We will never know the answer with precision.

This fascinating phenomenon plays itself out, to use a modern example, in the many variations of an accident that a police officer frequently hears from eyewitnesses. Or it reminds us of the tough choices that face a business leader who is trying to resolve conflicting points of view on a complex issue or situation. Everyone may have experienced more or less the same thing, or is looking at the same set of facts. Everyone is reporting honestly what they think they know, but no two stories are similar. This is the time-honored challenge for both the historical sleuth and today's leaders as well: which version of "the truth" do I believe?

THE LONGSTREET MEMORIAL:
GETTYSBURG BATTLEFIELD TOUR STOP
NUMBER SIX

The Longstreet Memorial sits on the Confederate or western side of the battlefield, just south of the majestic Virginia Memorial, off of West Confederate Avenue in Pitzer's Woods. A traveler needs to look carefully into the woods to see the statue of General Longstreet on his horse Hero; otherwise, the memorial would be easy to miss. Compared to the enormous size and grandeur of the Virginia monument, which depicts a gigantic General Lee on horseback peering off to the east, the Longstreet statue is humble indeed.

We need to remember that Longstreet was (and still is in some circles) long vilified in the South. The Gettysburg statue is apparently the first monument honoring Longstreet anywhere, and it was only dedicated a little more than a decade ago, on July 3, 1998 (the 135th anniversary of the last day of the battle). Longstreet's reputation has been rehabilitated in recent decades, especially with the favorable treatment he received in Michael Sharra's Pulitzer Prize winning book *The Killer Angels* (1974) and the movie *Gettysburg* (1993).

The statue itself is a curious piece of artwork. It depicts Longstreet reining in his horse as he arrives hurriedly on the scene in the midst of the battle. One of the animal's hooves is in the air, though

Longstreet was not wounded in the battle (he was seriously wounded the next year in the Battle of the Wilderness—like Stonewall Jackson, he was accidentally shot by his own troops). Apparently the sculptor received special permission from the National Park Service to deviate from perceived protocol in this way. Also, Longstreet's is the only equestrian statue at the park that rests on the ground. All other generals on horseback sit atop a pedestal. In contrast, visitors can look General Longstreet right in the eye. In addition, while Longstreet is depicted as life-size, his horse is shown at four-fifths size. In short, the man and the horse look somewhat out of proportion. Nevertheless, in studying this statue of Longstreet, one gets a very real sense of his physical vigor and the power of his personality. All of these factors contribute to making the Longstreet Memorial one of the most interesting and unique attractions at Gettysburg, and very much worth seeing.

CUSTER'S ADVANCE: LITTLE BIGHORN NATIONAL BATTLEFIELD MONUMENT TOUR STOP NUMBER TWO

From Battlefield Stop Number One describing the Indian Village, a visitor must drive three miles southeast along winding Battlefield Road to reach Stop Number Two, which is called Custer's Advance. From this elevated perch, which is just west of the position of the Reno-Benteen hill, the view is absolutely panoramic to the west and to the south. This spot contains not just one, but three tablets that describe Custer's approach to the field from the Crow's Nest to the south, Reno's advance down to the valley and into the southern end of the encampment and finally, Reno's retreat across the river to the bluffs on the east bank.

The Park Service once again does a superb job of depicting via colorful renderings what the various scenes must have looked like on June 25, 1876. The tablet for Custer's Advance shows the exact spot, with a tiny red circle on the tablet's picture of the Wolf Mountains to the east, of the Crow's Nest. It is fun to watch people study the tablet, then carefully scan the distant horizon and point to the notch in the hills (fifteen miles away) from which Custer's scouts, gazing toward the west, told him to "look for worms in the grass." One can then move to the next two tablets, view the pictures that depict the battle action that raged in the valley below, and develop a really good understanding of just what the men of Reno's command saw and went through during their incredibly arduous day of fighting on June 25.

CEMETERY HILL: GETTYSBURG BATTLEFIELD TOUR STOP NUMBER FOURTEEN

When a visitor arrives on Cemetery Hill (which sits just south of town) at the Gettysburg battlefield, it is a bit difficult to imagine what the spot must have looked like in July 1863. Today, there is a fair amount of commercial development nearby and within view and the traffic on Baltimore Street whizzes by at high speed. The hilltop is also covered with cannons, various unit markers, and statues of Union generals such as Winfield Scott Hancock and Oliver Otis Howard who fought there.

This combination of a bit too much commercial development and perceived crowding (both of people and monuments) is true not just at Cemetery Hill but elsewhere on the battlefield. There are approximately 1,400 commemorative markers and monuments of all types scattered about an area of ten square miles. There are 400 cannons, around the same number that the armies had with them in July 1863. Some of the guns that dot the landscape today were apparently used in the battle, but most of them were not. There are battery markers that show the location of the one hundred or so artillery batteries that fought. Union brigade markers (seventy in all) have a square base, while the fifty-six Confederate brigade markers can be differentiated by their round bases. Granite markers show the principal locations of the twenty-two Union and ten Confederate divisions that fought, and there are seven Union and three Confederate corps markers, plus a single cavalry corps marker for each side.

Some of the most interesting and eclectic monuments are the regimental markers, which were erected by the state governments or, more often, by veterans groups. There are many Union regimental monuments, and relatively few Confederate monuments. One can understand the reluctance of Confederate veterans to place markers on a battlefield that represented one of their most devastating losses of the war. But during World War 1, Southern veterans and states began to place monuments at various spots around the field—starting with the Virginia Memorial—many of which are incredibly beautiful and impressive.

At Cemetery Hill, one does get a sense of the potential importance of this piece of elevated terrain. The wooded and slightly higher Culp's Hill can be clearly seen to the southeast. The private Evergreen Cemetery, as well as the National Military Cemetery, sits nearby. Ironically, at the time of the battle, there was a sign posted on the gate of Evergreen Cemetery that read, "All persons found using firearms on these grounds will be prosecuted with the utmost rigor of the law."

MEDICINE TAIL COULEE: LITTLE BIGHORN NATIONAL BATTLEFIELD MONUMENT TOUR STOP NUMBER EIGHT

One of the fascinating features of the Little Bighorn battlefield is its very appearance. There are many places on the field where if one gazes off into the distance, it could easily be 1876 again. Medicine Tail Coulee—which is the low-lying area about one mile west of the Indian Village marker where Custer gave his men a break and dispatched Sergeant John Martin with the famous note telling Benteen to "come quick"—is just such a place.

There are many other locations on the field where hardscrabble nature predominates, and there is no visible commercial development whatsoever. Signs warn the traveler that to leave the beaten path is to risk being bitten by a rattlesnake. This is in contrast with Gettysburg. The National Park Service and the Gettysburg Foundation are striving honorably and mightily to restore the battlefield to its 1863 appearance, by doing such things as taking out some trees and planting others, and moving power lines underground. But, as was mentioned earlier, because of the volume of visitors (just under 2 million a year), the prevalence of development nearby, and the number of monuments (1,400), it is somewhat more difficult at Gettysburg to visualize what the scene may have actually looked like at the time of the battle. Granted, the Little Bighorn battlefield is in a substantially more remote location in southeastern Montana. It has fewer visitors (about 400,000 annually), and has a different monument scheme (aside from a couple of larger sculptures, there are only white marble markers approximating where soldiers fell and some red granite markers where Native American warriors fell). Nevertheless, the contrast is striking.

When I bring leadership teams to Medicine Tail Coulee, I always ask them to look off toward the horizon to the east, to take in the hard, unspoiled, and enduring beauty of the natural landscape, and to go back in time, even if only in their mind's eye.

THE PEACH ORCHARD: GETTYSBURG BATTLEFIELD TOUR STOP NUMBER TEN

The Peach Orchard sits just north of Wheatfield Road and east of the Emmitsburg Road, which is today designated as Business Route 15, and which leads gradually northeast into Gettysburg. As part of its restoration effort, the National Park Service is attempting to replant peach trees in the orchard, but the acreage dominated by farmer Joseph Sherfy's lush fruit trees was twice as expansive in 1863 as what we see today.

One-quarter-mile south of the Peach Orchard sits the Rose farm, and a half-mile east is the Trostle farm, which served as the headquarters for Union General Dan Sickles. Both locations were the scene of intense fighting on the second day of the battle. As we stand in the Peach Orchard and look east, we can see the low-lying terrain that Sickles was asked to defend along Cemetery Ridge, as well as the two Round Tops farther south.

Difficult though it may be to admit for those who would skewer Sickles for his unilateral decision to move his Third Corps forward, one can at least understand what he might have been thinking when he chose the elevated position of the Peach Orchard over the obstructed and somewhat vulnerable position along Cemetery Ridge. Nevertheless, even amateur tacticians, when presented with a choice of separating from the main force and occupying the Peach Orchard over occupying the commanding high ground of Little Round Top (which is today as it was then dominant in height, open, and presents clear fields of fire from its western face), have no trouble making the correct decision. Those visitors who closely study the terrain around the Peach Orchard will clearly see the folly of Dan Sickles's decision making on Day Two of the battle.

RENO-BENTEEN DEFENSE SITE: LITTLE BIGHORN NATIONAL BATTLEFIELD MONUMENT TOUR STOP NUMBER FIVE

The entire Little Bighorn battlefield sits on land that is part of an extremely large Crow Indian reservation. The Reno-Benteen Defense Site occupies the far southeastern edge of the battlefield on land that was purchased from the Crow tribe in 1930. Today, except for this parcel and the area around the visitor center and Last Stand Hill to the northwest, the entire surrounding acreage is owned not by the National Park Service but by the Crow Nation or other private landholders.

The first thing that a visitor to the Reno-Benteen Defense Site notices is that while the high and steep bluffs offer an excellent defensive position facing west toward the river down below, the rest of the terrain consists mainly of rolling contours that offer no particular protection from any other direction. In 1965, as part of a series of physical improvements at the battlefield, a parking loop was constructed at the Reno-Benteen location. Now, visitors can park their cars and walk the lengthy path that winds all the way around the site. Just at the beginning point for the walking tour sits a granite shaft, dedicated in 1929, which reads, "This area was occupied by troops A, B, D, G, H, K, and M, Seventh U.S. Cavalry, and the pack train when they were besieged by the Sioux Indians June 25th and 26th 1876."

Highlights of the walking tour include a view of numerous shallow entrenchments, still visible today, dug by the desperate soldiers to protect themselves from incoming fire. Medal of Honor Point marks the spot where a courageous group of soldiers raced down the ravine to the river, under great peril, to retrieve water for their unbearably thirsty comrades. In the distance 500 yards to the northeast is Sharpshooter Ridge. Though the majority of both the Indians and white soldiers were poor marksmen with a gun, several Indian riflemen exhibited great skill in sniping from Sharpshooter Ridge and were able to make life miserable for their enemy by picking off soldiers even from this seemingly great distance.

In walking the perimeter, a visitor does get a sense of desolation and loneliness, and how difficult and terrifying it must have been for soldiers to defend this ground against a determined enemy.

LITTLE ROUND TOP: GETTYSBURG BATTLEFIELD TOUR STOP NUMBER EIGHT

Little Round Top is the most visited location at the Gettysburg battlefield today. When I take leadership teams to this spot, we always start at the top of the hill, behind the famous statue of Gouverneur Warren—ever vigilant as he looks off to the west, forever in search of the approaching Confederate enemy. From this magnificent summit, which provides one of the most breathtaking views of any American battlefield, a visitor can see a number of critical landmarks.

To the south or left sits Big Round Top, higher in elevation than Little Round Top but densely vegetated today just as it was in 1863. Looking down into the valley to the south, the amazing granite boulders of the Devils' Den look gigantic—some of them seem as big as buildings—even from 500 yards away. It is hard to believe that marksmen from both sides hit each other with deadly accuracy from this distance, but they did. In the center of the vast open fields to the west, we see the Codori farm with its trademark red barn. This is the area from which a despondent George Pickett sat his horse and helplessly watched his beloved division be massacred on the battle's final day. Looking to the north or right, we see the line of Cemetery Ridge, dotted with monuments, with the especially immense and impressive Pennsylvania State Memorial standing out among all others.

On a clear day, South Mountain is visible a dozen or so miles to the west. I am always struck by the peacefulness of battlefields, and this is especially true for me at the crest of Little Round Top. From this quiet and lovely spot, I always ask my teams to consider the awesome beauty of the natural world around them and to try to reconcile that with the terrible events that we all know took place here. It is a difficult mental leap to make.

From the western face of the hill, we proceed to the southern ridge (known today as "Vincent's Spur") where Strong Vincent, Paddy O'Rorke, Joshua L. Chamberlain, William Oates, and all of the brave men who fought under their commands struggled desperately for control of that piece of ground. This position represented the very left flank of the line of the Army of the Potomac, and there is a small gray monument down in front that commemorates the courage and sacrifice of Chamberlain's Twentieth Maine Regiment.

The lightly wooded, rock-strewn ridge is isolated and very condensed, making it hard to believe that several hundred men fought in this relatively cramped space. When I have visited the battlefield during the off-season, I have on more than one occasion been physically alone on Vincent's Spur, yet somehow I have never felt completely alone. There is tremendous energy here. One can almost hear, faintly on the wind, the rumble of gunfire and the cries of anguish.

Historian James McPherson tells a sweet story about Little Round Top in his excellent book, *Hallowed Ground: A Walk at Gettysburg*. Over the years, McPherson has taken groups of students from Princeton University, where he teaches, to visit the battlefield. In 1987 he took a group and, he recalled, "This year one of those students had written her senior thesis on Chamberlain, but had never before actually been to Gettysburg. As we came to the place where the Twentieth Maine fought, she could no longer hold back the tears. Nor could the rest of us...."

CRAZY HORSE-KEOGH FIGHT: LITTLE BIGHORN NATIONAL BATTLEFIELD MONUMENT STOP NUMBER FOURTEEN

This battlefield stop is technically called the "Keogh-Crazy Horse Fight," but I reversed the order of names in this book for purposes of emphasizing the role of Crazy Horse at this place and during this stage of the battle. To get here, we need to drive north on Battlefield Road about a mile-and-a-half from Medicine Tail Coulee. We are now on property owned by the National Park Service, and Last Stand Hill is visible just a few hundred yards further to the northwest.

The striking visual element from here is the numerous white markers that lay scattered across the landscape in the gully below. They represent the men of Keogh's C and I Companies, with perhaps a smattering of men from Company L who may have made it this far north. There is a clump of markers that shows where Keogh fell, surrounded by his loyal staff. The rest of the white stones are generally strung along in a line, giving the clear impression of a group of individuals who were at this point panicked and on their own. They had been routed, and it was every man for himself in trying to reach the perceived safety that might be provided by Custer's soldiers at Last Stand Hill. Only twenty or so survived to get to Custer, and they did not last long.

This is the spot near where Crazy Horse recognized his tactical opportunity and with perfect timing completed his incredible bravery run. Keogh's command was split in two and destroyed piecemeal, and the end was no longer in doubt.

Pickett's Charge: Gettysburg Battlefield Stop Number Five

I actually begin the Pickett's Charge sequence of my seminar from Battlefield Stop Number Five, which is the Virginia Memorial. This magnificent, immense gray sculpture sits on the spot from which Robert E. Lee watched the progress of the famous assault across open ground against the determined Yankee enemy defending Cemetery Ridge to the east on the third day of Gettysburg. At the base of the monument, there are depictions of regular Virginians from all walks of life who found themselves caught up in the drama while serving as soldiers in Lee's Army of Northern Virginia. From the monument, we take a path east alongside a post-and-rail fence for several hundred yards to a battery of Confederate Napoleon cannons, sitting wheel-to-wheel, and aimed toward the well-known copse of oak trees three-quarters of a mile away, which Lee had identified as the aiming point for the attack. This is also supposed to be the spot where Lee met his beleaguered and bloodied men upon their return, telling them, "It's all my fault."

We talk as a group about the awesome but inaccurate bombardment that preceded the charge. I then ask each participant, in a word or a phrase, to share what the men of Pickett's and Pettigrew's divisions might have been thinking as they commenced their advance to destiny. We hear answers like "prayerful," "determined," "scared," "cursing," "thinking of home," "remembering family," and so on. I believe I have never had an answer that felt wrong because all of those thoughts could have (and probably did) race through the minds of those brave men.

We then step off and walk the ground of Pickett's Charge, through the tall grass, all the way across the Emmitsburg Road to the low stone wall and the notorious "Angle," where the battle came to its violent climax. It usually takes about twenty minutes, and people are struck by what a long, frightening, and exhausting traverse it must have been under constant artillery and, later, rifle fire. There is tremendous energy on this part of the field too. People are simply in awe of the courage it took for these men to keep going forward.

When we reach the Angle, we sit down on the stone fence for a rest. The group is usually pretty quiet at this point. I ask everyone this time, in a word or a phrase, to describe what they themselves are now thinking or feeling. We get answers like, "I had no idea," "humbled," "horrified," "saddened," "inspired," "perspective," "honored," and "unforgettable." Once again, all good answers.

Finally, we move to the National Cemetery, where I ask one of the participants to read the Gettysburg Address (see the full text in the appendix) near the spot where Abraham Lincoln delivered it in November 1863. I believe that this is always a "fitting and proper" way to end our day on the battlefield. All of us come away changed.

Last Stand Hill: Little Bighorn National Battlefield Monument Stop Number Sixteen

In July 1881 a granite monument, which weighed almost twenty tons and was transported to remote southeastern Montana only with great difficulty, was erected at the summit of Last Stand Hill. The disinterred remains of every enlisted trooper that could still be found on the field were reburied in a trench that surrounds all four sides of the monument. An interpretive marker near the monument explains, "The remains of about 220 soldiers, scouts, and civilians are buried around the base of this memorial. The white marble headstones scattered over the battlefield denote where the slain troopers were found and originally buried. In 1881 they were reinterred in a single grave on this site. The officers' remains were removed in 1877 to various cemeteries throughout the country. General Custer is buried at West Point."

Numerous eyewitnesses stated that Custer died and was found at the top of Last Stand Hill, along with nine other soldiers (including his brother Tom), within a few feet of the spot where the granite shaft now sits. Yet in looking from the top of the hill down the west slope, a visitor clearly sees a distinctive white marker with a black face sitting more than fifty feet away, which states that Custer "fell here." As with many of the other markers on this mystical field, it seems that the one that would generate the most interest is also in the wrong place. Apparently the explanation is that while Custer was found on the hilltop, he and the others were moved down the hillside for burial. In any event, the stark symbolic finality of Custer's fate, and of the men who followed him, is evident in looking at the abundant white stones that dot the desolate hillside.

When I take leaders to the Little Bighorn, Last Stand Hill is only our second-to-last stop. When we are done discussing Custer's demise, we move to the nearby Indian Memorial. Among other goals, the memorial was designed to express a theme of "Peace through Unity," to celebrate and honor the memory of the Indian men, women, and children who took part in the battle, and to rectify the imbalance over the years in the portrayal of the Indian role and sacrifice. The memorial was dedicated in 2003, and it is beautiful. It is constructed in a circular form, deep into the earth, and opens to the sky. An interpretive "living memorial" wall occupies the inner sanctum. The wall uses texts, quotations, and pictographs to tell the Indian side of the story. A large bronze tracing of three Indian warriors on horseback and an Indian woman on foot stands forever silhouetted against the harsh Montana landscape and the awesome, endless horizon.

I ask one of the team members to read the inspiring, bittersweet words of the Sioux chief Ohiyesa (see the full text in the appendix) who said of his people, "... our contribution to the nation and our world is not to be measured in the material realm. Our greatest contribution has been spiritual and philosophical...." Once again, just as at Gettysburg, no thinking, feeling citizen can experience a day on this sacred ground and fail to come away changed.

Appendix

Army Organization

Army
- 2/3 + Corps
- 72,000 men
- Major General (USA),
- General (CSA) commanding

Corps
- 2/3 Divisions
- 24,000 men
- Major General (USA), Maj. or Lieut. Gen (CSA) commanding
- CSA Corps sometimes contained four divisions

Division
- Three brigades
- 12,000 men
- Brigadier or Major General commanding
- CSA division sometimes contained four brigades

Brigade
- 4+ regiments
- 4000 men
- Col. (CSA); Brigadier General (CSA) commanding

❖ Cavalry: Union and Confederate cavalry units were attached to division, corps, or armies as required, but also frequently operated independently.

❖ Artillery: Field artillery batteries were attached to brigades, division, or corps, as required.

Army Organization

Regiment
- 10 companies
- 1000 men
- Colonel commanding

Company
- Two platoons
- 100 men
- Captain commanding

Platoon
- 50 men
- Lieutenant commanding

Squad
- Sergeant commanding

	Union	Confederate
Infantry	80%	74%
Cavalry	14%	20%
Artillery	6%	6%

Army units virtually never existed at full strength; they were typically at 1/3 to 1/2 strength.

Army of the Potomac

**Major General
George Gordon Meade
Commander**

I Corps	II Corps	III Corps	V Corps	VI Corps	XI Corps	XII Corps
Maj. General John Reynolds	Maj. General Winfield Scott Hancock	Maj. General Daniel Sickles	Maj. General George Sykes	Maj. General John Sedgwick	Maj. General Oliver Howard	Maj. General William Slocum

- Approximately 68,000 infantry
- Cavalry Corps, Maj. General Alfred Pleasonton commanding; three divisions
- 372 artillery pieces in 65 batteries (six guns each)
- Total strength approximately 95,000

Army of Northern Virginia

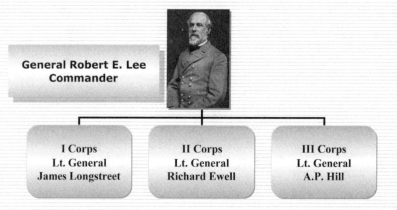

**General Robert E. Lee
Commander**

I Corps	II Corps	III Corps
Lt. General	Lt. General	Lt. General
James Longstreet	Richard Ewell	A.P. Hill

- Approximately 62,000 infantry
- Cavalry Division, Maj. General Jeb Stuart commanding; five brigades
- 265 artillery pieces in 60 batteries (four guns each)
- Total strength approximately 75,000

APPENDIX

THE GETTYSBURG ADDRESS

Four score and seven years ago our fathers brought forth on this continent a new nation, conceived in liberty and dedicated to the proposition that all men are created equal.

Now we are engaged in a great civil war, testing whether that nation or any nation so conceived and so dedicated can long endure. We are met on a great battlefield of that war. We have come to dedicate a portion of that field as a final resting-place for those who here gave their lives that that nation might live. It is altogether fitting and proper that we should do this.

But in a larger sense, we cannot dedicate, we cannot consecrate, we cannot hallow this ground. The brave men, living and dead who struggled here have consecrated it far above our poor power to add or detract. The world will little note nor long remember what we say here, but it can never forget what they did here. It is for us the living rather to be dedicated here to the unfinished work which they who fought here have thus far so nobly advanced.

It is rather for us to be here dedicated to the great task remaining before us—that from these honored dead we take increased devotion to that cause for which they gave the last full measure of devotion—that we here highly resolve that these dead shall not have died in vain, that this nation under God shall have a new birth of freedom, and that government of the people, by the people, for the people shall not perish from the earth.

Delivered by President Abraham Lincoln at the
Dedication of the National Cemetery, Gettysburg, Pennsylvania,
November 19, 1863.

THE GIFT OF MY PEOPLE

I am an Indian; and while I have learned much from civilization, I have never lost my Indian sense of right and justice.

When I reduce civilization to its most basic terms, it becomes a system of life based on trade. Each man stakes his powers, the product of his labor, his social, political, and religious standing against his neighbor. To gain what? To gain control over his fellow workers, and the results of their labor.

Is there not something worthy of perpetuation in our Indian spirit of democracy, where Earth, our mother, was free to all, and no one sought to impoverish or enslave his neighbor? Where the good things of Earth were not ours to hold against our brothers and sisters, but were ours to use and enjoy together with them, and with whom it was our privilege to share?

Indeed, our contribution to our nation and the world is not to be measured in the material realm. Our greatest contribution has been spiritual and philosophical. Silently, by example only, in wordless patience, we have held stoutly to our native vision of personal faithfulness to duty and devotion to a trust. We have not advertised our faithfulness nor made capital of our honor.

But again and again we have proved our worth as citizens of this country by our constancy in the face of hardship and death. Prejudice and racial injustice have been no excuse for our breaking our word. This simplicity and fairness has cost us dear. It has cost us our land and our freedom, and even the extinction of our race as a separate and unique people.

But, as an ideal, we live and will live, not only in the splendor of our past, the poetry of our legends and art, not only in the interfusion of our blood with yours, and in our faithful adherence to the ideals of American citizenship, but in the living heart of the nation.

The Sioux chief Ohiyesa (later known as Charles Alexander Eastman), from *The Wisdom of Native Americans*, edited by Kent Nerburn.

Acknowledgments

I need to thank, first, my editor Anne Hodgson. Anne was patient, kind, and solicitous of my feelings throughout the process of giving me really good and honest feedback. She need not have been so gentle; I was a Marine after all and am well-used to being corrected in all manner of things. Anne did a superb job, and the book is much, much better for her efforts. My good friends Jack El-Hai, Tom Siebold, and Mat Gjetson each read an early draft of the manuscript and offered extremely helpful suggestions. I must thank the incredibly talented Emily Yost, my creative guru, for her innovative jacket design and all the other insights she has provided in helping me to achieve my vision over the past couple of years. Emily's intern Danielle Melin did a wonderful job with the maps. I asked her when the project began if she had ever seen a battle map before and she said no, but that she loved the *Lord of the Rings* books. I said that was good enough for me. The Zen philosophers say that the expert mind sees few possibilities, but the beginner's mind sees endless possibilities. We used a number of different maps for guidance, but the maps of Hal Jespersen were particularly helpful. Danielle's hand-drawn maps are, as we used to say in the law, "sui generis" (one-of-a-kind) and have added so much to the story. Jeannie Androsoff has been my loyal administrative assistant, all-around helper, friend, and cheerleader for a couple of years now, and I want to thank her for all that she does to make me successful. The people at Beaver's Pond Press have been great in guiding a novice like me through the publishing process, and I have enjoyed working with them. I especially want to call out Dara Beevas, Jordan Wiklund, Jay Monroe, and April Michelle Davis for their patience, time, and attention.

I used myriad bibliographical resources to do my research, but six books in particular were very helpful to me, and I would highly recommend them to those who would seek to do additional reading. I want to thank the following scholar-historians for their profound analytical insights and high narrative skills: Stephen Sears, author of *Gettysburg*; Noah Andre Trudeau, author of *Gettysburg: A Testing of Courage*; James McPherson, author of *Hallowed Ground: A Walk at Gettysburg*; James Donovan, author of *A Terrible Glory: Custer and the Little Bighorn—the Last Great Battle of the American West*; James Brust, Brian Pohanka, and Sandy Barnard, authors of *Where Custer Fell: Photographs of the Little Bighorn Battlefield Then and Now*; and Gregory Michno, author of *Lakota Noon: The Indian Narrative of Custer's Defeat*. The knowledge and understanding I gained from these fine historians were critically important. I did not agree with everything they wrote; in many cases historians contradict one another, which is especially noticeable when comparing versions of the Little Bighorn battle. Historians should be forgiven, however, because even eyewitnesses frequently contradict one another. I sifted through the data from both primary and secondary sources and did my best to accurately piece the story together. All factual errors in *Sacred Ground* are, of course, my responsibility alone.

I want to thank the members of my Blue Knight Battlefield Seminars Board of Advisors whom I have not already mentioned for their support throughout this project: Ann Aronson, John Berge, Gail Dorn, Jenney Egertson, Bill Gjetson, Herschel Herndon, Jeff Johnson, Traci Petschl, Kris Rosen, Randy Ross, and Brent Siegel. They are an incredible bunch of leaders, and I have learned a lot from them.

I have a great network of friends. Space prohibits listing them all, but I do want to call out each of the following special people for being my allies and helpers, and for their support, encouragement, and friendship over the years: Danal and Wendy Abrams, Shari Ballard, Brian and Cathy Gauger, Samantha Hanson, Al and Jill Hatfield, Gayle Hayhurst, Ellen Hinrichs, John Magnusson, Shelly Malone-Vestal, Bill Miller, Matt Moran, Charlie Newman, Val Johnson, Tamara Reding, Julie Roemen, Pete and Nancy Ross, Chuck Schneider, Jack Uldrich, Paul and Kathy Vaaler, Joellyn Veninga, and John and Jennifer Youngblood.

I am blessed with a wonderful family. I dedicated the book to my dad, but also want to thank my mother, Doris, for a lifetime of unconditional love and endless encouragement. I am one of those guys who can honestly brag that his mother is a saint. Both of my parents have always been great readers, and they instilled a love of books and a passion for learning early in my life. My brother, Tom, and sister, Joan, are terrific, and I love them both very much. Finally, thanks to my beloved wife and best friend of almost a quarter-century, Faith, and to my daughters Anna and Lucia. They were extremely patient as I went into what business author Jim Collins calls "monk-mode," hunkered down in my study, to complete this book. My ladies, you are, all three of you, bright and beautiful and kind. I will love you always.

—Jeff Appelquist—

Bibliography

HISTORICAL SOURCES:

Ambrose, Stephen. *Crazy Horse and Custer: The Parallel Lives of Two American Warriors.* New York, Doubleday and Company, 1975.

Battles and Leaders of the Civil War: The Tide Shifts (Volume 3). Edison, New Jersey, Castle Books, New Edition, 1995.

Bray, Kingsley. *Crazy Horse: A Lakota Life.* Norman, University of Oklahoma Press, 2006.

Brown, Dee. *Bury My Heart at Wounded Knee.* New York, Henry Holt and Company, 1970.

Brust, James, Brian Pohanka, and Sandy Barnard. *Where Custer Fell: Photographs of the Little Bighorn Then and Now.* Norman, University of Oklahoma Press, 2005.

Catton, Bruce. *The Army of the Potomac: Glory Road (Volume 2).* New York, Doubleday and Company, 1952.

———. *The American Heritage New History of the Civil War.* New York, Viking, 1996.

———. *This Hallowed Ground: The Story of the Union Side of the Civil War.* Edison, New Jersey, Castle Books, New Edition, 2002.

Chamberlain, Joshua Lawrence. *"Bayonet! Forward": My Civil War Reminiscences.* Gettysburg, Pennsylvania, Stan Clark Military Books, New Edition, 1994.

———. *The Passing of the Armies: The Last Campaign of the Armies.* Gettysburg, Pennsylvania, Stan Clark Military Books, New Edition, 1994.

Clark, Champ. *Gettysburg: The Confederate High Tide.* Alexandria, Virginia, Time-Life Books, 1985.

Connell, Evan. *Son of the Morning Star: Custer and the Little Bighorn.* San Francisco, North Point Press, 1984.

Cowley, Robert (Editor). *With My Face to the Enemy: Perspectives on the Civil War.* New York, G. P. Putnam and Sons, 2001.

Cozzens, Peter (Editor). *Eyewitnesses to the Indian Wars, 1865–1890, Volume Four: The Long War for the Northern Plains*. Mechanicsburg, Pennsylvania, Stackpole Books, 2004.

_____. *Eyewitnesses to the Indian Wars, 1865–1890, Volume Five: The Army and the Indian*. Mechanicsburg, Pennsylvania, Stackpole Books, 2005.

Custer, George Armstrong. *My Life on the Plains or, Personal Experiences With Indians*. Norman, University of Oklahoma Press, New Edition Copyright 1962.

Davis, David Brion. *Inhuman Bondage: The Rise and Fall of Slavery in the New World*. New York, Oxford University Press, 2006.

Donovan, James. *A Terrible Glory: Custer and the Little Bighorn—The Last Great Battle of the American West*. Little, Brown and Company, 2008.

Faust, Drew Gilpin. *This Republic of Suffering: Death and the American Civil War*. New York, Alfred A. Knopf, 2008.

Foote, Shelby. *The Civil War: A Narrative—Fredericksburg to Meridian (Volume 2)*. New York, Random House, 1963.

Freeman, Douglas Southall. *Lee's Lieutenants: A Study in Command (3 Volumes)*. New York, Charles Scribner's Sons, 1942.

_____. *Lee: An Abridgment in One Volume of the Four-Volume R. E. Lee by Douglas Southall Freeman*. New York, Charles Scribner's Sons, 1961.

Gallagher, Gary. *The American Civil War*. Chantilly, Virginia, The Great Courses of The Teaching Company, 2000.

Goodwin, Doris Kearns. *Team of Rivals: The Political Genius of Abraham Lincoln*. New York, Simon and Schuster, 2005.

Gottfried, Bradley. *The Maps of Gettysburg: An Atlas of the Gettysburg Campaign, June 3–July 13, 1863*. New York, Savas Beatie, 2007.

Grinnell, George Bird. *The Fighting Cheyennes*. Norman, Oklahoma, University of Oklahoma Press, 1915.

Heidler, David and Jeanne Heidler (Editors). *Encyclopedia of the American Civil War: A Political, Social, and Military History*. New York, W. W. Norton and Company, 2000.

Hessler, James. *Sickles At Gettysburg: The Controversial Civil War General Who Committed Murder, Abandoned Little Round Top, and Declared Himself the Hero of Gettysburg*. New York, Savas Beatie, 2009.

Jones, Virgil Carrington. *Gray Ghosts and Rebel Raiders: The Daring Exploits of the Confederate Guerillas*. New York, Galahad Books, 1956.

Josephy, Alvin. *500 Nations: An Illustrated History of North American Indians*. New York, Alfred A. Knopf, 1994.

Kagan, Neil (Editor) and Stephen Hyslop. *Atlas of the Civil War: A Comprehensive Guide to The Tactics and Terrain of Battle*. Washington, D. C., National Geographic, 2009.

Linderman, Gerald. *Embattled Courage: The Experience of Combat in the American Civil War*. New York, The Free Press, 1987.

Longstreet, James. *From Manassas to Appomattox: Memoirs of the Civil War in America*. Secaucus, New Jersey, The Blue and Grey Press, 1896.

McPherson, James. *Battle Cry of Freedom: The Civil War Era*. New York, Oxford University Press, 1988.

————. *Abraham Lincoln and the Second American Revolution*. New York, Oxford University Press, 1991.

————. *Drawn With the Sword: Reflections on the American Civil War*. New York, Oxford University Press, 1996.

————. *For Cause and Comrades: Why Men Fought in the Civil War*. New York, Oxford University Press, 1997.

————. *Hallowed Ground: A Walk at Gettysburg*. New York, Crown Publishers, 2003.

Michno, Gregory. *Lakota Noon: The Indian Narrative of Custer's Defeat*. Missoula, Montana, Mountain Press, 1997.

Nerburn, Kent (Editor). *The Wisdom of Native Americans*. Novato, California, New World Library, 1999.

Nesbitt, Mark. *Through Blood and Fire: Selected Civil War Papers of Major General Joshua Chamberlain*. Mechanicsburg, Pennsylvania, Stackpole Books, 1996.

Nevin, David. *The Old West: The Soldiers*. New York, Time-Life Books, 1973.

Petruzzi, J. David and Steven Stanley. *The Complete Gettysburg Guide: Walking and Driving Tours of the Battlefield, Town, Cemeteries, Field Hospital Sites, and other Topics of Historical Interest*. New York, Savas Beatie, 2009.

Robertson, James, Jr. *Stonewall Jackson: The Man, the Soldier, the Legend*. New York, Macmillan Publishing U.S.A., 1997.

Sears, Stephen. *Gettysburg*. New York, Houghton Mifflin Company, 2003.

Shaara, Michael. *The Killer Angels*. New York, Random House, 1974.

Skelnar, Larry. *To Hell With Honor: Custer and the Little Bighorn*. Norman, University of Oklahoma Press, 2000.

Stackpole, Edward and Wilbur Nye. *The Battle of Gettysburg: A Guided Tour*. Mechanicsburg, Pennsylvania, Stackpole Books, 1998.

Symonds, Craig. *American Heritage History of the Battle of Gettysburg*. New York, HarperCollins Publishers, 2001.

Tanner, Robert. *Stonewall in the Valley: Thomas J. "Stonewall" Jackson's Shenandoah Valley Campaign, Spring 1862*. New York, Doubleday and Company, 1976.

Thomas, Emory. *Bold Dragoon: The Life of J. E. B. Stuart*. New York, Harper and Row, Publishers, 1986.

————. *Robert E. Lee: A Biography*. New York, W. W. Norton and Company, 1995.

Trudeau, Noah Andre. *Gettysburg: A Testing of Courage*. New York, HarperCollins Publishers, 2002.

————. "Did Lee Doom Himself at Gettysburg?" *Military History Quarterly* (Fall 2009): 14–25.

Trulock, Alice Rains. *Into the Hands of Providence: Joshua L. Chamberlain and the American Civil War*. Chapel Hill, North Carolina, University of North Carolina Press, 1992.

Utley, Robert. *The American Heritage History of the Indian Wars*. New York, American Heritage Publishing Company, 1977.

————. *The Lance and the Shield: The Life and Times of Sitting Bull*. New York, Henry Holt and Company, 1993.

————. *Custer: Cavalier in Buckskin*. Norman, Oklahoma, University of Oklahoma Press, 2001.

Viola, Herman. *Little Bighorn Remembered: The Untold Indian Story of Custer's Last Stand*. New York, Times Books, 1999.

Ward, Geoffrey, Ric Burns, and Ken Burns. *The Civil War: An Illustrated History*. New York, Alfred A. Knopf, 1990.

Weigley, Russell. *A Great Civil War: A Military and Political History, 1861–1865*. Bloomington, Indiana, Indiana University Press, 2000.

Wert, Jeffrey. *Custer: The Controversial Life of George Armstrong Custer*. New York, Simon and Schuster, 1996.

Williams, T. Harry. *Lincoln and His Generals*. New York, Gramercy Books, 1952.

Wills, Garry. *Lincoln at Gettysburg: The Words That Remade America*. New York, Simon and Schuster, 1992.

BUSINESS CASE STUDY SOURCES:

Bryant, Howard. "The Revolutionary: The A's are losing again, and Billy Beane's radical Moneyball legacy is suffering." *ESPN: Outside the Lines* (July 29, 2009).

Business: The Ultimate Resource. Cambridge, Massachusetts, Basic Books, 2006.

Byrne, John. *Chainsaw: The Notorious Career of Al Dunlap In the Era of Profit-At-Any-Price*. New York, HarperCollins, 1999.

Carr, David. "A Triumph of Avoiding the Traps." *The New York Times* (November 23, 2009).

Cendrowski, Scott. "Harley-Davidson: Bears vs. Bulls." *Fortune* (April 16, 2009).

Curry, Jack. "In Postseason, Book of Revelations Helps Guide Yanks: Girardi Seeks Statistical Edge." *The New York Times* (October 2, 2009).

Dunlap, Albert, and Bob Andelman. *Mean Business: How I Save Bad Companies and Make Good Companies Great*. New York, Fireside, 1996.

eBay Web Site. www.ebay.com. Accessed May 17, 2009.

BIBLIOGRAPHY

General Electric Web Site. www.generalelectric.com. Accessed March 27, 2009.

Girard, Bernard. *The Google Way: How One Company Is Revolutionizing Management As We Know It*. San Francisco, California, No Starch Press, 2009.

Google Web Site. www.google.com. Accessed August 21, 2009.

Gordon, John Steele. *The Business of America*. New York, Walker and Company, 2001.

Gross, Daniel. *Forbes Greatest Business Stories of All Time*. New York, John Wiley and Sons, 1996.

Gunnison, Liz, and Kevin Maney. "The Best (and Worst) CEOs (Ever)." *Conde Nast Portfolio* (May 2009).

Harley-Davidson Web Site. www.harley-davidson.com. Accessed September 9, 2009.

Helyar, John. "Will Harley-Davidson Hit the Wall?" *Fortune* (August 12, 2002).

Hof, Robert. "Meet eBay's Auctioneer-in-Chief." *Business Week* (May 29, 2003).

_____. "The Constant Challenge at eBay." *Business Week* (June 30, 2004).

Johnson, Earvin "Magic." *32 Ways to Be a Champion in Business*. New York, Crown Business, 2008.

Johnson and Johnson Web Site. www.johnsonandjohnson.com. Accessed June 17, 2009.

Kolhatkar, Sheelah. "Meg's Run." *Time* (December 14, 2009): 46–49.

Kroichick, Ron. "Heavy Hitter." *Diablo: The Magazine of the San Francisco East Bay* (August 2008).

Lashinsky, Adam. "Where Does Google Go Next?" *Fortune* (May 26, 2008): 105–108.

Lewin, Tamar. "Tylenol Maker Finding New Crisis Less Severe." *The New York Times* (February 12, 1986).

Lewis, Michael. *Moneyball: The Art of Winning an Unfair Game*. New York, W. W. Norton and Company, 2003.

Magic Johnson Enterprises Web Site. www.magicjohnsonenterprises.com. Accessed April 30, 2009.

Manjoo, Farhard. "The Search For a Rival." *Time* (August 31, 2009): 38–39.

Oprah Winfrey Web Site. www.oprah.com. Accessed July 1, 2009.

Pixar Animation Studios Web Site. www.pixar.com. Accessed June 12, 2009.

Price, David. *The Pixar Touch: The Making of a Company*. New York, Alfred A. Knopf, 2008.

Rafferty, Tod. *America Celebrates 100 Years of Harley-Davidson*. Osceola, Wisconsin, MBI Publishing, 2002.

Reid, Peter. *Well-Made In America: Lessons From Harley-Davidson On Being the Best*. New York, McGraw-Hill Publishing Company, 1989.

Reusse, Patrick. "Coaching icons are deserving of a special tribute in Prep Bowl." *StarTribune.com* (November 29, 2008).

Sellers, Patricia. "The Business of Being Oprah." *Fortune* (April 8, 2002).

—————. "Can Meg Whitman Save California?" *Fortune* (March 30, 2009): 64–74.

Stanley, Allesandra. "The Fine Art of Quitting While She's Ahead." *The New York Times* (November 21, 2009).

Stevenson, Richard. "Johnson & Johnson's Recovery." *The New York Times* (July 5, 1986).

Stewart, James. *Disney War*. New York, Simon and Schuster, 2005.

Stross, Randall. *Planet Google: One Company's Audacious Plan to Organize Everything We Know*. New York, Free Press, 2008.

Tannen, Deborah. "The Time 100: Oprah Winfrey." *Time* (June 8, 1998).

Vise, David, and Mark Malseed. *The Google Story*. New York, Delta (New Edition), 2008.

Walt Disney Company Web Site. www.disney.com. Accessed September 30, 2009.

Wheeler, Tom. *Take Command! Leadership Lessons From the Civil War*. New York, Doubleday, 2000.

Wiebner, Michael. "The Battle of Bull Run (Lobbying Against New Disney Historical Theme Park)." *Campaigns and Elections* 16 (December 1, 1994): 44–50.

Welch, Jack, and John Byrne. *Jack: Straight From the Gut*. New York, Warner Business Books, Inc., 2001.

Wyatt, Edward. "A Few Tremors in Oprahland." *The New York Times* (May 26, 2008).

Zinni, Tony, and Tony Koltz. *Leading the Charge: Leadership Lessons From the Battlefield to the Boardroom*. New York, Palgrave Macmillan, 2009.

Index

INDEX